Vladimir Nabokov

Lolita

EDITED BY CHRISTINE CLEGG

Consultant editor: Nicolas Tredell

ICON BOOKS

Published in 2000 by Icon Books Ltd.,
Grange Road, Duxford, Cambridge CB2 4QF
e-mail: info@iconbooks.co.uk
www.iconbooks.co.uk

Distributed in the UK, Europe, Canada, South Africa and Asia by the
Penguin Group: Penguin Books Ltd., 27 Wrights Lane, London W8 5TZ

Published in Australia in 2000 by Allen & Unwin Pty. Ltd.,
PO Box 8500, 9 Atchison Street, St Leonards, NSW 2065

Consultant editor: Nicolas Tredell
Managing editor: Duncan Heath
Series devised by: Christopher Cox
Cover design: Simon Flynn
Typesetting: Wayzgoose

ISBN 1 84046 173 X

Printed and bound in Great Britain by
Biddles Ltd., Guildford and King's Lynn

Contents

A NOTE ON REFERENCES AND QUOTATIONS

All page references to *Lolita* are given in brackets in the text of the Guide,
unless otherwise stated. Full details of the particular edition used by the
critic will be given in the first reference to appear in the endnotes.

In any quotation, a row of three dots indicates an editorial ellipsis within
a sentence or paragraph. A row of six dots indicates an editorial omission
of one or more paragraphs, or of a paragraph break or section break.

INTRODUCTION

'My Poor Lolita is Having a Rough Time': Creating Nabokov's *Lolita*

■ Q: This may be like asking a father to publicly declare which of his children is most loved, but do you have one novel towards which you feel the most affection, which you esteem over all others?

A: The most affection, *Lolita*; the greatest esteem, *Priglashenie na Kazn* [*Invitation to a Beheading*].[1] □

On 31 December 1956, Vladimir Nabokov wrote to Graham Greene in England, thanking him for his kind attentions to *Lolita*, and expressing concern about 'her' treatment in France and England.

■ My poor Lolita is having a rough time. The pity is that if I had made her a boy, or a cow, or a bicycle, Philistines might never have flinched. On the other hand, Olympia Press informs me that amateurs (amateurs!) are disappointed with the tame turn my story takes in the second volume, and do not buy it. I have been sent copies of the article, in which, about a year ago, a Mr. Gordon with your witty assistance made such a fool of himself. It would seem, however, that a clean vulgar mind makes Gordon's wonderfully strong, for my French agent tells me that the book (the English original) is now banned by governmental decree in France. She says: 'La réponse de James Gordon [*sic*] à l'article de M. Graham Greene a indigné certains puritains et . . . c'est le Gouvernement anglais qui a demandé au Ministre de l'Intérieur (of France) de prendre cette décision'.

This is an extraordinary situation. I could patter on like this till next year . . .[2] □

Clearly not one of Vladimir Nabokov's 'Philistine' readers, Graham Greene discovered for himself the literary values of the fiction between the notorious green covers of the Travellers Companion series, and named *Lolita* in the *Sunday Times* as one of the best books of 1955. In response to this open praise, John Gordon, the chief editor of the *Sunday Express*, attacked the book as 'sheer unrestrained pornography',[3] reviling it as 'about the filthiest book I've ever read'.[4] This public 'exchange' between Greene and Gordon was instrumental in respective campaigns to publish and to ban the book in England. In reply to Nabokov's best wishes, Greene confirmed that he was trying all out to get the book published, declaring boldly that 'in England one may go to prison, but there couldn't be a better cause!'.[5]

This brief correspondence in 1956 between Nabokov (Russian emigré, American academic, lepidopterist, translator and writer) and Graham Greene (British writer and critic) about a book unofficially 'banned' in Britain and America for want of publishers, and at the point of having English-language editions banned in France, is fascinating for a number of reasons. In the first place it registers the difficulties of publication, circulation and reception encountered by Nabokov between 1954 when publishers in America first turned down the manuscript and 1959 when *Lolita* was finally published by Weidenfeld and Nicolson in England. In the second place, Nabokov's letter articulates some of the dramatic, indeed melodramatic, terms in which disputes and debates about *Lolita* are conducted throughout the period. Is it literature or is it pornography? Is is morally uplifting or is it obscene? What is it about the novel that prompts these questions? Should it be banned? Lastly, the letter draws attention to some of the more complicated aspects of the critical response in regard to the character of Lolita, and to the ways in which a girl might be connected to the idea of cultural value that generates the public feud about 'filth' and fine writing.

In the exchange of letters, 'poor' Lolita passes between the devotions of Nabokov the author and Greene the reader in the name of literary virtue. However, while Greene is declaring his allegiance to the cause of '*Lollita*' [sic] and voicing the legal risks involved in trying to publish and circulate the book, Nabokov is lamenting the girl. 'The pity is that if I had made her a boy, or a cow, or a bicycle, Philistines might never have flinched.' In passing, we might note the surrealism in this naming of alternative object choices for H.H., the pseudonymous narrator of the fictional memoir, but the important point for Nabokov is that 'Philistines' cannot see beyond the fact of the girl Lolita. The connection between the girl and the book, which is explicit in Nabokov's letter to Greene, tends to disappear as a self-conscious concern once the critical response to *Lolita* starts to get established.

Although *Lolita* was banned three times in France, the novel was never 'officially' brought to trial. In place of *Lolita*, D.H. Lawrence's *Lady Chatterley's Lover* was selected as the test case in British law (1960).[6]

Throughout the course of the Chatterley trial, questions about the meaning of sex and the representation of sex in literature were much debated. The (literal) charges of obscenity were contested by literary counterclaims of artistic integrity and moral seriousness. Historically, novels have variously and scandalously challenged contemporary ideas of morals (from Flaubert's *Madame Bovary* and the idea of adultery in nineteenth-century France, to Radclyffe Hall's *The Well of Loneliness* and the unimaginable idea of lesbian love in early twentieth-century England). What is so notable about *Lolita* in comparison with *Lady Chatterley's Lover* is that it is still enmeshed in controversial debates about the literary representation of sexual acts and desires. The comparison between the two novels draws attention to the difference between the public response to the notion of adultery as consensual adult sex, and the idea of adult–child sex. One of the reasons *Lolita* remains a provocative text is that the subject of child sexuality and adult sexual interest in children continues to matter. Unlike adultery, the idea of adult–child sex retains a certain power to shock. In the 1950s Lionel Trilling suggested that the general response to the subject is 'visceral'. There may still be truth in that remark.

In the first instance, the question prompted by the manuscript of *Lolita* was deceptively simple. Is it literature or is it pornography? Deceptively simple because decisions and indecisions about the provenance of the narrative, the intentions of the author, the imagined desires of potential readers, as well as the possibility of legal charges, determined the publishing history of the book between 1955 and 1959. In different ways, *Lolita* has continued to court controversy since the initial publication in Paris by Olympia Press in September 1955. In a recent essay, Annette Michelson claims that 'the master no doubt spins furiously in his grave' to know that a 'Lolita' is now 'the generic, vulgate term for an item of what is known as child pornography'.[7] Vladimir Nabokov's twelfth and most famous novel made its appearance between the green covers of the Travellers Companion series, on a list that included *The Sexual Life of Robinson Crusoe*. The imprint was notorious for its erotic and sexually explicit subjects. Throughout his life Nabokov was vigilant concerning what was written about him and his work, and in 1959 he wrote to *Life International* correcting 'two little errors' in a recent issue:

■ And on p. 68 I am described as being 'startled . . . and indignant' when my Parisian agent informed me that the Olympia Press wanted 'to add *Lolita* to its list': I certainly was neither 'startled' nor 'indignant' since I was only interested in having the book published – no matter by whom.[8] □

In suggesting that the publishing connection was a matter of expediency since *Lolita* had nothing in common with erotica and pornography other than appearing together in a list of titles, Nabokov expresses a supreme confidence in the literary value of *Lolita* that was not entirely shared. The book raised difficult questions about the representation of sex and desire in fiction, and since it shaded the distinctions between the sexual fictions of literature and pornography, *Lolita* troubled, delighted and frustrated readers and critics alike, many of whom were not sure what they were reading. Andrew Field, one of Nabokov's literary biographers, is not alone in suggesting that as a Travellers Companion, *Lolita* was not pornographic enough. It was 'probably the most chaste book ever published by Olympia'.[9] In the introduction to *The Annotated 'Lolita'* (1970), the American critic Alfred Appel Jr, a former student of Nabokov's at Cornell, supplies an anecdote to illustrate what he refers to as the 'Instant Pornography Test'. Appel 'found *Lolita*' in a Left Bank bookstore on tour with the army in France. At the base 'the dirty book' was read aloud: '"Lo . . . lita, light . . . of my life, fire of my . . . loins. My sin, my soul . . . Lo-lee-ta: The . . . tip of the . . . tongue . . . taking . . . a trip . . ." – "Damn!" yelled Stockade, throwing the book against the wall. "It's God-damn Litachure!!"'.[10]

The early months of *Lolita*'s publication in France were fairly quiet, and the book was finding its way to England and America in the pockets of literary critics. In the following extract from Appel's introduction to *The Annotated 'Lolita'* he swiftly summarises events leading up to the American publication.

■ . . . But in the winter of 1956 Graham Greene in England recommended *Lolita* as one of the best books of 1955, incurring the immediate wrath of a columnist in the *Sunday Express*, which moved Greene to respond in the *Spectator*. Under the heading of 'Albion' (suggesting a quaint tempest in an old teapot), *The New York Times Book Review* of February 26, 1956, alluded briefly to this exchange, calling *Lolita* 'a long French novel' and not mentioning Nabokov by name. Two weeks later, noting 'that our mention of it created a flurry of mail', *The Times* devoted two-thirds of a column to the subject, quoting Greene at some length. Thus began the underground existence of *Lolita*, which became public in the summer of 1957 when the *Anchor Review* in New York devoted 112 of its pages to Nabokov.[11] □

This is a familiar and not inaccurate version of the rise of *Lolita*, and Appel is right, I think, to see Graham Greene's public sponsoring of the book in England as pivotal to understanding the events leading up to the astonishing success of *Lolita* in America. However, it does seem to leave out Nabokov's intensive efforts to promote the book as a literary cause. Nabokov's correspondence throughout the period (1955–8) testifies to the arduous business of extricating *Lolita* from the unsatisfactory contractual arrangements with Maurice Girodias of Olympia Press, and negotiating with potential publishers in America. On 14 December 1956, for instance, a few weeks before the letter to Greene, Nabokov wrote to Girodias:

■ You and I understand perfectly well that *Lolita* is not the kind of book that should appeal to the kind of people you euphemistically call 'amateurs'. In fact, my friends here are waging an intensive campaign to establish the book as a literary achievement of artistic value and lasting importance, and to counteract the unfortunate publicity it received at the outset. Only after this has been achieved can one hope to have *Lolita* published in this country.[12] □

The American success of *Lolita*, which eventually removes the novel from the original taint of obscenity and pornography, is not simply a question therefore of spontaneous literary recognition. It is also to do with the careful garnering of substantial critical support. Implicit in this letter is the circular sense that the right critical conditions must be created in advance of the right critical recognition. Influential criticism in the 1950s from Lionel Trilling, Fred Dupee and Kingsley Amis is relevant here not only for its important contribution to interpretations of *Lolita*. It also demonstrates the ways in which 'literature' is created and recreated by critical decisions about what 'literature' can be and how we will recognise it. In the same letter to Girodias, Nabokov discusses the selections from *Lolita* that are to appear in the *Anchor Review* in June 1957: 'These excerpts will be accompanied by a wonderful article written by a well-known literary critic, F. Dupee, who thinks very highly of *Lolita*. On my part, I am contributing to the same issue . . . an essay explaining the author's point of view'. The essay specially written for the *Anchor Review* issue is 'On a Book Entitled *Lolita*'. This will later be reprinted as the Afterword to *Lolita* in future publications of the book.

It was several years before Nabokov was able to place the novel with a British publisher, but *Lolita* was finally published in America by Putnam's in August 1958. The American edition of *Lolita* was launched with a lavish display of critical approvals and authoritative literary claims. These credentials represent the strong support Nabokov received in anticipation of the successful American publication of the novel. This really was an immediate success. Walter Minton of Putnam's sent Nabokov the following telegram on 18 August:

■ EVERYBODY TALKING OF *LOLITA* ON PUBLICATION DAY YESTERDAYS REVIEWS MAGNIFICENT AND NEW YORK TIMES BLAST THIS MORNING PROVIDED NECESSARY FUEL TO FLAME

300 REORDERS THIS MORNING AND BOOK STORES REPORT
EXCELLENT DEMAND CONGRATULATIONS ON PUBLICATION
DAY[13] □

The status of the text as literature was assured, and *Lolita* remained at the
top of the best-seller lists for six months until displaced by Boris
Pasternak's *Dr Zhivago* (a book famously disliked by Nabokov). The widespread success of *Lolita* certainly secured the novel from official charges
of pornography and obscenity, and gave Nabokov the financial security
to devote his time to writing, but critical controversy about the meaning
of the content was not abated, it was just beginning.

Literary criticism of *Lolita* turns on the problem of how to respond
'seriously' to the ostensibly 'ironic', sometimes 'comic', and often 'tragic'
representation of a man's sexual obsession with an adolescent girl: the
problem that had marked the novel out as dubious in the first place.
Furthermore, since the novel generates a debate about the relationship
between aesthetic form and sexual content, in terms of *Lolita*'s moral
value there is an implicit demand that critics declare their allegiances.
The problem of where critics place themselves in relation to the question
of morality and art is central to the unfolding of the critical history of
Lolita. Frederick Whiting's incisive and informative discussion of the
social, sexual and critical context of *Lolita*'s American success (1998) sees
this as related also to the confessional form of the narrative itself: 'professional critics and casual readers alike felt compelled not only to reveal
where they stood with respect to Humbert and his strange desire but to
deliver as well their own literary loyalty oaths and pledges of aesthetic
allegiance'.[14]

When the idea of artistic form is in the ascendent and aesthetic practice is the focus of attention, as in the period of literary criticism into
which *Lolita* issues forth, the content is more readily disposed of. Indeed,
it is argued by many critical commentators, most forcefully Whiting
(1998), that the apparent disposal of the social content in literary criticism
is a measure of the effect of political anxieties and concerns in the post-
war, cold-war period of 1950s America. 'At one extreme is a quite
remarkable sort of critical repression that leads not only to a denial of
any effective linkage between art and political anxiety but to a denial of
the political anxiety itself.'[15] Looking back at *Lolita* criticism of the 1950s
and 1960s the critical scene cannot be neatly formalised. Formalism itself
risks becoming an overdetermined description of a practice that is variable and contradictory, as can be seen particularly in chapter one of this
Guide. It is fair to say, for example, that Lionel Trilling, the influential
American critic of *Lolita* in the 1950s, pays considerable attention to the
formal features of romantic parody and the literary invocations of courtly
love: an attention that allows him to pass lightly over the question of

what happens to the girl. At the same time, Trilling also offers a sharply drawn critique of the eroticisation of little girls in mid-twentieth-century American culture, which anticipates later feminist concerns with the social construction of femininity and gender roles. For Whiting, the problem with formalist criticism is the way in which it serves as a distraction from what is 'really' at stake in the text. His interpretation of *Lolita* represents the shift in emphasis that appears in *Lolita* criticism from around the 1980s, broadly from the aesthetics of literary form to the politics of literary representation. But one of the abiding fascinations of *Lolita* criticism is the way in which any attempt to map out shifts, trends and tendencies is disturbed by contradictions that create surprising affiliations over time.

The early chapters of this Guide reveal a struggle to resolve certain questions about the relation between the aesthetics of literary form and the 'reality' of an unacceptable content. What we start to see from the beginning of the 1980s is a sense that the attempt to resolve the question is itself a problem. Now refigured in terms of a relation between the ethics of literature, and the ethics of human relations, the old opposition between morality and art starts to undergo a transformation. In part this can be attributed to the status of *Lolita* as a canonical literary text. In the terms of academic institutions and the discourses of literary criticism, *Lolita* is clearly here to stay. Given this security, the 'unacceptable' content of the novel need no longer be defended up to the hilt. Thus, attention to the content and the representations of *Lolita* starts to make its presence felt. The feeling now is that difficult questions can be asked about what happens to the girl in the text (and the book will still be literature). The return to the question of ethics in the 1980s is prompted in part by the sense that readers and critics alike have been seduced by the literary persuasions of H. H., a perversely ambiguous narrator.

It is self-evident that all texts are subject to further interpretations and new readings. In this sense the response to *Lolita*, like the response to any other canonical text, is also a charting of the history of developments in literary criticism; from the residual formalisms of American New Criticism, to the broader humanist concerns of New York Intellectuals, to the influence of psychoanalysis, feminism, semiotics, and deconstructive criticism. If there are defining moments in the critical histories of canonical texts, there can be no definitive readings. In this light, *Lolita* moves into a new century as an exemplary text in debates about the literary representation of sexual acts and desires, the politics of literary criticism, and the ethics of reading.

Finally, a word about origins. In the Afterword to *Lolita*, Nabokov refers to the 'initial shiver of inspiration' he experienced in relation to a 'newspaper story about an ape in the Jardin des Plantes' which resulted in *Volshebnik*.[16] *Volshebnik* was written in Russian when Nabokov was living in Paris in 1939. Considering the story 'a dead scrap', and on the point of leaving France with his wife Vera and their young son Dmitri to live in America, he thought to destroy it.[17] However, the manuscript turned up in 1959, at which time Nabokov reappraised it as 'a beautiful piece of Russian prose' and gave it an English title, *The Enchanter*. Nothing came of the idea to publish it as a 'very limited edition' with Putnam's and once again the manuscript was put aside. After Nabokov's death in Switzerland in 1977, *The Enchanter* was rediscovered amongst a shipment of belongings from America. It was translated into English by the author's son, Dmitri Nabokov, and eventually published by Picador in 1986. Echoing Nabokov's earliest comment on the work, the novella was alighted upon as 'the first little throb of *Lolita*'.

The fictional scene may have shifted between the novella and the novel, from the barest sketch of a pre-war European city in *The Enchanter* to the elaborate iconography of post-war America in *Lolita*, but the lay-out of desire in the narrative is unmistakeable. How *does* a childless man with a sexual interest in girls of a certain age bring a particular girl within his reach? In the Afterword to *The Enchanter* ('On a Book Entitled *The Enchanter*'), Dmitri Nabokov fervently dismisses the claim that *Lolita* is based on 'Havelock Ellis's transcription, circa 1912, of a Ukrainian pedophile's confessions' (p. 126).[18] Further speculations have led readers to a footnote appended to the poem 'Lilith', originally written in 1928 in Russian and translated for the English-language edition of *Poems and Problems* in 1972.

■ Composed more than forty years ago to amuse a friend, 'Lilith' could not be published in any of the sedate *émigré* periodicals of the time. Its manuscript turned up only recently among my old papers. Intelligent readers will abstain from examining this impersonal fantasy for any links with my later fiction.[19] □

What is most intriguing about this instruction to look no further is that the 'links' between 'Lilith', *Lolita* and *The Enchanter* are plainly there to see. In the event of a critical oversight, the footnote serves as a timely reminder to look again.[20] In one sense this note can be read in the same register as Nabokov's famous contempt for psychoanalysis in general and Freudianism in particular. It functions as an authoritarian warning to readers not to trespass beyond the lines laid down. Looking again at the close thematic relations between the formally different narratives of the poem, novella and novel, which respectively chart a masculine subject's fantasies about sex with a young girl, it is difficult to read Nabokov's pre-scripts and postscripts as anything other than a ruse.[21] The reappearance of 'Lilith', which in common with *The Enchanter* was also lost and found, would seem to proclaim the poem as 'the first little throb of *Lolita*', but it has not created much of a stir. It is *The Enchanter* that is recognised as the (belated) conceptual template for *Lolita*.

Lolita is implicated in a controversial critical history. It is a history that represents changing attitudes towards the idea of literary texts and the ways in which literature might also be a touchstone for ethical concerns and critical responsibilities. Questions about how far criticism can go with a text are complicated in the case of *Lolita* by how far the text can go with its subject – before it is no longer literature.

CHAPTER ONE

'The Weird Shapes of Sexuality that *Lolita* Assumes': Art and Morality, Literature and Life; The Making of *Lolita* in the 1950s

*L*OLITA COMES into the world as a book that challenges the idea not only of what literature is, but what literature can be about in the 1950s. Since the idea of literature involves notions of distinction in both writing and reading, it is self-evident that *Lolita* is what readers and reading have made of it. In his invaluable introduction to *Nabokov: The Critical Heritage*, Norman Page emphasises the diversity of contemporary responses to the novel: '*Lolita* is a complex work which presented different faces to different readers; and reviewers naturally varied considerably in the emphasis they placed on various elements – on the novel as a love story, a parody, a psychological study of obsessional behaviour, an evocation of certain aspects of American life, a book that makes for morality or immorality – as well as in their judgement of its success or failure, its pretensions and achievements'.[1] Trying to make a selection from the overwhelming number of contemporary reviews, articles, correspondence in the press, as well as letters, is also complicated by the contemporary time span of the publication history of *Lolita*, which travels for five years in a circuitous route between America, France and Britain before finally coming home to rest.

In 1967, Jackson R. Bryer, and Thomas J. Bergin, Jr, published a bibliography of Nabokov criticism for a special issue of *Wisconsin Studies* that was devoted to the author's work. Alfred Appel's influential article on 'Parody', which is discussed in the following chapter, also appeared in this important issue. For Bryer and Bergin, the response to Nabokov's work in the 1950s is marred by the massive attention paid to *Lolita* that effectively isolates the novel from the full range of his literary output.

What is fascinating about this brief discussion of *Lolita* included in the essay 'Vladimir Nabokov's Critical Reputation in English: A Note and a Checklist' is the way in which Nabokov studies can be seen to construct an extremely selective critical canon of contemporary writing at a key moment of retrospection in the 1960s. The vast majority of the reviews on *Lolita* are simply dismissed as worthless.

■ But by far the single most notable – and deplorable – characteristic of Nabokov criticism is the disproportionate amount of attention devoted to *Lolita* and the resultant lack of serious comment on the other fiction, poetry, and translations. Vladimir Nabokov is the author in English of eleven novels, two collections of short stories, a volume of poetry, a play, and two translations, one of which, a four-volume edition of *Eugene Onegin*, he calls 'the great work of my life'. Yet, aside from book reviews, well over two-thirds of the criticism prompted by his work deals with *Lolita*, which very few serious critics consider his most significant book. Further, a good deal of this comment on *Lolita* can at best be described as quasi-literary, dealing as it does with the question of whether the novel is pornographic or not.

To be sure, important essays and reviews on *Lolita* are in print. F. W. Dupee's famous 'Preface' to the first appearance of the work in a 1957 issue of the *Anchor Review* and Lionel Trilling's 'The Last Lover' (*Griffin*, August 1958) certainly rank with the best of Nabokov criticism to date; while reviews by John Hollander (*Partisan Review*, Fall 1956), Kingsley Amis (*The Spectator*, November 6, 1959), Howard Nemerov (*Kenyon Review*, Spring 1957), Richard Schickel (*The Reporter*, November 28, 1957 and *The Progressive*, November 1958), and Rebecca West (London *Sunday Times*, November 8, 1959) are of much greater value than all but a very few of the critical essays published.

The last situation, as suggested earlier, is one of the several peculiar aspects of Nabokov criticism: most of the serious and incisive commentary has appeared in the form of book reviews. Given this fact, it is not surprising that Richard Kostelanetz, when faced with the task of selecting three pieces on Nabokov for his 1964 anthology *On Contemporary Literature* chose to do a short essay himself rather than choose any of the articles then available to him. As Kostelanetz must have discovered very quickly, there is a great dearth of worthwhile critical essays on Nabokov . . .[2] □

The significance of this extract is threefold. First of all, it can be seen how the field of Nabokov studies is attempting to 'contain' *Lolita*, a single book that is getting too much of the wrong sort of attention. Secondly, there is a revisionist history at work here in the identification of *Lolita*'s first appearance in *Anchor Review*. To be sure, this is the first public glimpse of the book in America, but the first publication of the book in Paris with Olympia Press seems to have been effectively displaced for the moment. This is linked to the third point, which is the attempt to distance the book from 'quasi-literary' commentaries that raise the spectral question of pornography. There is an assumption in the 1950s, which also extends into the 1970s, that the subject of pornography has no bearing on the discussion of literature. Literature is seen as a quality of writing (and reading) which is already there. What is then so fascinating about *Lolita* is the ways in which the contemporary reception demonstrates the very process through which a text is created as literature.

More than thirty years on from Bryer and Bergin's complaint, there is a wealth of 'serious' and 'worthwhile' critical writing on *Lolita*. Dearth is no longer a word that could be used to describe this substantial body of work. But in regard to what is worthwhile in the 1950s and what has continued to be essential, one would have to agree with the bibliographers' limited selection. Hence this chapter will largely focus on extracts from the reviews by Trilling, Dupee and Amis. Amis is a fascinating figure in this context. He is often cited as a kind of maverick voice in the canon. Indeed, it is worth noting that his is the one dissenting voice that receives 'serious' critical credence, when others are treated as no more than charming curiosities. Alfred Appel, for example, in his introduction to *The Annotated 'Lolita'* (1970) automatically removes 1950s dissenters from the category of literary history into social history.

■ Although [*Lolita*] never ran afoul of the law in this country, there were predictably some outraged protests, including an editorial in *The New Republic*; but, since these at best belong to the social rather than literary history, they need not be detailed here, with one exception. Orville Prescott's review in the daily *New York Times* of August 18, 1958, has a charm that should be preserved: '*Lolita*, then, is undeniably news in the world of books. Unfortunately, it is bad news. There are two equally serious reasons why it isn't worth any adult reader's attention. The first is that it is dull, dull, dull in a pretentious, florid and archly fatuous fashion. The second is that it is repulsive'.[3] □

There is much more to Amis's critique of the novel than Prescott's. Amis gives a strong indication of the differences between prevailing literary discourses in Britain and America at the time. His reading is also remarkable for revealing the ways in which emergent concerns about the content of the novel in relation to aesthetics have not only made their presence felt in different ways but reappear over time in various forms. I will return towards the end of the chapter to the extract from Amis. For now let us continue with the American context. In 1958 *Lolita* finally secured a contract with the American publisher Putnam's. The homecoming success of the book immediately guaranteed its standing in the interests of literature.

Lionel Trilling's review article, 'The Last Lover: Vladimir Nabokov's *Lolita*', first appeared in *Griffin* (August 1958), was reprinted in *Encounter* (October 1958) and is the longest of the selected reviews in *Nabokov: The Critical Heritage* (1982). It is not only one of the most influential commentaries of the 1950s, it also continues to make its presence felt as a starting point for investigations into the critical history of the novel. The significance of Trilling's reading as something still to be reckoned with can be seen most strikingly in Linda Kauffman's extensive feminist reading of the sexual politics of literary criticism of *Lolita* in the 1980s (see chapter four), and Frederick Whiting's impressive study of the cold-war cultural context of the reception of *Lolita* in the 1990s (see chapter five). Whiting sees Trilling as a crucial figure not only for what he has to say about Lolita, but for the confessional mode in which he says it.

Trilling was a leading American critic who spent most of his academic career at Columbia University, and his books include *The Liberal Imagination* (1950). Trilling's approach to literature belongs to a critical formation that can be broadly described as humanist and historical. Trilling, Edmund Wilson, Alfred Kazin and a number of other eminent male critics tend to be grouped as the New York Intellectuals. In regard to the place of Trilling in *Lolita* criticism, it is important to note the concerns of this 'group' of critics with what M. H. Abrams describes as 'the moral and imaginative qualities [of the work] and its consequences for society'.[4] Bearing this in mind, let us now turn to the first extract from Trilling's article, in which he deliberates on the story of *Lolita* and the ways in which it challenges cultural understandings of sexuality and sexual relations.

■ . . . In a tone which is calculatedly not serious, [*Lolita*] makes a prolonged assault on one of our unquestioned and unquestionable sexual prohibitions, the sexual inviolability of girls of a certain age (and compounds the impiousness with what amounts to incest).

It is all very well for us to remember that Juliet was fourteen when she was betrothed to Paris, and gave herself, with our full approval, to Romeo. It is all very well for us to find a wry idyllic charm in the story of the Aged David and the little maid Abishag. And to gravely receive Dante's account of Beatrice. And to say that distant cultures – H. H. gives a list of them to put his idiosyncrasy in some moral perspective – and hot climates make a difference in ideas of the right age for female sexuality to begin. All very well for us to have long ago got over our first horror at what Freud told us about the sexuality of children; and to receive blandly what he has told us about the 'family romance' and its part in the dynamics of the psyche. All very well for the family and society to take approving note of the little girl's developing sexual charms, to find a sweet comedy in her growing awareness of them and her learning to use them, and for her mother to be open and frank and delighted and ironic over the teacups about the clear signs of the explosive force of her sexual impulse. We have all become so nicely clear-eyed, so sensibly Coming-of-Age-in-Samoa. [A reference to the widespread influence of Margaret Mead's anthropological study, which was first published in 1928. The full title of the work will give a clear indication of the link Trilling is making: *Coming of Age in Samoa: A study of Adolescence and Sex in Primitive Societies*. The book was reprinted for the third time in 1954.[5]] But let an adult male seriously think about the girl as a sexual object and all our sensibility is revolted.

The response is not reasoned but visceral. Within the range of possible heterosexual conduct, this is one of the few prohibitions which still seem to us to be confirmed by nature itself. Virginity once seemed so confirmed, as did the marital fidelity of women, but they do so no longer. No novelist would expect us to respond with any moral intensity to his representing an unmarried girl having a sexual experience, whether in love or curiosity; the infidelity of a wife may perhaps be a little more interesting, but not much. The most serious response the novelist would expect from us is that we should 'understand', which he would count on us to do automatically.

But our response to the situation that Mr. Nabokov presents to us is that of shock. And we find ourselves the more shocked when we realise that, in the course of reading the novel, we have come virtually to condone the violation it presents. Charles Dickens, by no means a naive man, was once required to meet a young woman who had lived for some years with a man out of wedlock; he was dreadfully agitated at the prospect, and when he met the girl he was appalled to discover that he was not confronting a piece of depravity but a principled, attractive young person, virtually a lady. It was a terrible blow to the certitude of his moral feelings. That we may experience the same loss of certitude about the sexual behaviour that *Lolita* describes is perhaps suggested by the tone of my summary of the story – I was plainly not able to muster up the note of moral outrage. And it is likely that any reader of *Lolita* will discover that he comes to see the situation as less and less abstract and moral and horrible, and more and more as human and 'understandable'. Less and less, indeed, do we see a *situation*; what we become aware of is people. Humbert is perfectly willing to say that he is a monster; no doubt he is, but we find ourselves less and less eager to say so. Perhaps his depravity is the easier to accept when we learn that he deals with a Lolita who is not innocent, and who seems to have very few emotions to be violated; and I suppose we naturally incline to be lenient towards a rapist – legally and by intention H.H. is that – who eventually feels a deathless devotion to his victim![6] □

Not surprisingly, this particular aspect of Trilling's defence of H.H. is troubling for modern readers and critics. One of the important aspects of Trilling's contribution to literary criticism and its relation to broader cultural concerns is his engagement with psychoanalysis in general, and Freudian theory in particular. In 1955, the year of *Lolita*'s publication in France, Trilling gave the Freud Anniversary Lecture of the New York Psychoanalytic Society and the New York Psychoanalytic Institute. The title of the paper was 'Freud: Within and Beyond Culture', and one of the topics discussed was Freud's abandonment of the seduction theory.

■ . . . We recall, for instance, that dramatic moment in the development of psychoanalysis when Freud accepted as literally true the stories told him by so many of his early patients, of their having been, as children, sexually seduced or assaulted by adults, often by their own parents. We know how his patients rewarded his credulity – scarcely any of them were telling the truth. They had betrayed Freud into constructing a hypothesis on the basis of their stories. Hypotheses are precious things and this one now had to be abandoned, and so Freud had reason to think very harshly of his patients if he wished to. But he did not blame them, he did not say they were lying – he willingly suspended his disbelief in their fantasies, which they themselves believed, and taught himself how to find the truth that was really in them.[7] □

What crucially connects the Freud lecture with Trilling's defence of H.H. is the rhetorical terms in which the abandonment of the seduction theory is represented. (Freud initially believed that sexuality was introduced from the outside, and that his hysterical patients suffered from real childhood seductions. He later proposed a theory of infantile sexuality and unconscious fantasy. This apparent shift from a theory of violent seduction to the sexual fantasies of women has continued to be controversial, especially for feminist debates about child sexual abuse in the 1970s and 1980s.[8]) Trilling's retelling of the seduction story in the form of a fantasy that turns little girls into betrayers (however unwitting) and Freud into a forgiving, indulgent father has a very clear resonance for the ways in which the idea of 'seduction' comes to be popularised and understood in 1950s America. It also has a particular bearing on what Michael Wood will later describe (in the 1990s, see chapter five of this Guide) as the 'lazy tolerance' of early critics of *Lolita* in response to H.H.'s 'seduction' of Lolita. Let us now return to Trilling's discussion of the conflict between the representation of violation in the novel, and the narrative sway of obsessive passion.

■ But we have only to let the immediate influence of the book diminish a little with time, we have only to free ourselves from the rationalising effect of H.H.'s obsessive passion, we have only to move back into the real world where twelve-year-olds are being bored by Social Studies and plagued by orthodonture, to feel again the outrage at the violation of the sexual prohibition. And to feel this the more because we have been seduced into conniving in the violation, because we have permitted our fantasies to accept what we know to be revolting.

What, we must ask, is Mr. Nabokov's purpose in making this occasion for outrage?

I have indicated that his purpose cannot be explained by any interest in the 'psychological' aspects of the story; he has none whatever. His novel is as far as possible from being a 'study of' the emotions it presents. The malice which H.H. bears to psychiatry is quite Mr. Nabokov's own; for author, as for character, psychiatric concepts are merely occasions for naughty irreverence. Psychiatry and the world may join in giving scientific or ugly names to Humbert's sexual idiosyncrasy; the novel treats of it as a condition of love like another. [Trilling is not alone in arguing for a reading of the obsession for Lolita as symptomatic of obsessive love *per se*. In the 1990s, both Michael Wood and Rachel Bowlby evoke similar suggestions; see chapter five of this Guide.]

And we can be sure that Mr. Nabokov has not committed himself to moral subversion. He is not concerned to bring about a sexual revolution which will make paedophilia a rational and respectable form of heterosexuality. Humbert's 'ferocity and jocularity', what we might call his moral facetiousness reaching the point of anarchic silliness, make the pervasive tone of the narrative, and that tone does have its curious influence upon us, as does the absoluteness of Humbert's passional obsession. Yet any anarchic power to which we may respond in the novel is quite negated when, near the end of the history, H.H. reflects, in a tone never used before, on the havoc he has made of Lolita's life.

It is of course possible that Mr. Nabokov wanted to shock us merely for shocking's sake, that he had in mind the intention of what might be called general satire, the purpose of which is to make us uneasy with ourselves, less sure of our moral simplicity than we have been: this he brings about by contriving the effect I have described, of leading us to become quite at ease with a sexual situation that should outrage us and then facing us with our facilely-given acquiescence.

And then of course Mr. Nabokov may be intending a more particular satire, upon the peculiar sexual hypocrisy of American life. I have in mind the perpetual publicity we give to sexuality, the unending invitation made by our popular art and advertising to sexual awareness, competence, and competition. To what end is a girl-child taught from her earliest years to consider her brightness and fragrance of her hair, and the shape of her body, and her look of readiness for adventure? Why, what other end than that she shall some day be a really capable air-line hostess? Or, that she shall have the shining self-respect which, as we know, underlies all true virtue and efficiency? Or that her husband and her children shall not be ashamed of her, but on the contrary, proud to claim her as their own? So say the head-mistresses, the principals, the deans of women, the parents. But in every other culture that Mr. Nabokov is aware of, which is a good many, the arts of the boudoir were understood to point to the bed, and if they were taught early, they were understood to point to the bed early. [Trilling is offering here what amounts to a formidable critique of the eroticisation of little girls in American culture, with the family as a significant site of collusion in the process. The terms of this criticism of the construction of femininity seem to anticipate Betty Friedan's worries in *The Feminine Mystique* (1963) about what girls in the 1950s were being trained for.[9]]

But I think that the real reason why Mr. Nabokov chose his outrageous subject matter is that he wanted to write a story about love. [The following space, which appears in the original text, gives the sense of an important section break.]

Lolita is about love. Perhaps I shall be better understood if I put the statement in this form: *Lolita* is not about sex, but about love. Almost every page sets forth some explicit erotic action and still it is not about sex. It is about love.

This makes it unique in my experience of contemporary novels. If our fiction gives accurate testimony, love has disappeared from the western world, just as Denis de Rougemont said it should. The contemporary novel can tell us about sex, and about sexual communion, and about mutuality, and about the strong fine relationships that grow up between men and women; and it can tell us about marriage. But about love, which was once one of its chief preoccupations, it can tell us nothing at all.

My having mentioned Denis de Rougemont and his curious, belated, supererogatory onslaught on love will indicate that I have in mind what I seem to remember he calls passion-love, a kind of love with which European literature has dealt since time immemorial but with especial intensity since the Arthurian romance and the code of courtly love. ['Supererogatory' means 'pay in addition'. Given the rather derogatory manner in which Trilling summons up de Rougemont's account of myths of love in the western world, I think we may take supererogatory to mean 'excessive'. There is an extract from de Rougemont in the following chapter, and a discussion of the insights of de Rougemont's analysis of parody in relation to love and *Lolita*.] **Passion-love was a mode of feeling not available to everyone – the authorities on the subject restricted it to the aristocracy – but it was always of the greatest interest to almost everyone who was at all interested in the feelings, and it had a continuing influence on other kinds of love and on the literary conventions through which love was represented.**[10] □

After outlining the significance of passion-love in western culture, and the way in which it could exist 'only apart from and more or less in opposition to marriage', Trilling goes on to elaborate the argument that 'one of the most interesting and important of cultural revisions was when the middle-classes assimilated the idea of passion-love to marriage'. The following extract takes up the argument at the point at which Trilling starts to make the connections between *Lolita* and the older literary conventions of passion-love in which 'lovers were conceived of much as we conceive of the artist'.

■ If a novelist wanted, for whatever strange reason, to write a novel about the old kind of love, how would he go about it? How would he find or contrive the elements that make love possible?

For example, if love requires scandal, what could the novelist count on to constitute a scandal? Surely not – as I have already suggested – adultery. The very word is archaic; we recognise the possibility of its use only in law or in the past. Marital infidelity is not thought as necessarily destructive of marriage, and, indeed, the word *unfaithful*, which once had so terrible a charge of meaning, begins to sound quaint, seeming to be inappropriate to our modern code . . . A contemporary writer would not be able to interest us in a situation like Othello's because, even if he had proof in his own experience of the actuality of jealousy, he could not give intellectual credence, or expect his readers to give it, to an emotion which in Shakespeare was visceral, unquestionable, of absolute authority.

But the breaking of the taboo about the sexual unavailability of very young girls has for us something of the force that a wife's infidelity had for Shakespeare. H.H.'s relation with Lolita defies society as scandalously as did Tristan's relation with Iseult, or Vronsky's with Anna. It puts the lovers, as lovers in literature must be put, beyond the pale of society.

Then the novelist, if he is to maintain the right conditions for a story of passion-love, must see to it that his lovers do not approach the condition of marriage. That is, their behaviour to each other must not be touched by practicality, their virtues must not be of a kind that acknowledges the claims of the world. As soon as mutuality comes in, and common interests, and co-operation, and tolerance, and a concern for each other's welfare or prestige in the world, the ethos of the family, or marriage, has asserted itself and they lose the status of lovers. Their behaviour to each other must be precisely not what we call 'mature' – they must see each other and the world with the imperious absolutism of children. So that a man in the grip of an obsessional lust and a girl of twelve make the ideal couple for a story about love written in our time. At least at the beginning of his love for Lolita there are no practical moral considerations, no practical personal considerations, that qualify H. H.'s behaviour. As for Lolita, there is no possibility of her bringing the relation close to the condition of marriage because she cannot even imagine the female rôle in marriage. She remains perpetually the cruel mistress; even after her lover has won physical possession of her, she withholds the favour of her feeling, for she has none to give, by reason of her age, possibly by reason of her temperament.

Then the novelist must pay due attention to making the lover's obsession believable and not ridiculous. Nowadays we find it difficult to give credence to the idea that a man might feel that his reason and his very life depended on the response to him of a particular woman . . . But our doubts are allayed if the obsession can be accounted for by the known fact of a sexual peculiarity, an avowed aberration. Pathology naturalises the strange particularity of the lover's preference.

I may seem to have been talking about *Lolita* as if in writing it Mr. Nabokov had undertaken a job of emotional archaeology. This may not be quite fair to Mr. Nabokov's whole intention, but it does suggest how regressive a book *Lolita* is, how, although it strikes all the most approved modern postures and attitudes, it is concerned to restore a foregone mode of feeling. And in nothing is *Lolita* so archaic as in its way of imaging the beloved. We with our modern latitude in these matters are likely to be amused by the minor details of his mistress's person that caught the lover's fancy in the novels of the 19th century – the expressiveness of the eyes, a certain kind of glance, a foot, an ankle, a wrist, an ear, a ringlet; with our modern reader's knowledge of the size and shape of the heroine's breasts, thighs, belly, and buttocks, these seem trifling and beside the point. Yet the interest in the not immediately erotic details of the female person was not forced on the lover or the novelist by narrow conventions; rather, it was an aspect of the fetishism which seems to attend passion-love, a sort of synecdoche of desire, in which the part stands for the whole, and even the glove or scarf of the beloved has an erotic value. [In the 1990s several critics take up this notion of fetishism, in particular Elisabeth Bronfen who views it in more violent terms than Trilling.] This is the mode of H. H.'s adoration of Lolita, and against the background of his sexual greed, which he calls 'ape-like', it comes over us as another reason for being shocked, that in recent fiction no lover has thought of his beloved with so much tenderness, that no woman has been so charmingly evoked, in such grace and delicacy, as Lolita; the description of her tennis game, in which even her racket has an erotic charm, is one of the few examples of rapture in modern writing.

It seems to me that it is impossible to miss the *parti pris* in Mr. Nabokov's archaeological undertaking, the impulse to mock and discredit all forms of progressive rationalism not only because they are stupid in themselves but because they have brought the madness of love to an end. But Mr. Nabokov is not partisan to the point of being dishonest about the true nature of love. It is H.H., that mixture of ferocity and jocularity, who reminds us that 'Love seeketh only self to please . . . And builds a Hell in Heaven's despite'. The passages in which Humbert gives voice to this judgment [*sic*] are not as well done as one might wish; they stand in an awkward relation to the tone and device of the book. Yet perhaps for this very reason they are the more startling and impressive (if we do not read them in a mood which makes them seem to verge on the maudlin).

And in the end H.H. succumbs, and happily, to the dialectic of the history of love. I have represented passion-love as being the antithesis of marriage and as coming to an end when the conditions characteristic of marriage impose themselves, by whatever means, upon the lovers. Yet it is always to marriage that passion-love aspires, unique marriage, ideal marriage, marriage available to no other pair, but marriage nonetheless, with all the cramping vows and habitualness of marriage. And it is just this that H.H. eventually desires. Mr. Nabokov is, among his other accomplishments, an eminent entomologist and I shall leave it to some really rigorous close reader of fiction to tell us what an entomological novelist wants us to do with the fact that *nymph* is the name for the young of an insect without complete metamorphosis. Probably nothing. But he is also a scholar of languages and he knows that *nymph* is the Greek word for *bride*.[11] □

Trilling seems to forget the radical disjunction between Lolita and H.H. here: a forgetting that allows him to focus on H.H.'s narrative of desire and loss. By assimilating the two characters with Anna and Vronsky, and Tristan and Iseult, he elides the very specific differences between these sets of couples. It is precisely in the attempt to recover such 'parodic' differences that Denis de Rougement's intervention into *Lolita* criticism makes its mark. Trilling risks making Lolita and H.H. into star-crossed lovers: risks forgetting that they are lovers technically, but not in any of the senses suggested by the romantic evocations (other than in H.H.'s imagination, and arguably not even then). Trilling ends his analysis by settling for the ambiguity of the novel, concluding that '*Lolita* gives us no chance to settle and sink roots. Perhaps it is the curious moral mobility it urges on us that accounts for its remarkable ability to represent certain aspects of American life'.[12] Admitting ambiguity and mobility is one thing, but there is a paradox here that critics will alight on in the 1980s and 1990s. Trilling's reading relies on the fixing of certain 'realistic' aspects of the text such as Lolita's lack of innocence, and her lack of recognisable emotions. Finally then, Trilling is not entirely uncritical of the novel, pointing to something regressive about the narrative desire for an older version of passion-love.

Concerning the reviews reprinted in *The Critical Heritage*, it is important to note that 'plot summaries' in the longer selections have been edited out. Given the controversial subject matter of *Lolita* the elisions raise a question about the way in which the representation of the plot informs the analysis of the novel. Trilling, for example, later recalls the 'tone' of his summary of the story, and the fact that he was 'plainly not able to muster up the note of moral outrage'.[13] We can retrace this implied absence – a tone of moral outrage that never was. It is there in the original text of the review as it appears in both *Griffin* and *Encounter*. More to the point is that Trilling's confession turns on the very problem of representing the plot: the story of what happens in *Lolita*. As we will see throughout this Guide, critical positions start to turn more or less on the implied question of what happens to Lolita. For Trilling, the story of *Lolita* solicited a moral tone that he could not muster because of the way in which he was seduced by the narrative. His surrender to H.H.'s obsessive narrative of passion-love is contingent on the critical judgement that Lolita 'is not innocent'.

According to H.H., Lolita is not a virgin, and technically she makes the first advance:

■ Frigid gentlewomen of the jury! I had thought that months, perhaps years, would elapse before I dared to reveal myself to Dolores Haze; but by 6 she was wide awake, and by 6.15 we were technically lovers. I am going to tell you something very strange: it was she who seduced me (p. 132).[14] □

Throughout the narrative of *Lolita*, adult versions of childhood and adolescent sexuality are persistently parodied and ironised. But the question of who seduced whom in this scene is not only pivotal to the publishing history and to the critical history, it also challenges cultural understandings of sexual boundaries between adults and children, and in particular the question of what sex and sexuality might be to this adult and this girl. What is notable about H.H.'s recollection of the scene is the way it draws attention to the enactment of Lolita's sexual fantasies as a kind of 'play', a schoolgirl performance of what she knows about sex. If this is a seduction, then it is not in the same register as H.H.'s seduction of her. And it is this difference of context and meaning that problematises the way in which the one term is used to describe what she does to him, and what he does to her, as if those events had an equivalence. As many critics of the novel will later argue, Lolita's prior sexual experience is not assimilable to Humbert's sexual advances. That is, her experiences of summer camp sex with 'Charlie boy', or perhaps 'a little lesbian', do not place her on an equal sexual footing with H.H. The following extract from F.W. Dupee's commentary on the novel, which first appeared as an introduction to selections of *Lolita* in the *Anchor Review*, takes up the question of what happens at the Enchanted Hunters motel.

■ The scene at the Enchanted Hunters, the suburban hotel where Humbert and Lolita finally seduce each other, is one long spasm of comic horror – though now with a different drift from the Charlotte scenes – and Nabokov spares us nothing of Humbert's soft misery and dubious triumph. The famous scene in Proust in which Charlus pays to have himself flogged by personable young men who are only turning an honest penny in the interim of caring for their families and fighting for *la Patrie* – that scene appears heroically comic, almost like some adventure of Falsaff or Don Quixote, compared to the mean ironies that beat upon Humbert Humbert through the long night, while a religious convention is in progress in the hotel, and the corridors creak and toilets groan familiarly, and Lolita refuses to give up her restless spirit to sleep.

Their historic night at the Enchanted Hunters is an initiation into the impostures and discomfitures of the motel-hopping life that awaits them. '"The name", I said coldly [to the room clerk], "is not Humberg, and not Humbug, but Herbert, I mean Humbert, and any room will do, just put in a cot for my little daughter. She is ten and very tired"'. Humbert's guilty fears constantly stalk him. An Inspector at the state line peers suspiciously into the car and says, 'Any honey?' Tires go flat with an accusing plap-plap beneath them. All hostelries seem hostile, whether they are merely called the Kumfy Kabins or are elaborate affairs with notices on the wall that read:

> We wish you to feel at home while here. All equipment was carefully checked upon your arrival. Your license number is on record here. Use hot water sparingly. We reserve the right to eject without notice any objectionable person. Do not throw waste material of ANY kind in the toilet bowl. Thank you. Call again. The Management. P.S. We consider our guests the Finest People in the World.[15]

In the course of this insane journey, Humbert undergoes a reversal of roles and in so doing registers more and more sharply the real horror and the real significance of his partnership with Lolita. He first impersonates her father in order to elude the authorities, but in time he comes to feel more and more like her actual father. Towards the end he begins to reflect on the whole affair in the spirit of a parent who has disappointed his child and been disappointed by her in turn. 'I often noticed that, living as we did, she and I, in a world of total evil, we would become strangely embarrassed whenever I tried to discuss anything she and an older friend, she and a parent, she and a real healthy sweetheart . . . might have discussed . . . She would mail her invulnerability in trite brashness and boredom, whereas I, using for my desperately detached comments an artificial tone of voice that set my own last teeth on edge, provoked my audience to such outbursts of rudeness as made any further conversation impossible, oh, my poor, bruised child'.

Humbert's remorse is more effective for not clothing itself in abstractly moral terms. He feels, not that he has betrayed a 'trust' of the kind that traditionally inheres in parenthood, but that he has horribly let Lolita down as lover, friend, and fellow human being, as well as in his capacity as father. The consequence has been a complete sundering of human relations with her. Lolita herself, we learn at their last meeting, has not been destroyed; indeed she has exhibited the strange capacity of the young to survive the worst abuses (other things being equal). Nor is any forgiveness of him on her part in question at this final meeting. Her career with him, so painfully vivid in his own memory, has for her fallen into place in a world of experience which she views as 'just one gag after another'. If she originally called him Dad in bitter irony, she now calls him Dad in sad earnest. But she doesn't mean anything by it, any real affection, and it's too late anyway. His betrayal, not of a trust but of her, has done its work. For of course he did betray her unspeakably. It did not constitute any justification of Humbert that she was his willing mistress at first and already knew the ropes. On the contrary this only deepened and complicated his guilt. Outright rape would conceivably have counted for less than this queasy collusion, especially considering the orphaned state of Lolita, to whom he was after all her only excuse for a parent.

In all this, the distorting mirrors have been continuously at work, giving back a monstrous picture of what is again, like the grim sexual comedy of the Charlotte episode, a desperately common experience. The perverse partnership of Humbert and Lolita reflects some of the painful comedy of family relations in general. There is, on Lolita's side, the recurrent childhood feeling of being misunderstood, abused, betrayed by one's parents until at last – if one is lucky enough to grow up to that stage – one can accept them as part of the gag that life is, or even love them if one is luckier than Lolita. From Humbert's point of

confuser *plaisant*

view, which is the predominating one, the situation is even more complicated, in fact, quite hopeless. He is the parent who sadly suspects that communication has broken down between himself and his child. Instead of conversation there is only a weary compulsive banter. Mutual trust is replaced by a shameful system of bargains and bribes: the 'normal' man's form of collusion with his child. Desiring an affectionate and willing compliance with his wishes, he is fortunate if he can purchase a temporary docility with gifts of money, clothes, or chocolate sundaes. In his own eyes he becomes a mere purveyor of such material favors, and day after day he pays the too large bills at the endless motels of life. All the time, his suffering over the failure of love in his child is enhanced by his suspicion that it is all his fault. While trying to count up the blessings he has bestowed on her he remembers, as he fears *she* remembers, only his acts of cruelty or indifference. [Emphasis Dupee's.] He attempts now and then to repair the damage, restore communications. But he is quickly rebuffed in some unexpected way which confirms his original fears. '"A penny for your thoughts", I said, and she stretched out her palm at once'. Those inaccessible thoughts, that outstretched palm! Such are the cares of a family man.

Considering the weird shapes of sexuality that *Lolita* assumes, the novel might appear to invite Freudian interpretations of the usual kind. Fathers want to sleep with their daughters, daughters with their fathers. [This is another example of the way in which Freud's seduction theory is evoked as a general term of understanding. The further Freudian gloss might be that daughter's only 'wish' to sleep with their fathers, and, in psychoanalytic terms, wishing does not mean wanting in any straightforward translation.] The reverse of any such intention is the burden of *Lolita*. By parading the theme of incest, with drums and banners, Mr. Nabokov makes it ridicule itself out of existence so far as *Lolita* is concerned; and the same holds for the other evidences of popular Freudianism with which the tale is strewn. *Lolita*, far from being mythic, is anti-mythic in this respect. Mr. Nabokov cultivates the groans and guffaws of the recalcitrant fact, the embarrassment that yields to neither myth nor clinic, the bitter commonplaces of life's indestructible surface.

To say this, however, is to take *Lolita* at its best. The novel has its less than superlative moments, when the ribald fantastication gives way to a thin facetiousness or a pastiche of Joyce. In confessional novels of the intensity of *Lolita*, moreover, there is frequently a disquieting note of unresolved tension. It is present even in the great narratives of this character by Constant and Proust. The hero of such self-scrutinizing novels is both the culprit and the judge, an unlikely situation, and he must strain and strain to persuade us that he is at once bad enough to sin and good enough to repent. Humbert's 'world of total evil' seems out of character, or at least in conflict with his idiom. It is the author intervening on Humbert's behalf and playing the role straight in order to make a vital point. So, too, with Humbert's belated love cries for his Lolita, which seem to be dictated by some principle of compensation and ring a little false (to me). 'I was a penta-pod monster, but I loved you. I was despicable and brutal and turpid, and everything, *mais je t'aimais, je t'aimais*!' *Lolita* is partly a masterpiece of grotesque comedy, partly an unsubdued wilderness where the wolf howls – a real wolf howling for a real Red Riding Hood.[16] □

Dupee's indispensable insight in the previous extract can be directly located in his sense of what the narrative must do in order to work: '[Humbert] must strain and strain to persuade us that he is at once bad enough to sin and good enough to repent'. Dupee indicates the extent to which the narrative demands a full recognition from its readers of the worst that H.H. is capable of, and finally a recognition from H.H. of the worst that he has done. This is exactly the moment of tension in the narra-tive that critics in the 1980s, such as Ellen Pifer (see chapter four of this Guide) will return to as a way of recovering an ethical reading of *Lolita*. In a review that, like Dupee's, also precedes the American publication of *Lolita*, the poet, novelist and critic Howard Nemerov underscores the view that 'Nabokov's own artistic concern . . . has no more to do with morality than with sex'. In this brief extract, Nemerov follows Dupee's reading of the confessional structure of sin and repentence, albeit in the slightly different terms of sin and retribution.

■ *Lolita* is nevertheless a moral work, if by morality in literature we are to understand the illustration of a usurious rate of exchange between our naughty desires and virtuous pains, of the process whereby pleasures become punishments, or our vices suddenly become recognizable as identical with our sufferings. In some dream-America, *Lolita* would make a fine test for the Producers' Code, for if Humbert Humbert is a wicked man, and he is, he gets punished for it in the end. Also in the middle. And at the beginning.[17] □

Nemerov is not abandoning the question of morality. In reading the novel as an exemplary text in which the punishment is made to fit the crime, he finds *Lolita* to be 'a moral work'. If the entrance of *Lolita* into the modern canon appears to leave behind the blatant question of pornography, the difficulties of subject matter and the ambiguities of rep-resentation that prompted the 'original' question do not simply disappear. On the one hand, as key signs of literariness, the characteristic difficulty and ambiguity of the novel are held up as decisive proofs of

Nabokov's erudition. On the other hand, the problem of what it might mean to represent the sexual desire of a man for a girl as ambiguous is easily displaced by the conventions of criticism into which *Lolita* is born, particularly in America. What is the cost of insisting on the aesthetic value of *Lolita*? Is it possible that the earlier question of literature or pornography is transformed into a complicated narrative encounter between the literary and the literal? Following on from the British publication of the novel in 1959 by Weidenfeld and Nicolson, a highly critical and contentious review by poet, novelist and critic Kingsley Amis appeared in *The Spectator* (6 November 1959). What is particularly fascinating about this review is not just the intelligent articulation of fierce criticism of the novel amid the flow of veneration, but the surprising ways in which Amis's criticisms seem to anticipate the emergence of feminist approaches to the novel in the 1980s. In voicing concern about H.H.'s treatment of Lolita, Amis also prefigures a number of key interpretations of the novel in the 1980s and 1990s in which the question of ethics in the practice of writing and reading, and in the process of human relations, is paramount. I should also add that the range of cultural references invoked here is not just an example of literary erudition, it is invaluable for thinking through the state of 'English literature' in the 1950s.

■ Few books published in this country since the King James Bible can have set up more eager expectations that *Lolita*, nor, on the other hand, can any work have been much better known in advance to its potential audience. The interest of this first British issue, indeed, is likely to be less in what the thing is actually like – you and I had already got hold of it somehow, hadn't we? – than in what 'they' will say about it. 'They' in this case covers a far wider spectrum than usual, all the way from the inevitable big-review-plus-leader-plus-interminable-correspondence in the *Times Literary Supplement* to the stern clashes of personality and taste round the local Boots counter; and somewhere in the middle will come Richard Hoggart, Cassandra, Lord Montgomery, two or three bishops, Dame Edith Sitwell, the chairman of the Bournemouth East Conservative Association, Dr. Bronowski, Professor Ayer, John O'London, Mr. Bevan and every last one of the couple of hundred thousand people in Britain who have, or can scrounge, access to some public medium. [The critic Richard Hoggart was a key witness for the defence in the trial of *Lady Chatterley's Lover* (1960).] It is encouraging to see all this concern for a book of serious literary pretension, even if some of the concern, while serious enough, is not literary in the way we ordinarily think of it. One would be even more encouraged if the book in question were not so thoroughly bad in both senses: bad as a work of art, that is, and morally bad – though certainly not obscene or pornographic.

At that last qualification I suspect I shall lose quite a number of my readers, even if they are *Spectator* readers – though I cannot see anything wrong in enjoying the kind of hot book that so many acquirers of *Lolita* will have found to their chagrin that it is not. But I take it as fairly probable that these are the kind of people who kept the book at the top of the American best-seller lists week after week, and who will doubtless do the same or better over here. Perception of this probability, together with an understandable desire to protect serious literature from the assaults of official and unofficial wowsers, has had its share in evoking the wild hosannas of praise for *Lolita* that have been ringing round the civilised world. As things are, it is not enough that such a book should be declared non-obscene in the eyes of any reasonable person; it must be declared great as well if it is to be quite safe. The issue is further complicated by the fact that what really offends the wowsers is not just presumptive obscenity, but this in combination with an insufficiently reverent attitude in sexual matters. Thus in the case of 'The Philanderer', an instructive semi-precedent to that of *Lolita*, what got the thing into the courts was the theme of philandering as such, rather than any corruptive power imaginable as residing in individual passages and expressions. Actually there can have been few books of overtly sexual content written out of stronger moral conviction or in purer terms (or with duller impact). If only the hero had been properly 'in love', his bedroom antics could have been detailed down to the last twitch without anyone taking much notice.

Lolita, accordingly, reaches the British public preceded by a sort of creeping barrage of critical acclaim: I expect great things from the jacket, which I have not yet seen. Meanwhile, I note a nine-page appendix in which thirty-one critics from nine countries fire off their commendatory salvoes. Only a few of these are content to assert the mere inoffensiveness of the work; the majority, from Lord Boothby via Heikki Brotherus in the Finnish *Soumen Kuvalehti* down to Dorothy Parker, go on to extol its high moral seriousness and/or (usually and) its outstanding literary merits: distinguished – beauty – beauty – brilliant – great – major – masterpiece – power – great – beautiful – beautiful – masterpiece. That ought to be enough to roll up both flanks of any local bench or libraries committee of even the highest wowser morale, not to speak of more elevated powers, and this is fine as far as it goes. But it would be a pity if all the 'masterpiece' stuff got treated seriously, especially in view of the critical direction it takes. *Beauty* and *beautiful* and their synonyms set the tone here, and there is much talk of style. [Emphases Amis's.] The long battle against style still hangs in the balance, and a reverse over *Lolita* could be damaging.

Style, a personal style, a distinguished style, usually turns out in practice to mean a high idiosyncratic noise level in the writing, with plenty of rumble and wow from imagery, syntax and diction: Donne, Pater, Virginia Woolf. There is, however, a good deal of nostalgia for style nowadays among people of oldster age-group or literary training; it shows in snorting accusations of gracelessness levelled against some younger novelists and merges into the hankering for 'experiment' that still dies hard.[18] Those interested will have noticed a connection here with that yearning for uplift, or a rich man's Billy Graham, which masquerades as reasoned antipathy to modern British philosophy. If we have not got Kant or Nietzsche, at least we have Colin Wilson. And if we have not got Ruskin or Carlyle at least we have Nabokov:

> She adored brilliant water and was a remarkably smart diver. Comfortably robed, I would settle down in the rich post-meridian shade after my own demure dip, and there I would sit, with a dummy book or a bag of bonbons, or both, or nothing but my ting-ling glands, and watch her gambol, rubber-capped, bepearled, smoothly tanned, as glad as an ad, in her trim-fitted satin pants and shirred bra. Pubescent sweetheart! How smugly would I marvel that she was mine, mine, mine, and revise the recent matitudinal swoon to the moan of the mourning doves, and devise the late afternoon one, and slitting my sun-speared eyes, compare Lolita to whatever other nymphets parsimonious chance collected around her for my anthological delectation and judgement; and today, putting my hand on my ailing heart, I really do not think that any of them ever surpassed her in desirability, or if they did, it was so two or three times at the most, in a certain light, with certain per-fumes blended in the air – once in the hopeless case of a pale Spanish child, the daughter of a heavy-jawed nobleman, and another time – *mais je divague*.[19]

No extract, however, could do justice to the sustained din of pun, allusion, neologism, alliteration, *cynghanedd*, apostrophe, parenthesis, rhetorical question. French, Latin, *anent, perchance, would fain, for the nonce* – here is style and no mistake. [Emphases Amis's.] One will be told, of course, that this is the 'whole point', that this is the hero, Humbert Humbert, talking in his own person, not the author, and that what we are getting is 'characterisation'. All right; but it seems ill-advised to characterise logomania by making it talk 120,000 words at us, and a glance at Nabokov's last novel, *Pnin*, which is not written in the first person, establishes that this is Nabokov talking (there is non-stylistic evidence too). The development of this *émigré*'s euphuism is a likely consequence of Nabokov's having had to abandon his natural idiom, as he puts it, his 'untrammelled, rich and infinitely docile Russian tongue for a second-rate brand of English, devoid of any of those apparatuses – the baffling mirror, the black velvet backdrop, the implied associations and traditions – which the native illusionist, fractails flying, can magically use to transcend the heritage in his own way'. This, which enacts the problem with characteristic tricksy indirection, also implies its solution as the laborious confection of equivalent apparatuses in the adoptive language: the whole farrago of imagery, archaism, etc., which cannot strike even the most finely tuned foreign ear as it strikes that of the native English-speaker. The end product sadly invokes a Charles Atlas muscle-man of language as opposed to the healthy and useful adult.

We know well enough that every style has a way of infiltrating what is being presented, so that, offered as the vehicle of Humbert's soliloquy, this style is involved with the entire moral tenor of the book. Thus Humbert is not only decadently sophisticated and tortuously imaginative and self-regardingly detached, he is also all of these things as he describes his seduction of the twelve-year-old Lolita and his long history of cohabitation with her. All this is arguably Humbert himself, and so is his account, 'delightfully witty' in implication, of his murder of a rival; but the many totally incidental cruelties – the bloody car wreck by the roadside that brings into view the kind of shoe Lolita covets, the wounding of a squirrel, apparently just for fun – bring the author into consideration as well, and I really don't care which of them is being wonderfully mature and devastating when Lolita's mother (recently Humbert's wife) is run over and killed . . . . . .

There comes a point where the atrophy of moral sense, evident throughout this book, finally leads to dullness, fatuity and unreality. Humbert's 'love' for Lolita is a matter of the senses, even of the membranes; his moments of remorse are few, brief and unconvincing; it never really occurs to him to ask himself just what the hell he thinks he is up to. There is plenty of self-absorption around us, heaven knows, but not enough on this scale to be worth writing about at length, just as the mad are much less interesting than the sane. And – here again the author heaves into view – the human circuit of *Lolita*, for all its geographical sweep, is suffocatingly narrow: the murderee is Humbert over again, Humbert's old queer pal is Humbert and unnecessary, Lolita's mother talks like Humbert, writes letters in Humbert's style, so does Lolita's girl-chum – the whole affair is Humbert gleefully meditating about Lolita, looking up to be ever so European about some American thing, then gleefully meditating again. There is, further, an appalling poverty of incident and even of narrative: the central episode of the book, a long illicit motel tour round the States, is related in catalogue, without scenes, as near as possible without the singling-out of individual occasions; meditation again, an exercise in the frequentative imperfect tense – there's one you missed, Nabokov/Humbert boy.

The only success of the book is the portrait of Lolita herself. I have rarely seen the external ambience of a character so marvellously realised, and yet there is seldom more than the necessary undertone of sensuality . . . The pity is that Humbert could not care less about the darkness of her life at home, and although the teenage vulgarity of Lolita's behaviour is caught with an equal precision he could not care less either about what she was really like. She is a 'portrait' in a very full sense, devotedly watched and listened to but never conversed with, the object of desire but never of curiosity. What else did she do in Humbert's presence but play tennis and eat sundaes and go to bed with him? What did they talk about? What did they actually get up to? Apart from a few sentences of elegant hot-book euphemism – reminding us that the work first saw the light under the imprint of the Olympia Press, Paris – we are not even told that. Do not misunderstand me if I say that one of the troubles with 'Lolita' is that, so far from being too pornographic, it is not pornographic enough.

As well as *moral* and *beautiful*, the book is also held to be *funny*, often *devastatingly* so, and *satirical*. As for the funny part, all that registered with me were a few passages where irritation caused Humbert to drop the old style-scrambler for a moment and speak in clear. [Emphases Amis's.] The satirical thing is a bit better, but it has been rather foisted on to *Lolita* as a result of the eagerness of Americans to hear the worst of themselves. V.S. Pritchett's comparison with *The Loved One* is apt in a different way from that intended: both books score the expected points with great gusto, neither is nearly as devastating as dozens of books by Americans, neither is acceptable as a picture of America. Perhaps only native-born Americans can provide this, which leads one to reflect that Nabokov's tragedy has been his separation from Europe, the source of his natural subject-matter as well as of his natural language. There is nothing in *Lolita* as fine as the seven pages of Colette, a story of his dating from 1948 in which the germ of *Lolita* is clearly discernible. Here is the same little monkey with the long-toed bare feet and the bruise on her tender skin, inciting the author to a reminiscence of *Carmen* – in *Lolita* this reappears in the eerie modernised disguise of a pop song. The Biarritz world of pre-1914 is evoked with a tender intensity that none of the Middle West travelogues or Virginia moteliana can match; and here the hero, being like the heroine ten years old, allows his love to slip away from him down a path which Humbert, out of solipsistic brutality, and Nabokov, out of a deficiency of good sense, denied to Lolita . . . [20] □

Amis's critique of the fancy words of *Lolita* gives a sense of the fashion in 1950s Britain for language that is stripped down rather than elaborately played up. As we will see in greater detail throughout this Guide, particularly in the 1960s and 1970s, the one thing on which all critics are more or less agreed is that Lolita (to borrow Alfred Appel's apposite phrase) is one of the 'significant realities of the novel'. This reality is directly connected to the way in which she appears to speak and act like a typical teenage girl in 1950s America. In spite of disagreeing with almost everything else approved of by Nabokov's adoring fans, Amis agrees that Nabokov gets something absolutely right in the representation of his 'poor Lolita'. More to the point though is what critics make of the 'significant reality' of the girl, and how that affects the response to the text as literature. Amis is moved, not by Humbert's narration of his desire for Lolita, but by the representation of Lolita herself, and it is this uncompromising identification with the girl that makes his reading so striking. The paradoxical question for Amis is this: given the narrative structure of the fictional memoir, how is it possible to recover a 'real' representaton of Lolita from Humbert's desiring narrative?

In his conviction that there is no distance between Humbert's narration and Nabokov's novel-writing, Amis is close to Julia Bader's argument in the 1970s (see chapter three of this Guide). For Bader, reading *Lolita* is inseparable from the question of reading the fictional *memoir* of H.H. Amis also notes the cruelty and the incuriosity of Humbert in his dealings with Lolita. In this he clearly prefigures Ellen Pifer and Richard Rorty in the 1980s (see chapter four of this Guide), and Michael Wood in the 1990s (see chapter five of this Guide). Indeed, what is perhaps remarkable is the way in which Amis seems to 'find' Lolita, in the sophisticated sense that Wood will later urge that all readers must do. Finally, Amis's insight is to see that the claims of high moral worth are the real terms on which the book will be secured for 'art'. It will not be enough to show that *Lolita* is not pornographic.

In a review published in the *New Statesman* the following day (7 November 1959), novelist and critic Walter Allen, who in 1960 would become the Literary Editor of the *New Statesman*, suggests in opposition to Amis that a distinction must be made between Humbert's narration and Nabokov's gift for language. Allen's review begins by acknowledging the claim that certain scenes in the book may be obscene.

■ Inevitably, character and subject being what they are, there are two or three passages, of varying length, which some people might consider obscene. Now that we are allowed under the Jenkins Act to consider the book 'as a whole', these surely fall into their proper perspective. [Roy Jenkins (at the time, a member of the Labour Party) was one of the sponsors of the Obscene Publications Act of 1959. The new act offered the defence of literary merit to the 1868 definition of obscenity as 'the tendency to deprave and corrupt'. The act stated that there would be no conviction *if* it could be proved that publication served 'the public good on the ground that it is in the interests of science, literature, art, or learning, or of other objects of general concern'.[21] **The novel is told with sparkling brilliance. But here one must distinguish between Nabokov's brilliance and that which is postulated to Humbert. On Nabokov's part the creation of Humbert is a feat of impersonation only comparable in our time, it seems to me, with Joyce Cary's turning himself into the crotchety, dotty, semi-senile lawyer, Tom Wilcher, in** *To Be a Pilgrim*. **But Humbert's brilliance, the insolent ease with which he manipulates the English language, is part of his character. It becomes at times almost a form of exhibitionism, a manic showing off.**[22] □

For Allen, writing in the spirit of the new Act, any possible charges of obscenity, official and otherwise, are clearly cancelled out by the brilliant exhibitionism of the language. Allen is explicit in suggesting that scenes which *could* be read as obscene are absorbed or contained by the brilliance of the book 'as a whole'. That brilliance relies first of all on the manipulations of Humbert's narration, and in the second place on the reader's identifications with it. In other words, by coming under the sway of the brilliance 'postulated to Humbert', problematic scenes will be rendered unproblematic. What we can start to see here is the range of oppositions and the terms of criticism in the early reviews. Added to this is the way in which certain kinds of readers and readings are invoked and revoked. The final review to be considered in this chapter is from the British writer and critic V. S. Pritchett. What is especially revealing about Pritchett's contribution, and it is one that has not yet been fully explored, is the way in which he raises the question of reading *Lolita*. Writing in the *New Statesman* (10 January 1959) about a book still unpublished in Britain at that moment, Pritchett insists that *Lolita* is 'not a pornographic novel'. His efforts to prove this turn on a rudimentary sociology of reading in which he differentiates between three kinds of reader.

■ I can imagine no book less likely to incite the corruptible reader; the already corrupted would surely be devastated by the author's power of projecting himself into their fantasy-addled minds. As for the minors, the nymphets and schoolboys, one hardly sees *them* toiling through a book written in difficult style, filled on every page with literary allusions.[23] □

What can this mean for the question of pornography that haunts *Lolita* criticism without being seriously addressed? As far as Pritchett is concerned, readers like Humbert cannot read the novel: recognising their image would simply drive them mad, presupposing they are not mad already. Readers like Lolita, and the young boys who are potential subjects of desires such as Humbert's, cannot read the novel: they will not understand it. What Pritchett does not explicitly address is the reader who is taken for granted: the literary reader in his own image, the ideal 'critical reader' whose writing is the subject of this Guide.

By the end of the 1950s the entry of *Lolita* into the modern American canon of literature is assured. One of the fascinating aspects of the initial critical response to the book is the diversity of intelligent criticism. In the 1960s there is a notable lack of dissent as American critics (in particular) pore over the aesthetic form of the novel, seeking to unravel the abundance of literary references in the text.

CHAPTER TWO

'An Idealistic Obsession with the Never-to-be-had': Parody, Perversion and the Meaning of Style; Interpretations of *Lolita* in the 1960s

MANY CRITICS feel compelled to 'take on' Nabokov's own critical commentary on *Lolita*. In one sense this is not surprising, since novelists may be known also as literary critics, both of their own writing and that of others. We need look no further than Henry James and Virginia Woolf to appreciate that novelists have fascinating critical insights into their writing. This is not to suggest, of course, that the author is the source of all knowledge of his or her own text, or the last word on it. Since the idea of 'the disappearance of the author' was famously signalled by French writers and cultural critics, Michel Foucault ('What is an Author', 1969), and Roland Barthes ('The Death of the Author', 1968), it is no longer tenable to regard the writer as supreme governor of the meaning of his or her own text. For Barthes, the effect of this 'death' is not to mourn, but to celebrate. Readers will be liberated from the impossible constraints and restrictions of authorial intention and meaning. Ideally, the text belongs to the reader, and the meaning of the fiction becomes whatever the reader makes of it.

As the author of *Lolita*, however, Nabokov complicates this proposition from the outset in interesting ways. It is not just the force and influence of Nabokov's own remarks on *Lolita* that make the difference, it is the fact that the concentrated effects of those remarks are destined to accompany the novel throughout its life. As evidenced by the amount of attention it has received, Nabokov's Afterword, 'On a Book Entitled *Lolita*', is considerably more than an authorial postscript to the novel. Although it is that too, since it was written *after* the Olympia Press publication of *Lolita*, appearing in the American edition of the novel (1958), but as we have noted in the previous chapter, the essay was occasioned by the publication of selections from *Lolita* in the *Anchor Review* in 1957. It is the place in which Nabokov elaborates his uncompromising theories about the relation between art and life. It is where he sets out his version of the genealogy of *Lolita* (where the novel comes from). And if his forbidding presence is there to advise readers of the creative process that brought forth this controversial novel, it is there also to remind us that the author is a reader too. Indeed, as Richard Rorty's fascinating discussion of *Lolita* will show in the 1980s (see chapter five of this Guide), Nabokov may be present as an exemplary reading lesson to inattentive readers. In one of the most influential readings of *Lolita* in the 1960s, which because of its extended publishing history also spans the 1970s, Gabriel Josipovici sets out in very clear terms the kinds of constraints and problems with which critics approaching the work of Nabokov are confronted. '*Lolita*: Parody and the Pursuit of Beauty' was originally published as an article in *Critical Quarterly* in 1964. It was then reprinted as a chapter in a book by Josipovici, *The World and the Book: A Study of Modern Fiction*, published in 1971. The book remains in print, the third edition appearing in 1994, and continues to be a valuable critical resource. The following extract is taken from the essay's opening section in which Josipovici charts the difficult position of critics, including himself, in relation to the book, and to the author of the book, *Lolita*.

■ To comment in print on the work of Vladimir Nabokov one must be either very foolish or very daring. For Nabokov has never made a secret of his contempt for critics; in preface and postscript, in interviews with the papers, on radio and television, he has poured scorn on all those who would try to 'place' him in relation to his contemporaries, who would examine his 'themes' or decipher the 'messages' his novels contain. In the preface to his son's translation of *Invitation to a Beheading* he tells us that critics have found in his work the influence of Cervantes, Kafka, Tolstoyevsky and many others. He himself denies it. The only influence he will admit is that of the French writer Pierre Delalande, whom he has invented. And in his essay 'On a Book Entitled *Lolita*' he asserts that critics who have not read his earlier novels – the best of which, he claims,[1] have not been translated from their original Russian – are in no position to pass judgement upon him. He has, moreover, no message, nothing to communicate, and writes 'with no other purpose than to get rid' of a book – to get it out of his system.

In the face of this onslaught there seems little for the sympathetic critic to do except praise the author's mastery of invective and self-protective irony and turn to more amenable writers. And such an attitude would seem to find justification in the novels themselves, and in Nabokov's way there of destroying the pretensions of all those he hates and despises: the Goodmans, the Paduks and all the shallow and pretentious bores who throng his pages, talking of Freud or Marx, Ball Zac or Doll's Toy. Yet it is just such passages as these which should make the critic pause in his understandable desire to escape as quickly and silently as possible. For is there not more in Nabokov's personal attitude than a simple dislike of the critical profession as such? The theme of the critic as buffoon, of the academic mind run mad, of the moral perversion involved in explaining human beings in terms of heredity or environment and books in terms of mechanism or organism – these themes are so central to Nabokov's work that it is impossible not to see his attitude towards his own critics as an extension into real life of the preoccupations of his novels. Indeed by an irony which cannot have failed to appeal to him, the patterns of misrepresentation established in his novels have been faithfully reproduced in the critical reception accorded to these novels. Perhaps if we look at *Lolita* as, among other things, a model of the relationship between the writer and his book and the reader and the writer we may come closer to grasping its real nature. As Nabokov knows – it is one of the reasons for his profound melancholy – it is the critic's prerogative always to have the last word.[2] □

The last word on *Lolita* for Josipovici (and for critics 'the last word' is always contingent) is that the unattainable beauty that Humbert Humbert longs for, and believes he will find in Lolita, 'is beautiful *just because* it is unattainable'.[3] It is in crossing the threshold from the fantasies of his desire for Lolita to the physical enactment of those desires that Humbert Humbert finds himself 'in a realm where values have ceased to exist'.[4] In the following extract from Josipovici's conclusion he brings together the connections between Humbert's fatal attempt to 'possess' Lolita, and the reader's attempt to grasp the book.

■ For the reader to ask what the novel is 'about', for him to try and extract its 'theme' or 'message' is for him to be guilty of Humbert's initial error: to try and possess carnally what can only be apprehended imaginatively. The novel does not reveal its secret once and for all; the imaginative effort must be renewed each time it is reread. Ultimately the theme is the imaginative effort itself, that progress towards inevitable failure and loss which is the pattern of success. In the end Humbert does fail. The beauty is not there for us to behold. Lolita has once again slipped through his hands. In the actuality of the fiction he is about to die and all that is left of his story is a pile of paper: art is only a *local* palliative, it will not save anybody's life. He has had a vision, made his effort, and now it is the turn of life, of the ordinary, of

that which is silent and without meaning. Despite Humbert's dis-
claimer, he was not one of nature's faithful hounds, his initial act was
not natural, no matter how much he desired it. Just as Nabokov's first
act, his choice of subject-matter and of how and when to start, was not
natural. And for this unnatural act life will have its revenge . . . When
the novel comes to an end there is nothing there for us to hold. The
palliative of art works only while Humbert is actually writing, or the
reader actually reading. But the miracle of art lies in the fact that we
can reread this novel as often as we like.[5] □

Page Stegner's study of five English novels by Nabokov in 1966 (*Escape
into Aesthetics: The Art of Vladimir Nabokov*) has been widely engaged with,
and his reading of *Lolita* is one of the key critical readings of the 1960s.
With similar concerns to Josipovici, Stegner confronts the problem of
how to 'place' Nabokov in relation to other writers, given Nabokov's
consistent refusal to identify either himself or his work with any group,
movement, or artistic purpose. An important aspect of Stegner's enterprise is to show that 'Nabokov is not an isolated artist working in a void'.[6]
To this end, Stegner 'uncovers' the various ways in which the novel is
engaged with the conventions of literature and other influential cultural
forms: 'In one sense *Lolita* might be considered an extensive parody of
Freudian myths and Freudian explanations for psychological aberration'
(p. 103); 'Quilty seems to be a parody of the psychological "double" that
E. T. A. Hoffman, and Dostoevsky, made into a popular literary tradition'
(p. 104); 'the Hollywood–Mickey Spillane melodramatic brutal ending'
(p. 105); 'And, Quilty, in the best Shakespearian tradition, takes his time
to die' (p. 105).

In keeping with most critics of the novel, since the references and
allusions are more or less obvious, Stegner comments on the abiding
connections between the text of *Lolita* and the works of Edgar Allan Poe:
'[Nabokov] chooses first of all Edgar Allan Poe's "Annabel Lee" for the
name and theme of Humbert's story of Lolita's precursor in that prince-
dom by the sea . . . Humbert's mother, like Poe's, died when he was
three' (p. 105).[7] Stegner frames this discussion of *Lolita* by suggesting that
critics with specific intentions towards the novel invariably and necessarily
overlook other important features. For example, F. W. Dupee points to
the 'comic horror' but does not go into the 'extensive games that the
author plays with his readers'. Lionel Trilling, on the other hand, is so
concerned with the 'poignant and touching love story' that he forgets
the comic aspects of the narrative. Admittedly, this focus on the over-
sights and omissions of previous critics is a typical critical procedure by
which the path is cleared for new insights, but what is especially pertinent about Stegner's use of such a focus is the way in which he declares
the omissions of his own essay. Although Stegner seems to take his

distance from Trilling, they share an anxiety about the broad implications of the novel's content. We may recall Trilling's 'confession' that the narrative literally seduced him away from the moral response he might have had. Stegner is much more explicit in making the connection between the idea of the moral content and the seductions of the literary narrative. This extract is taken from the second and final section of Stegner's discussion of *Lolita* in which it is suggested that only by suspending 'moral repugnance for pederasts' can the 'total artistic effect' of the novel be fully appreciated. For Stegner, the key to aesthetic appreciation is obtained through a sympathetic identification with Humbert Humbert's story.

■ The conjuror's hand jerking the strings and producing private jokes, clues, false scents, word plays, allusions, illusions and sleights of hand constitutes only a part of art – primarily the comic art – of *Lolita*. But readers who are able to transcend their socially conditioned response to sexual perversion, to suspend for the time being their moral repugnance for pederasts and nympholepts, find in Humbert's story something that is touching and most un-comic in the destructive power of his obsession. For Humbert Humbert is not a monster; he is not simply grotesque and absurd. Unlike Rousseau, whose confessions his sometimes resemble, Humbert evokes our sympathy and pity.

While Humbert is a sexual pervert and a murderer, he is not a rapist; not a seducer of adolescent girls in dark alleys. He looks, but, except for Lolita, he has not touched, and does not. Judging from the come-on that Lolita gives him while he is a boarder in her mother's house, his statement that it is she who seduced him seems very possibly true – though it can never be forgotten that all this is reported by Hum. And the man whom Humbert kills is, himself, a despicable creature; in the melodramatic terms that the extravaganza murder scene seems to parody, he 'needs killing'. None of this, of course, should excuse Humbert, but it does certainly mitigate the degree of his culpability. It is useful to recall T. S. Eliot's admonition to the critics of *Hamlet* that it is the play that is at issue, not the man. *Lolita* amounts to a good deal more than Humbert's tragic flaw.

Humbert is invested with considerable charm and wit. He has a keen eye for the phony and the absurd, and we agree with him in his judgements about the Miss Pratts, the Gaston Godins, and the Clare Quiltys of the world. His traveler's guide to the American motel and restaurant is a marvel of what 'oft was thought, but ne'er so well expressed':

We passed and re-passed through the whole gamut of American roadside restaurants, from the lowly Eat with its deer head (dark trace of long tear at inner canthus), 'humorous' picture post cards of the posterior 'Kurort' type, impaled guest checks, life savers, sunglasses, adman visions of celestial sundaes, one half a chocolate cake under glass, and several horribly experienced flies zigzagging over the sticky sugar-pour on the ignoble counter; and all the way to the expensive place with the subdued lights, preposterously poor table linen, inept waiters (ex-convicts or college boys), the roan back of a screen actress, the sable eyebrows of her male of the moment, and an orchestra of zoot-suiters with trumpets. (p. 157)[8]

And his disgust for the false front of the gum-chewing American teenager makes any parent nod in agreement. Moreover, Humbert has a great deal of honesty about himself, and while he occasionally wallows in self-pity and self-justification, he just as often expresses great self-loathing. For his sick obsession with nymphets, Humbert suffers.

Hum's candor and straight-faced reporting (almost naïve at times) of the ridiculous in his own life is what makes him, like Huck Finn, both comic and human. For example, in the great seduction scene at The Enchanted Hunters, he is bothered by curiously mundane obstacles. 'Deep-throated' toilets cascade all night, trucks roar past, a drunk is sick next to his room, a staple of the teen-age diet is tearing up his stomach, but worst of all Lolita has taken both pillows. 'I had no place to rest my head', he moans, 'and a fit of heartburn (they call those fries "French", *grand Dieu*!) was added to my discomfort' (p. 131). All night he burns with desire and dyspepsia. When Lolita, life of his life, fire of his loins, wakes up and demands a cup of water, Humbert sneaks back his pillow.

I do not mean to suggest that Humbert is a put-upon, misunderstood pervert who never did anybody any harm. I do mean to suggest that, unattractive as he can be, he is given by his creator a certain persuasiveness and charm that all of his crimes cannot wipe out, and it is an inaccurate reading that places all the attention on Humbert's aberration and neglects his suffering and his comedy.

But there is a more important reason than Humbert's candor for our sympathetic involvement with him. Through the surface of his perversion I think we glimpse a longing for something lost that goes well beyond his first love, Annabel: a kind of nostalgic, hopeless yearning for some intangible element in that private universe of childhood, that 'island of entranced time' in which Humbert lived before being sent at the age of thirteen 'to a *lycée* in Lyon'. Humbert hungers after an ideal state that nymphets represent, a quality that exists beyond space and time.

Nabokov goes to some pains at the beginning of the novel to point out the supernatural qualities of nymphets. 'Between the age limits of nine and fourteen there occur maidens who, to certain bewitched travelers, twice or many times older than they, reveal their true nature which is not human, but nymphic (that is demoniac)' (p. 18). They are different, he points out, from ordinary 'essentially *human* little girls'. [Emphasis Stegner's.] Humbert admits that he is able to have relations with 'terrestrial women', but he complains that these 'human females . . . were but palliative agents'. Humbert's Freudian explanation for his sexual deviance – his coitus interruptus with Annabel on that enchanted island of entranced time of his childhood – suggests (in view of Nabokov's hatred for things Freudian) that Hum is playing with his reader here. But there is perhaps a reason beyond the simple joke for his making this the opening scene of the book. For one thing, The Enchanted Hunters hotel with Lolita echoes the 'enchanted island' with Annabel and suggests a search for the timeless, immortal, uncomplicated, never-never land in which preadolescents seem to live, rather than an obsession with the physically real little girl.

The notion of timelessness becomes extremely important in Humbert's description of nymphets and nympholepts. 'It will be marked that I substitute time terms for spatial ones. In fact, I would have the reader see "nine" and "fourteen" as the boundaries' (p. 18). Humbert describes the characteristics: 'the fey grace, the elusive, shifty, soul-shattering, insidious charm that separates the nymphet from such coevals of hers as are incomparably more dependent on the spatial world of synchronous phenomena than on that intangible island of entranced time where Lolita plays with her likes' (p. 19). 'Furthermore', he says, 'since the idea of time plays such a magic part in the matter, the student should not be surprised to learn that there must be a gap of several years, never less than ten I should say, generally thirty or forty, and as many as ninety in a few known cases, between maiden and man to enable the latter to come under a nymphet's spell' (p. 19). As Humbert points out about his first love, 'When I was a child and she was a child, my little Annabel was no nymphet to me; I was her equal, a faunlet in my own right, on that same enchanted island of time . . . ' (pp. 19–20).

While Humbert is sitting on a park bench, his 'rack of joy' under which a nymphet is groping for a marble, an old woman sits down and asks him if he has a stomach ache. And he wails to those interrupters, 'Ah leave me alone in my pubescent park, in my mossy garden. Let them play around me forever. Never grow up' (p. 23). Humbert remarks about the three years that pass between Lolita's disappearance and his rediscovery of her as Dolly Schiller: 'the general impression I desire to convey is of a side door crashing open in life's full flight, and a rush of roaring black time drowning with its whipping wind the cry of lone disaster' (pp. 255–6).

Humbert makes a curious remark about peeping at nymphets through his window:

> There was in the fiery phantasm a perfection which made my wild delight also perfect, just because the vision was out of reach, with no possibility of attainment to spoil it by the awareness of an appended taboo; indeed, it may well be that the very attraction immaturity has for me lies not so much in the limpidity of pure young forbidden fairy child beauty as in the security of a situation where infinite perfections fill the gap between the little given and the great promised – the great rosegrey never-to-be-had. (p. 266)

In short, it is the image of 'fairy child beauty' taken over and acted upon by the imagination that Humbert chases. 'The great promised' can only exist in the imagination and can only be *infinite* in the imagination. [Emphasis Stegner's.] Reality is deception and change. The consummation of desire quenches its source.

At the end of the book, when Humbert has run his car up a bank and is waiting for his capture, he conjures up a final memory of a late summer afternoon just after Lolita has left him for Quilty. Nauseated, he pulled off on a mountain road high above a small mining town, and as he looked over the precipice, he recalls, 'I grew aware of a melodious unity of sounds rising like vapor . . . ' In the valley below he sees the street patterns and roofs of the houses, 'but even brighter than those quietly rejoicing colours . . . both brighter and dreamier to the ear than they were to the eye, was that vapory vibration of accumulated sounds that never ceased for a moment, as it rose to the lip . . . ' Humbert suddenly realizes that these sounds are all of a kind. 'Reader! What I heard was but the melody of children at play, nothing but that', and the air is so clear and light 'that within this vapor of blended voices, majestic and minute, remote and magically near, frank and divinely enigmatic – one could hear now and then, as if released, an almost articulate spurt of vivid laughter, or the crack of a bat . . . ' As Humbert stands on the slope listening to the 'musical vibration' from below he suddenly understands; 'and then I knew that the hopelessly poignant thing was not Lolita's absence from my side, but the absence of her voice from that concord' (pp. 309–10).

There is, perhaps, another echo from Poe in this passage – the narrator of 'The Imp of the Perverse' speaking on perversity: 'We stand upon the brink of a precipice. We peer into the abyss – we grow sick and dizzy . . . By slow degrees our sickness, and dizziness, and horror become merged in a cloud of unnamable [*sic*] feeling . . . this cloud assumes shape, as did the vapor from the bottle out of which arose the genius in the Arabian Nights'. The narrator of Poe's story discusses perverseness (whose ultimate form is self-destruction, and through whose promptings 'we act, for the reason that we should *not*') in order to explain to the reader why he is in prison for murder. 'Had I not been thus prolix, you might either have misunderstood me altogether, or with the rabble, have fancied me mad'. Humbert Humbert, also an inhabitant of the murderer's cell, might have offered the same explanation for his memoir. Certainly he desires that we not misunderstand him or think him mad. But here the parallel between the two narrators seems to stop. Perversity might explain why Humbert, leaving the scene of his crime, deliberately drives on the wrong side of the road. 'In a way, it was a very spiritual itch'. But it won't do as a motivation for his nympholepsy. There is no indication in his narrative that he acts 'for the reason that [he] should *not*', acts simply to flout the laws and mores of a social structure that he despises. There is strong indication, in fact, that his actions are affirmative rather than negative; that they are attempts to recapture and petrify for eternity a piece of the cherished past.

In *Speak, Memory* Nabokov makes two seemingly contradictory remarks – that he does not believe in time, and that the nostalgia he has 'been cherishing all these years is a hypertrophied sense of lost childhood' (pp. 40–1).[9] Humbert Humbert clearly cherishes the same nostalgia for the past that his creator does (a *genderless* nostalgia in the final analysis) [emphasis Stegner's], but human mutability (his own and Lolita's) stand in the way of his attempts to reverse time. The paradox can only be resolved, Humbert suggests (and Nabokov too), through art. This is what we are left with in *Lolita*. The only treatment for Humbert's yearning for 'the impossible past' is the 'very local palliative of articulate art'. To his memory of Dolly Haze, Humbert writes, 'I am thinking of aurochs and angels, the secret of durable pigments, prophetic sonnets, the refuge of art. And this is the only immortality you and I may share, my Lolita' (p. 311). The immortality of *Lolita*, Humbert the artist's immortality, exists in the telling, in the farce and the anguish of his narrative, and not in the bizarre facts of the story told. It is the telling that matters. In an early part of the book when Humbert justifies his passion-obsession by pointing out that 'Dante fell in love with his Beatrice when she was nine', that Petrarch fell in love with Laura when she was twelve, that 'marriage and cohabitation before the age of puberty are still not uncommon in certain East Indian provinces', Nabokov is attempting to show that there is nothing *intrinsically* remarkable about an older man falling in love with a twelve-year-old girl. [Emphasis Stegner's.] What happens in *Lolita* is that Humbert *makes* it remarkable by the terms he puts it in, by the telling, because he makes an art out of perversion. Humbert's eye confronts vulgarity (his own and the world's) and converts it through imagination and subsequently language into a thing of beauty. Lolita is in reality a rather common, unwashed little girl whose interests are entirely plebian, though, in certain respects, precocious. [It is in this comment that Stegner registers the division between the literally 'real' vulgarity of Lolita versus the literary transformations that H.H. is able to perform on her. Such divisions, and the deeply embedded assumptions about cultural value and femininity they expose, are the subject of Rachel Bowlby's interpretation of the rhetoric of the novel in the 1990s (see chapter five of this Guide). For Stegner, as we see in his conclusion, Lolita's grubbiness and vulgarity are not an adequate defence against H.H.'s ultimate failure 'to distinguish the reality of his imagination from the reality of physical life'.] But the real irony is that Humbert's power to turn rough glass into sparkling crystal eventually subsumes him, and he is reduced to a servant of his art. Humbert sitting in his cage talking about the salvation afforded by the writing of his memoirs suggests, in fact, his imprisonment in art. Humbert perverts life, and art eventually perverts him because his life *becomes* art. [Emphasis Stegner's.] He has aesthetic vision but his moral vision is very seldom operative. Ultimately, distinctions have to be made, if one is to function in this world, between aesthetics and morality – between art and life. Humbert loses the ability effectively to distinguish the reality of his imagination from the reality of physical life, and in so doing removes himself from the combined reality that is the source of art.

But what makes *Lolita* a truly great novel is the incredible fusion of all the aesthetically admirable components of Nabokov's art. The conjuring, the parody, the irony and humor, and the real pathos of Humbert's situation combine in a forceful articulation of a real and meaningful experience that moves us, not (as John Ray suggests) to watch our daughters more closely, but to a compassionate understanding of the suffering produced by an idealistic obsession with the never-to-be-had.[10] □

Stegner's sense of a critical 'trade-off' between aesthetics and morality is not just a closing statement, a conclusion to his own argument. It is important as a commentary on the dominant forms of literary criticism in the 1960s. With Stegner's insight in mind, it becomes possible to see that trade-off in process. Carl R. Proffer's book-length study of 'some of the technical puzzles' in *Lolita* in 1968,[11] amply demonstrates the ways in which attempts to 'isolate' the wonderful linguistic qualities of the novel not only displace other important considerations, but also *rely* on that displacement. More to the point, the particular practice of close reading associated with this phase of formalist criticism suggests that *Lolita*, with all its puns, parodies and paradoxes, is a potentially endless playground for readings that need never go beyond repeating patterns of words on the page. The following extract is taken from the chapter on 'Style'.

■ Few writers have ever paid more attention to the 'instrumentation' of their prose than Nabokov.[12] Every page of Lolita provides dozens of examples of alliteration and assonance. But Nabokov's style is never meretricious in this respect – as is often the case in the work of more orthodox poets, infinitely less talented people, like Swinburne in England or Balmont in Russia, who hide with ornaments their want of art – and if the phonetic combinations ever become amusing, it is because they are supposed to be amusing (Humbert mocks himself occasionally). I have found that even where an epithet appears to have been chosen because of its sound, it usually turns out that phonetic deftness is complemented by novelty of expression and precision of meaning.

Nabokov's sound play in Lolita runs through the entire phonetic and written alphabet from 'abrupt attack' and an 'active Adam's apple, ogling Lo'[13] to 'zigzagging zanies'.[14] The variety of acoustically coupled epithets is vast. Sometimes it is a simple matter of alliteration on the initial phoneme:

> *a*ging *a*pe, *b*londe *b*itch, *c*olumbine *k*isses, *d*iaphonous *d*arling, *f*ilthy *f*iend, *g*hastly *g*rin, *h*umiliating *h*assack, *l*imp *L*o, *m*oaning *m*outh, *p*ubescent *p*ark, *r*aw *r*ose, *s*ubtle *s*pine, *t*ruculently *t*ight, *v*aguely *v*isualized, *w*elcoming *w*hine

Or the first two sounds may be reiterated:

> *bl*azing *bl*ack, *cr*iminal *cr*aving, *di*smal *di*strict, evolving even, flame-flower, gritty grey, humming hush, loquacious Lo, must and the mud, probably protruding, roughly rubbing, scorching scrawl, tremendous truck, veined vase, whined why . . . [15] □

The chapter continues in this way offering more of these combination groups of alliteration and assonance: two words, three words, four words, two verbs, noun and verb, adverb and verb, two adverbs, two or three adjectives. Looking back at this reading now, it is not difficult to see its potential for interminable analysis, and all the limitations this implies. As the history of *Lolita* criticism demonstrates, questions begin to be asked about the context and the meaning of this kind of textual analysis: What is its significance? How does it further our understanding of the novel and the ways in which it has been responded to? However, it is important to note that Proffer does draw attention to the idea of literary language as either a fancy embellishment covering a want of talent

('Swinburne'), or a fancy literary language that has substance ('Nabokov'). The very fact that this Guide exists is a clear indication that Proffer is right, since the debate surrounding *Lolita* is also a struggle about the relation between the fancy words on the page, what they may or may not represent, and the relation between the world of the novel and other realities. Whilst insisting that all these sparkling linguistic patterns mean something, Proffer's stylistic analysis falls short of saying what that something might be. But, again, this appears to be consistent with the contemporary critical drive to enclose and contain meaning within the world of the book. Proffer's work has clear links with Alfred Appel Jr's critical approach to *Lolita*. Alfred Appel Jr has a special place in the history of *Lolita* criticism since he was also a student of Nabokov's at Cornell in 1953–4. Appel discovered the original Olympia edition of *Lolita* whilst stationed in France, and in this sense bears witness to the remarkable transformation of Nabokov's status from professor of literature, translator, and writer with a modest reputation, to famous author. Appel himself achieved a certain critical status with the publication of *The Annotated 'Lolita'* in 1970. The substantial introduction to that work is largely based on articles written by Appel in the 1960s, in particular '*Lolita*: The Springboard of Parody', which was published originally in the Spring 1967 issue of *Wisconsin Studies in Contemporary Literature*. The issue was later reprinted as *Nabokov: The Man and his Work*, edited by L. S. Dembo.

Appel's approach to *Lolita* is quite specific. Indeed, as the title indicates, the article is primarily concerned with parody. At the same time, Appel is keen to sponsor 'a comprehensive view of *Lolita*'.[16] The effect of this is to situate Appel with Stegner, on the grounds that both critics are concerned with addressing 'gaps' in the criticism of *Lolita*. The importance of this positioning in regard to the critical history of the novel is that it indicates the scope of the critical field by the 1960s, and the sense of what needs to be done. For Stegner, it is the comic aspect of *Lolita* that is usually missed. For Appel, it is the question of morality and the way that it may be linked to certain literary conventions and tropes, namely parody: 'Many readers overlook the deep moral resonance of [Nabokov's] work, for characters hopelessly imprisoned within themselves must submit to Nabokov's irony, parody, or, most significantly, self-parody'.[17] As can be seen from the following extract, Appel identifies parody as the keyword, not only in regard to reading *Lolita* but in regard to Nabokov's entire oeuvre.

■ Parody is in *Lolita* the major means by which Nabokov breaks the circuit of reader-character identification one associates with the conventional novel. In his other novels this is accomplished by a complicated sequence of interacting devices which, by constantly reminding the reader of the novelist's presence in and above his book as a puppeteer in charge of everything, establishes the fiction as total artifice. In this sense 'mask' *is* the 'keyword' in Nabokov and one is continually aware of Nabokov's masked participation in his fiction, whether as chess player, actor, ventriloquist, conjurer, or as what Nabokov calls 'an anthropomorphic deity impersonated by me' – the intruding authorial consciousness which eventually takes over the novel altogether, involuting it, denying it any reality except that of 'book'. There is intrusive direct address to the reader in *Lolita*, and it is important, but it is still in the narrator's voice rather than in the distinctively different voice of the 'deity', as in *Invitation to a Beheading, Bend Sinister*, and *Pale Fire*. Even when Humbert momentarily loses control and lets the mask slip, one glimpses his despair, but not the 'real' Humbert nor the manipulative author. As Nabokov says in chapter five of *Gogol* (1944), analogously discussing Akaky Akakyvich and 'holes' and 'gaps' in the narrative texture of *The Overcoat*: 'We did not expect that, amid the whirling masks, one mask would turn out to be a real face, *or at least the place where that face ought to be*' [emphasis Appel's].

Because *Lolita* is Nabokov's only uninterrupted narrative since *Despair* (1934) and Humbert his most 'humanized' character since Luzhin (1930) – more so even than Pnin, who is the narrator's re-creation of other people's impersonations of Pnin – readers must consider the esthetic [*sic*] implications of parody, or they are liable to approach *Lolita* as if it were *The Turn of the Screw*. By definition, parody and self-parody suspend the possibility of a fully 'realistic' fiction, since their referents are either other literary works or themselves, and not the world of objective reality which the 'realist' or 'impressionist' tries to reproduce. Only an authorial sensibility, outside the book, can be said to have ordered the texture of parody; the dizzying, multiform perspectives it achieves are beyond the capacities of any 'point of view' within the book. In the terms of Henry James or Percy Lubbock, Humbert's is finally *not* a credible point of view. [Emphasis Appel's.] Aubrey McFate, who is following Humbert, turns up in the middle of the neatly alphabetized Ramsdale class list which Humbert incorporates in his narrative, thus undercutting the inviolable 'reality' of much more than that list (p. 54).[18] The 'coincidences', as has already been suggested, are not simply a matter of McFate's ominous work, since McFate only 'exists' insofar as he has been invented.

Nabokov has laid into the parodic design of *Lolita* an elaborate system of involutions which, like a network of coincidences, helps to close the circuits by demonstrating that everything is being manipulated, all is a fiction, thus parodying the reader's desire for verisimilitude. Typical of these inlays is Clare Quilty's entry in *Who's Who in the Limelight* (a mother lode of involutions), where he is listed as the author of *The Lady Who Loved Lightning* (p.33). Almost two hundred pages later, during a thunderstorm, Lolita comments gratuitously, 'I am not a lady and do not love lightning' (p.222), an involuted cross-reference which reveals a capacity for organization and order that is completely beyond the possibilities of Humbert's alleged unrevised 'first draft' manuscript, which has supposedly been composed furiously over a period of less than two months. ['Involuted' means 'complicated', 'abstruse', 'intricate'.] While he recounts his first night with Lolita he tries not to lose control of the language, but at the same time manages to tell how he was served by Mr. Swine, the room clerk, who is assisted by Mr. Potts, who can't find any cots because Swine has dispatched them to the Swoons (p.20). Like the presence in the novel of Quilty's anagrammatic mistress, 'Vivian Darkbloom' (Vladimir Nabokov), the verbal patterning points beyond his anguish to 'Someone else [who] is in the know', to quote an intruding voice in *Bend Sinister*.

Since it is Nabokov and not Humbert who is the expert lepidop-terist, the most significant authorial patterning in *Lolita* is the butterfly motif; it enables Nabokov to leave behind on Humbert's pages a trail of his own phosphorescent fingerprints. Nabokov himself casually underscored its considerable esthetic relevance when I visited him in Switzerland to interview him for this issue and in regard to my study of his work. [Appel is referring to his interview with Nabokov, which first appeared in the special issue of *Wisconsin Studies* on Nabokov, along with this article. Both are reprinted in *Nabokov: The Man and his Work*, edited by L.S. Dembo, from which this extract is taken.] As an example of the kind of humorous but telling detail whose significance critics often miss, I singled out the moment in the Humbert-Quilty con-frontation when Quilty notes that he is known as 'the American Maeterlinck', but quickly adds, 'Maeterlinck-Schmetterling, says I' (p.303). Nabokov nodded and with complete seriousness said, 'Yes. That's the most important phrase in the chapter'. At first this may seem to be an extreme statement, but in the context of the involuted pattern-ing it is perfectly just, for by mentioning the German word for *butterfly*, Quilty has superimposed the author's watermark on the scene, and it is the sole butterfly reference in the chapter.

Nabokov thus appears everywhere in the texture of *Lolita* but never in the text, although he 'com[es] damn close to it' as he lures the reader on. As Humbert says of 'Detective Trapp' (Quilty):

> . . . he succeeded in thoroughly enmeshing me and my thrashing anguish in his demoniacal game. With infinite skill, he swayed and staggered, and regained an impossible balance, always leaving me with the sportive hope – if I may use such a term in speaking of betrayal, fury, desolation, horror and hate – that he might give

himself away next time. He never did – though coming damn close
to it. We all admire the spangled acrobat with classical grace meticu-
lously walking his tight rope in the talcum light; but how much
rarer art there is in the sagging rope expert wearing scare-crow
clothes and impersonating a grotesque drunk. I should know.
(p. 251)

'Trapp's' balancing act lucidly describes the performance of both the
narrator and his creator, whose novels, by virtue of their delusive,
parodic form, are in themselves vast and grotesque 'impersonations'.
To take them literally is possibly to suffer feelings of 'betrayal, fury,
[or] desolation', for the parody-novel fashions a self-contained world
in a book; but the reader, in trying to make this kind of novel conform
to his vision, is continually manipulated by the book, trapped by the
parodies which reveal the speciousness or superficiality of his
assumptions, the commonplace qualities of his expectations.[19] At the
conclusion of his dramatic reunion with Lolita, Humbert says, 'Then I
pulled out my automatic – I mean, this is the kind of fool thing a reader
might suppose I did. It never even occurred to me to do it' (p. 282). By
creating a reality which is a fiction, but a fiction that is able to mock
the reader, the author has demonstrated the fiction of 'reality',[20] and
the reader who accepts these implications may even have experienced
a change in consciousness.

The detachment created by parody and self-parody ultimately
defines a way of viewing and judging the self. Characters (and their
creators) can never objectively observe their own existence, but self-
imitation is one way towards self-reflection and an expanded
consciousness. Humbert describes this process and maintains an
appropriately Nabokovian equilibrium between the 'truth and a cari-
cature of it' when he summarizes the essay he published in the *Cantrip
Review*, 'Mimir and Memory' (a 'cantrip' is a charm, spell or trick, and
describes Lolita's hold on him, while 'Mimir' is a giant in Norse
mythology who lived by the well at the roof of Yggdrasill, the great
tree symbolizing the universe. By drinking its water, he knew the past
and future). The essay suggests a 'theory of perpetual time based on
circulation of the blood and conceptually depending (to fill up this
nutshell) on the mind's being conscious of its own self, thus creating a
continuous spanning of two points (the storable future and the stored
past)' (p. 262).

Although Nabokov has called attention to the elements of parody
in his work, he has repeatedly denied the relevance of satire. One can
understand why he says 'I have neither the intent nor the temperament of a moral or social satirist', for he eschews the overtly moral
stance of the satirist who offers 'to mend the world' . . . Nabokov's

denials notwithstanding, Humbert's observations of American morals and mores *are* satirical, the product of his maker's moral sensibility, although this 'satire' is over-emphasized by readers who fail to recognize the extent of the parody, or its full implications.

In the course of showing us our landscape in all its natural beauty and meretricious glory, Humbert satirizes American songs, ads, movies, magazines, products, tourist attractions, summer camps, Dude Ranches, hotels, and motels, as well as the Good Housekeeping Syndrome (*Your Home is You* is one of Charlotte Haze's essential volumes) and the cant of progressive educationists and child guidance pontificators. Nabokov offers us a grotesque parody of a 'good relationship', for Humbert and Lo are 'pals' with a vengeance; *Know Your Own Daughter* is one of the books which Humbert consults. Yet Humbert's terrible demands notwithstanding, she is as insensitive as children are to their actual parents; sexuality aside, she demands anxious parental placation in a too typically American way, and affords Nabokov an ideal opportunity to comment on the Teen and Sub-Teen Tyranny. It is poetic justice that Lolita should seduce Humbert at The Enchanted Hunters hotel; the irony is obvious, but telling. Nabokov underscores his point with a resonant pun, characteristic of both himself and Joyce. The seduction takes place in the town of Briceland (note the *i* rather than *y*). Anyone over thirty should recall the popular weekly radio program of the forties, 'Baby Snooks', starring the late Fanny Brice. The show featured only Baby Snooks, a sappy but demanding little girl of indeterminate age, who spoke a patois of baby talk and teen jargon and her helpless, ineffectual Daddums (twice Humbert calls himself this). Year after year the program celebrated the various ways the tyrannical Baby Snooks could victimize her poor Daddy. The town of Briceland is well named. Nabokov's book is Baby Snooks and Daddums in apotheosis; Lolita is a Baby Snooks who looms threateningly high above us all. No one would deny that ours is a child-centered culture in deep trouble. 'Tristram in Movielove', remarks Humbert, and Nabokov has responded to those various travesties of behaviour which too many Americans recognize as tenable examples of significant reality. A gloss on this aspect of *Lolita* is provided by 'Ode to a Model', a poem which Nabokov published the same year as *Lolita* (1955).

Yet Nabokov's attitude towards both America and Lolita are similarly ambivalent; 'there is a queer, tender charm about that mythical nymphet', he said in an interview, and Humbert's satires are effected with an almost loving care. But there is nothing ambivalent about Nabokov's parody of the 'Viennese witch doctor'. Proclaiming himself 'King Sigmund the Second', Humbert mounts a frontal attack on many orthodox Freudian views, and the parodies are easily discerned.

Nabokov burlesques the case study by purposely providing the childhood 'trauma' which supposedly accounts for Humbert's nympholepsy: the incomplete coitus which the thirteen-year-old Humbert experienced on the French Riviera with Annabel, who died four months later (p.15). The incident seems to be a sly fictive transmutation of Nabokov's own considerably more innocent childhood infatuation with Colette (chapter six, *Speak, Memory*). When earnest readers nurtured on the 'standardized symbols of the psychoanalytic racket' (p.287) leap to make the association between the two episodes – as several have done – and immediately deduce that *Lolita* is surely autobiographical, then the trap has been sprung: their wantonly reductive gesture justifies the need for just such a parody as Nabokov's. With a cold literary perversity, Nabokov has demonstrated the falseness of their 'truth'; the implications are considerable. Even the exegetic act of searching for the 'meaning' of Lolita by trying to unfold the butterfly pattern becomes a parody of the expectations of the most sophisticated reader, who finds he is chasing a mocking inversion of the 'normal' Freudian direction of symbols which, once identified, may still remain mysterious, or explain very little.

The reader who has been unhappily deceived by the autobiographical trap or the butterfly motif may justifiably feel that he has been checkmated, for by reading *Lolita* carefully he is involved in a game, in the fullest and most serious sense. 'Darling, this is only a game!' says Humbert at the outset (p.22), and the pun on his name includes the game of *ombre*.[21] The readers who say they admire Nabokov in spite of his games are only demonstrating the failure of their responses. A hard distinction between the play and seriousness would vitiate the effect of *Lolita*,[22] and the central importance of the game-element in Nabokov is expressed in *Speak, Memory* when the description of his composition of chess problems turns out to serve as well for his fiction: 'Themes in chess, it may be explained, are such devices as forelaying, withdrawing, pinning, unpinning and so forth . . . Deceit, to the point of diabolism, and originality, grading into the grotesque, were my notions of strategy' (p.219). He explains that 'competition in chess problems is not really between White and Black but between composer and the hypothetical solver', just as in first-rate fiction 'the real clash' is between the author and the reader, rather than between the characters (p.220). The 'delusive opening moves, false scents, [and] specious lines of play' which characterize the chess problem are effected by parody in *Lolita*. The subject matter of *Lolita* is in itself a bravura and 'delusive opening move' – a withdrawn promise of pornography. The first one hundred or so pages of Lolita are often erotic – Lolita on Humbert's lap, for instance – but starting with the seduction scene, Nabokov withholds explicit sexual descriptions, at which point Humbert, trying to draw the reader into the vortex of the parody, exhorts us to 'Imagine me: I shall not exist if you do not imagine me' (p. 131). 'I am not concerned with so-called "sex" at all', Humbert says (p. 136); on the contrary, Nabokov is very much concerned with it, but with the reader's expectations rather than Humbert's machinations. 'Anybody can imagine those elements of animality', he says, and yet a great many readers wished that he had done it for them, enough to have kept *Lolita* at the top of the bestseller list for a year, although librarians reported that many readers never finished the novel. The critics and readers who complain that the second half of Lolita is less interesting are not aware of the possible significance of their admission. Their desire for highbrow pornography is doubled in Clare Quilty, whose main hobby is making pornographic films. At the end of the novel, Lolita tells Humbert that Quilty forced her to star in one of his unspeakable 'sexcapades', and more than one reader has unconsciously wished that Quilty had been the narrator, his unseen movie the novel. Two of Quilty's pseudonymous hotel guestbook registrations list his home as 'Larousse, Ill.' and 'Hoaxton, Eng.,' but the acute way in which Quilty parodies the reader's voyeurism suggests that the elements of ruse and hoax are deserved and entirely in earnest. Puns thus summarize the function of parody as game: 'Lolita was playing a double game', says Humbert, referring to Lolita's tennis and to the *Doppelgänger* parody, and Humbert's search for his Double, Quilty, whom he at first believes to be 'Detective Gustave Trapp', turns out to be the detective trap. The novel becomes a gameboard on which, through parody, Nabokov assaults the conventions and the worst pretensions of his readers.[23] □

What is so striking in the 1960s, and can be seen running very clearly into the 1970s, is the rhetorical structure of an argument that can be traced back to Trilling's reading in the 1950s. Appel's sentence casts this in recognisable terms, 'Yet Humbert's terrible demands notwithstanding, she is as insensitive as children are to their actual parents . . . '. Thus a predominant critical commentary in the 1960s and 1970s works by acknowledging H.H.'s impropriety, and then turns to the 'fact' of what Lolita is, what Lolita does, to mitigate his actions. In these terms, Lolita is a lippy, gum-chewing, vulgar, insensitive American teenager who wants and wants. In these terms, Lolita seduces her step-father. For Appel, Lolita is one of the 'tenable' examples of 'significant reality' in the novel. At the same time, he is at pains to demonstrate the ways in which the use of parody in the novel persistently undermines and disturbs 'reality', to the point that 'reality' is more or less a fiction. This is an important observation in the 1960s. Although Appel does not extend this argument we will see different versions of it appearing in the 1980s and 1990s: the 'real girl' Lolita is also a 'fictional' effect. In comparing Lolita with the radio character 'Baby Snooks', Appel effectively consolidates a strand of critical thought that can be traced back to Trilling in the 1950s, and forward to Douglas Fowler's reading in the 1970s: it is the sense that ultimately Humbert Humbert is both captive to (and victim of) a demanding teenager who is herself a 'victim' of a child-centred culture of mass consumption. Let us now return to Appel's conclusion in which he brings the question of morality into his discussion of parody.

■ What is extraordinary about *Lolita* is not the presence or absence of the author's 'moral position', but the way in which Nabokov enlists us, against our will, on Humbert's side. 'Pity is the password', says John Shade, speaking for his creator. Nabokov purposely takes a shocking subject in *Lolita*, and when we are sympathetic to Humbert, Nabokov has successfully expanded our potential for compassion, and has demonstrated that the certainty of our moral feelings is far more tenuous than we ever care to admit. We know exactly what Nabokov means about the contest between the author and the reader when we almost find ourself wishing Humbert well during his agonizing first night with Lolita at The Enchanted Hunters, or appreciating Humbert's situation when the drugged Lolita occupies an 'unfair amount of pillow' (p. 131). 'Mesmer Mesmer' is one of the pseudonyms Humbert considered but rejected. It would be a fitting cognomen, given the power and effect of his rhetoric, since Humbert has figuratively made the reader his accomplice in both statutory rape and murder. Needless to say, the rhetoric of morality can be just as manipulative, and what is worse, it may not connect meaningfully with emotion of any kind. Because Lolita seduces Humbert she might seem to be the agent of immorality, but the irony is another trap in the game; this is just the kind of easy release from culpability which we are too ready to accept; it does not mitigate the existence of their ensuing two years together, nor the fact that Humbert has denied Lolita her youth, whatever its qualities may be. It should be clear that when Nabokov says that there is 'No moral in tow' in *Lolita*, he is not denying it any moral resonance, but simply asserting that his intentions are not didactic (p. 316).[24] □

For Appel, 'Humbert's is finally not a credible point of view'. How, then, does it come to be taken as credible by many critics? I have referred above to Douglas Fowler's perception of Humbert as a 'victim' of Lolita. As we will see in the next chapter, Douglas Fowler discusses at some length the idea of Humbert Humbert as a fantasist, transforming everything he sees around him – America merges with Lolita from this perspective. At the same time, Fowler's argument is so enamoured with

H.H.'s point of view, and so sympathetic to the way in which his story turns out, that a credibility of sorts is granted. For Fowler, that credibility resides in H.H. as the sensitive soul of literary consciousness looking out onto the vulgar world of America that Lolita is believed to represent. The relevance of this for Appel's discussion of parody as a literary convention is that parody is unremittingly anti-realist, and therefore works against the representation of 'reality'. Since by all accounts Lolita is taken to be the 'reality' on which readings of the novel must inevitably stumble, both the figure of Lolita and the 'realist' narrative that surrounds her (the narrative of sexual abduction and suffering) must always be at risk of disappearing. At the same time, as critics such as Elisabeth Bronfen will point out in the 1990s (see chapter five of this Guide), with its 'framed' convention of a 'found' narrative, both *Lolita* the novel and Lolita the girl are already parodies of 'realist' forms.

From a rather different (European) perspective is Denis de Rougemont's insightful reading of the representation of romantic love in the novel. In drawing attention to the lack of reciprocity between Humbert Humbert and Lolita, and the ways in which H.H.'s 'love' for Lolita is different to the mythical love between Tristan and Iseult that the narrative invokes, de Rougemont anticipates the contextual concerns of later readings of the novel in the 1980s and 1990s. In this sense, de Rougemont's discussion of *Lolita* (which is quite short and appears as one section in a chapter entitled 'New Metamorphoses of Tristan' in *Love Declared: Essays on the Myths of Love* (1963)) also acts as a useful gloss on the idea of parody and intertextuality. It goes beyond simply pointing out the extratextual references and their function as forms of parody and so forth, attempting instead to show the *significant effects* of difference on the way the narrative unfolds. In the particular instance with which de Rougemont is concerned here, it is the very lack of reciprocity between H.H. and Lolita that defines a narrative torn between the 'poetic' desire of its narrator and, to borrow Appel's phrase, the 'significant reality' of Lolita as both object of and subject to a desire that is neither shared nor returned.

■ . . . Lolita, twelve years and seven months old, has the disturbing charm, the innocent shamelessness, and the touch of vulgarity that characterize the nymphet. Humbert Humbert, a European in his late thirties, who has been in America only a short time, discovers her in a small town where he is taking his vacation. Love at first sight. Lunatic plot to possess the child, whose mother he marries first. This unfortunate creature soon dies, run over by an automobile. H.H. takes Lolita away with him to a hotel called The Enchanted Hunters. He gives her a sleeping pill, but dares not take advantage of her slumbers. In the morning, it is she who seduces him! Then begins the long flight of the stepfather and daughter, tracked by their secret guilt, across the entire expanse of the United States,[25] until the day Lolita escapes, seduced by another middle-aged man whom Humbert will eventually kill. At seventeen, married to a brawny young mechanic, she dies in childbed, a few weeks after Humbert, who is spared capital punishment by a coronary thrombosis.

I do not mean to veil or to excuse the novel's scandalous character, for it appears to be essential, and the author misses no opportunity to underline and accentuate it, either by reproaching his hero in a preface attributed, moreover, to an American psychiatrist; or, more convincingly, by the cynical flippancy of Humbert Humbert's style. If loving nymphets was not, in our day and age, one of the last surviving sexual taboos (with incest), there would be neither true passion nor true novel, in the 'Tristanian' sense of these terms. For the necessary obstacle would be missing between the two protagonists, the necessary *distance* by which the mutual attraction, instead of being mitigated or exhausted by sensual gratification, is metamorphosed into passion. [Emphasis de Rougemont's.] It is first and foremost the evident scandal, the profaning character of H.H.'s love for Lolita that betrays the presence of the myth . . . . . .

. . . We are left with two sexual taboos, strangely respected by our mores in rapid transition from a primitive sense of the sacred to a scientific hygiene: nymphet-love and incest. Are these two loves *contra naturam*? We find them widely practiced in the animal world and in the great majority of human societies, the Western bourgeoisie constituting the most notable exception. Such practices are less against nature than against civilization. 'I found myself maturing amid a civilization which allows a man of twenty-five to court a girl of sixteen but not a girl of twelve'. Humbert describes, at the beginning of his memoirs, the love he conceived at the age of thirteen for a child of twelve whom he called Annabel and who died soon after – an evocation of Poe. Thus the Eros of this adult, otherwise sexually normal male is fixated on the child-woman, rendered doubly inaccessible by the difference in age and by the idea of death. This is how the nymphet becomes the mainstay of passion – that is, of the infinite desire which escapes the natural rhythms and plays the role of an absolute preferable to life itself. The possession of this inaccessible object then becomes ecstasy, 'the supreme joy' . . .

Yet those who have read *Lolita* with more perverse amusement than emotion will be entitled to suspect the legitimacy of so solemn an interpretation.

Of course, from the initial *coup de foudre* to the death of the separated lovers – the consequence of a forbidden love that exiles them from the community and consumes without truly uniting them – the great moments of the Myth are easily identifiable. Has the author been aware of them? [Tristan is the hero of Celtic legend who fell in love with Iseult, the bride he was sent to claim on behalf of his uncle. The story of Tristan and Iseult is part of the Arthurian cycle. Over time, it has been reworked in many different forms, most famously perhaps in Wagner's opera, *Tristan und Isolde*.] Certain episodes of the novel would suggest that this was the case, allusions to the most typical situations and peripeties of the Tristan legend. [Peripeteia, of which 'peripeties' is a derivative, means 'a sudden change of fortune in a drama or in life'.] But it is curious to note that on each occasion a touch of irony accompanies the allusion. Thus the hero's mother dies very early (as in Tristan), but this is the tone of the narrative: 'My very photogenic mother died in a freak accident (picnic, lightning) when I was three'. (We remember the lugubrious tone of fate, the *alte Weise* that marks the mother's death in *Tristan*!) The name of the hotel where the seduction occurs obviously recalls the state of trance of the avowal scene in *Tristan*, but the entire description of the place aims precisely at disenchanting it. The episode of the love-philter is present, but made absurd by its failure: it is only a sleeping pill which H.H. makes Lolita take by a ruse, and which moreover turns out to be too weak, the doctor who provided it having erred as to its ingredients or having bilked his client. ['Bilked' means 'cheated'.] . . . As in *Tristan*, it is true, the attack on marriage in the name of passion animates the entire narrative. As in *Tristan*, we feel that the author is not interested by the sexual aspect of his story, but solely by the magic of Eros, and he says as much: 'I am not concerned with so-called (sex) at all. Anybody can imagine those elements of animality. A greater endeavor lures on: to fix once and for all the perilous magic of nymphets'. As in Tristan, 'the lovers flee the world, and the world them'. Lastly, as in Tristan, they die within a short time of one another, separated. But their death is as sordid as the death of the legendary lovers was triumphant in the twelfth-century and Wagnerian versions.

This is because in reality H.H. and Lolita have never known what I call 'unhappy reciprocal love'. Lolita has never responded to the fierce and tender passion of her elder lover. Hence the failure of the Myth and the 'savagely facetious' tone of the novel, its pitiless realism and its somewhat mad jokes saved (just barely, on occasion) from vulgarity by a dazzling verbal virtuosity. If Lolita had loved the narrator, if she had been Iseult, the realistic novel would have given way to the poem, and the social satire to an inner lyricism. The hypothesis is not an arbitrary one . . . the absence, here very striking, not only of any kind of emotional impurity, but also of any spiritual horizon, reduces the novel to the dimensions of a genre-study of mores in the manner of Hogarth. We share the author's irritations, we acclaim his syntax and his vocabulary, we laugh often, we are never moved.

Such as it is, this perfect work remains, too, a *Tristan manqué*. And this is consonant with the immaturity of the very object of the passion described; yet without this immaturity there would be no obstacle, hence no passion. Perhaps the book, after all, is vicious only with regard to this circle.[26] □

As suggested, de Rougemont's reading seems to offer a way out of the enclosed formalist readings of the 1960s, in part because of the way in which his reading remains focused on the *differences* between the text and its intertexts. Coming from a critical tradition outside the American academy seems to grant de Rougemont a refreshing shift in perspective. He is not so seduced by the brilliance of form in Humbert's narrative. de Rougemont's reaction to the seductions of the text is compelling precisely because it allows us to see that it is Lolita who literally comes between the lyricism and the potential poetry of the novel. Lolita and her realism interrupt the achievement of literary bliss; the achievement that confines many of the 1960s readings. Clearly de Rougemont is not unique in observing the lack of reciprocity in Humbert's 'romance'. As we have seen already in the readings of both Stegner and Appel, the absolute disjunction between Humbert's desire for Lolita, and Lolita as subject to the enactment of those desires, cannot be overlooked. But it can be set aside, and it can be displaced at the point at which 'reality' threatens full appreciation and valorisation of the novel as esteemed literary object. In simple terms, what makes de Rougemont's position so tangential to the dominant American readings of the 1960s is his failure as a reader to come under the spell of H.H.'s confessional. Finally, he remains unmoved by the 'fancy prose style' to which so much attention is paid in the 1960s, and to which so many critics are in thrall.

In a brilliant and impressive reading of *Lolita*, which starts with a comparison of Nabokov and Tolstoy in regard to their respective philosophies of artistic purpose and value, Martin Green also takes up this question of romance and romantic love from a position thoroughly informed by a post-war, cold-war 'American' perspective of freedom and democracy. In many ways, Green takes on all of the important positions in the debate about *Lolita* up to this point, and complicates them. He refuses to entertain the binaries and oppositions that have haunted the response to *Lolita* since the novel appeared: art and pornography, fantasy and reality, romance and brutality. It is not just that Green allows for the oppositional terms, it is rather that he insists they are found together and it is because they are found together that *Lolita* is both great art and a work of morality. In this sense, Green anticipates later deconstructive practices of literary criticism. The following extract is taken from the conclusion to Green's argument in which he brings together his reading of 'romance' with what he sees as the 'morality of *Lolita*'.

■ . . . Let me just say now that this theme [of romantic love] is developed and resolved according to the pattern of the novel. That is, the major instance of love taken (the American instance, the Lolita instance) is very painful, ugly, unassimilable to romance; it is explicitly contrasted with the minor, perfect instance, and then described in insolent and brutal detail; but the total picture created is of a necessary interaction of very beautiful moments with very ugly ones. It is a development from idyllic romanticism to realistic romanticism, by means of interweaving the grotesque with the idealized in a convincing pattern.

It is only in this sense that I can understand Nabokov's sentence about aesthetic bliss. The novel gives us the sense of being connected with other states of being where art is the norm; and art he either identifies with or groups with curiosity, tenderness, kindness, ecstasy. *Lolita* obviously creates moments for us in which curiosity, tenderness, ecstasy, beauty, art itself are radiantly realized, and it creates a world within which we can rely on such moments recurring. But, to justify a man in entering such a mental world, he needs to be sure that it is 'realistic' – that he has taken adequate account of the ugliness of actual experience, and of the human impulse merely to make up such pretty dreams, merely to make itself see roses and hear violins. So *Lolita* must contain also moments of ugliness and pain as bitter and burning as any Nabokov could devise. And it must be infinitely skeptical about its own search for beauty, infinitely ironic about every mode of romanticism and idyll. Moreover, these anti-romantic modes of the imagination must be allowed to interpenetrate the romantic. Hence all the pornographic-seeming detail of the orgasm on the couch, so ugly and shocking as well as so brilliant and gay. Hence too all the trickery, all the warning against believing the narrator, against any unguarded response, throughout the novel. Only by giving full free play to both these anti-romantic tendencies, and by building a world that will contain them too, can the author justify those moments of perfect beauty and win for himself 'aesthetic bliss'.

This is the moral structure of *Lolita*, and it surely is strong enough to support and contain the anti-moral material the novel allows itself. A novel is not pornographic (except in the sense that it can be used as pornography) when its interest in sexual excitement is a necessary part of such large and serious interests. It is not anti-cultural when its cynicism (Humbert's cynicism) dramatizes an alienation which is so movingly, though unobtrusively, placed and judged.

But none of this contradicts Tolstoy's assumed condemnation of the novel. [Green is referring to his introduction, where it is suggested that Tolstoy would have loathed *Lolita*: 'Nabokov stands in immediate and intimate relationship to that symbolist tradition Tolstoy was denouncing, which replaced Tolstoy's own tradition in Russian literature'.[27]] All we have been saying is true only from a point of view completely sympathetic with the author, a view taken from a point, so to speak, inside the novel. This is the perfect reading of the novel, and novels do not exist only in that form. Culturally speaking, they exist much more in the form of imperfect readings – as understood from outside the novel, in very imperfect sympathy with the author's intentions. *Lolita can* be used as pornography; in fact it will be, and almost must be, and by highly trained readers as well as the untrained. It will also have, in its measure, an anti-cultural effect of weakening taboos and fostering cynicism. There is something powerfully disintegrative in Nabokov's sensibility, and, though the novel's form contains and transmutes that something, the total effect of reading it – even on highly trained readers – is not likely to be controlled by the form. *Lolita is* in fact the product and the agent of a corrupt culture.

If then we, like Tolstoy, were ready to judge art primarily by cultural criteria, we could, and would have to, condemn *Lolita*. Tolstoy followed Plato, and said better no art than bad art, which means better aesthetically bad art than morally bad. But we, presumably, are committed to using primarily aesthetic criteria, and to preferring aesthetically good art. We are committed to judging a novel primarily on its perfect reading, seeing it in perfect sympathy with the author's intentions, understanding it from inside; however rare, in cultural fact, such a reading may be; however little that reading may coincide with the book's effective meaning; however 'exclusive', to use Tolstoy's term, the audience for that version of the book.

This obligation on the critic is a necessary correlative of the freedom of the artist, and we of the liberal tradition are presumably committed to that freedom. Nabokov is a fine example of the free artist, and a fine symbol of what we are committed to. He is free first in the sense of refusing all allegiance to non-aesthetic schemes of value, and aggressively, positively refusing, as well as negatively; he affronts and injures those schemes of value; he is not only non-ideological, he is anti-ideological. And this freedom he so fully takes necessitates the other freedom we were discussing – his claim, his right, to be judged only from inside the special world he has created. His justification of those freedoms, and what they cost us in affronts and injuries to our personal and collective sensibilities, is the novel itself. Given its perfect reading, *Lolita* is a brilliant and beautiful experience, satisfying our most purely moral sense as well as all the others. What is there in Tolstoy's 'art of the future', Soviet literature, that can compare with it? But that comparison is not the point. It is the contrast, within our own case, between what we gain and what we lose, by our effective philosophy of art, which seems to me so interesting.[28] □

At the end of the 1960s, then, Green suggests the possibility of a 'perfect reading' of *Lolita* that will satisfy the desire for literature to be both morally and aesthetically pleasing. In an obvious sense, this fantasy of what an ideal reading can be, and can do, would effectively render reading redundant. As Stegner's analysis reveals, however, the practice of criticism and interpretation works from the principle of 'imperfect' reading. Turning to the 1970s, we can see the ways in which critics are both consciously and unconsciously clearing the way for new interpretations that would bring them even closer to the true text in hand – *Lolita*.

CHAPTER THREE

'The Manifold Recesses of Literary Possibility': Comparative Criticism of America's *Lolita* in the 1970s

ONE OF the most important publishing events in the critical life of *Lolita* is at the beginning of the decade. Edited by Alfred Appel Jr, with a substantial introduction based on two of his critical articles, *The Annotated 'Lolita'* appeared in 1970. The text contains 'some nine hundred notes' although, as Appel says in his preface, 'the initial annotated edition of a work should never be offered as definitive'. This event is so significant because it is the first annotated edition of a modern novel to be published in the lifetime of its author. In the space of fifteen years *Lolita* has travelled from uncertain charges of pornography and obscenity to a secure place in the American literary canon. In the corrections he made to Appel's notes, Nabokov's reputation as a meticulous reader is clearly justified, and his immediate response to the initial proposal for an annotated edition of *Lolita* is typical of his writerly precision: 'Theoretically the idea is splendid but specifically it is a great pity that the three first notes of this display batch are wrong'. He then goes on to correct them, and at the end of this letter to Appel makes a pointed reference to Diana Butler as a critic who had incurred his disapproval. Butler had written an article, '*Lolita* Lepidoptera' (1960), which Nabokov thought pretentious: 'I shall check all your notes but please do leave out all references to lepidoptera, a tricky subject (which led the unfortunate Diana so dreadfully astray). There are a couple of passages where lep notes are quite necessary but these I shall supply myself'.[1] In awe of Nabokov's expertise and vast literary and cultural knowledge, Appel also finds the author unique as a writer: 'Although other writers have created involuted works, Nabokov's self-consciousness is supreme; and the range and scale of his effects, his mastery and control, make him unique'.[2] As we noted in the extract from Appel's article on parody in the previous chapter, 'involuted' is one of his key terms for describing the technical brilliance of *Lolita*. Involuted means 'complicated', 'abstruse', or 'intricate'. Appel suggests that Nabokov achieves involution (or 'intricacy') in his writing in seven closely interrelated ways. These are 'Parody', 'Coincidence', 'Patterning', 'Allusion', 'The Work-Within-the-Work', 'The Staging of the Novel' and 'Authorial Voice'. Under each of these headings Appel qualifies the term, giving examples. Later in the introduction, Appel takes up the topic of intricacy under the heading, 'The Artifice of *Lolita*'. The following extract shows Appel elaborating some of these themes, both as a general argument for what is missing in *Lolita* criticism (to date) and as support for the view that the novel is unique.

■ Although *Lolita* has received much serious attention . . . the criticism which it has elicited usually forces a thesis which does not and in fact cannot accommodate the total design of the novel. That intricate design, described in the Notes to this edition, makes *Lolita* one of the few supremely original novels of the century. It is difficult to imagine, say, that *Lord Jim* could have been achieved without the example of Henry James's narrative strategies, or that *The Sound and the Fury* would be the same novel if Faulkner had not read *Ulysses*. But like *The Castle, Remembrance of Things Past, Ulysses, Finnegans Wake*, and *Pale Fire, Lolita* is one of those transcendent works of the imagination which defy the neat continuum maintained so carefully by literary historians. At most, it is one of those works which create their own precursors, to use Jorge Luis Borges's winning phrase.

Because Nabokov continually parodies the conventions of 'realistic' and 'impressionistic' fiction, readers must accept or reject him on his own terms. Many of his novels become all but meaningless in any other terms. At the same time, however, even Nabokov's most ardent admirers must sometimes wonder about the smaller, more hermetic components of Nabokov's artifice – the multifarious puns, allusions, and butterfly references which proliferate in novels such as *Pale Fire* and *Lolita*. Are they organic? Do they coalesce to form any meaningful pattern? Humbert's wide-ranging literary allusions more than 'challenge [our] scholarship', as H.H. says of Quilty's similar performance. Several of Humbert's allusions are woven so subtly into the texture of the narrative as to elude all but the most compulsive exegetes. ['Exegetes' means interpreters.] Many allusions, however, are direct and available, and these are most frequently to nineteenth-century writers; an early Note will suggest that this is of considerable importance. But unlike the allusions, which are sometimes only a matter of fun, the patterned verbal cross-references are always fundamental, defining a dimension of the novel that has escaped critical notice.

The verbal *figurae* in *Lolita* limn [illuminate] the novel's involuted design and establish the basis of its artifice . . . The following remarks on artifice and game are not intended to suggest that this 'level' of the novel is the most important; they are offered because no one has fully recognized the magnitude of this verbal patterning, or its significance.[3] □

It is worth pausing to ask here if this is something of an overstatement, a rhetorical claim for a critical project, since Appel is clearly not alone in the 1960s and 1970s in finding himself dazzled by the language of *Lolita*. Indeed, this is the very reason for the annotated version. Appel's schematic approach to the verbal fireworks in *Lolita* seems especially close to that of Carl R. Proffer in *Keys to Lolita* (1968), which was discussed in the previous chapter. Appel completed the first edition of his Notes in 1968, and he acknowledges earlier in the Preface to *The Annotated 'Lolita'* that while his own work was in progress, and awaiting publication, Proffer's book was actually published. 'Two enchanted hunters . . . working independently of each other, Mr. Proffer and I arrived at many similar identifications and, excepting those which are readily apparent, I have tried to indicate where he anticipated me.'[4] What the extract above clearly indicates is that whilst Appel views the Notes as an immediate aid (another key) to reading a deeply allusive novel, he also hopes it will be a further scholarly resource for the closure of certain critical gaps. The final extract from the Introduction to *The Annotated 'Lolita'* concerns the narration of *Lolita*. Appel takes the argument forward in interesting ways raising the question of narrative desire and the structure of reality in the novel.

■ A great deal has been written about 'unreliable narrators', but too little about unreliable readers. Although editor John Ray, Jr., serves fair enough warning to those 'old-fashioned readers who wish to follow the destinies of "real" people beyond the "true story"', virtually every 'move' in the 'true story' of *Lolita* seems to be structured with their predictable responses in mind; and the game-element depends on such reflexive action, for it tests the reader in so many ways. By calling out 'Reader! Bruder!' (p. 262),[5] Humbert echoes *Au Lecteur*, the prefatory poem in *Les Fleurs du Mal* ('Hypocrite reader! – My fellow man – My brother!'); and, indeed, the entire novel constitutes an ironic upending of Baudelaire and a good many other writers who would enlist the reader's full participation in the work. 'I want my learned readers to participate in the scene I am about to replay', says Humbert (p. 57), but such participation will find the reader in constant danger of check, or even rougher treatment: 'As greater authors than I have put it: "Let readers imagine" etc. On second thought, I may as well give those imaginations a kick in the pants' (p. 65).[6] □

Julia Bader takes up this problem of Humbert Humbert's imagination, and the implications of participating in his narrative of perversity, in one of the most influential readings of *Lolita* in the 1970s. Bader's reading appears as a chapter on *Lolita*, 'The Quest for Ecstasy', in a book-length study of Nabokov, *Crystal Land: Artifice in Nabokov's English Novels* (1972). The first extract to be considered is taken from the introduction to the chapter. The essence of Bader's argument is that 'artistry and perversion' are inseparable in the novel[7] because the central question of artististic creation is filtered through the perverse desires of Humbert Humbert. Hence, the 'quest' of Bader's chapter title refers not only to Nabokov's authorial enterprise, but also to Humbert's obsessive desire for Lolita, and the creation of *Lolita*/Lolita in the form of the memoir that constitutes the fiction(s).

■ The form and movement of *Lolita* are shaped by a dual task: to record the emotional apotheosis of the narrator's passion for a nymphet, and to transform his story into a work of art which will immortalize that passion. Thus the question of the nature of artistic creation is posed directly by the witty pedant, obsessive pervert, and ecstatic lover whose personality and motivation constitute one of the implicit themes of his memoir. Humbert Humbert is constantly conscious of the difficulties of creating a vehicle adequate to his adored subject and to his purpose of explaining, justifying, and condemning his role in Lolita's life.

Although the novel is a memoir narrated in the first person, there are themes and revelations of which Humbert is not fully in control. The striking verisimilitude which Nabokov creates through the mask of Humbert is only one aspect of a shifting tale. Despite the sharpness of observation, the flawless ear for dialogue, the detailed evocation of everyday American scenes, Humbert attempts to manipulate his readers; and he is manipulated in turn, without being aware of it. Critics have posed the question: 'Is there a voice behind Humbert?' and have answered in the negative. But 'point of view' need not be expressed through a separate voice; in Nabokov's case it is more a network of details behind and around Humbert which is not of his conscious making, and of which he may be unaware. After all, Aubrey McFate, the dramatization of destiny as decreed by the omniscient author, is not Humbert's agent; and Humbert himself, when Lolita reveals the name of her abductor, bows to a larger fictional necessity.

In significant and easily recognizable ways *Lolita* is rooted in a realistic convention, a lifelike density which is one of its most pleasurable achievements. Humbert, too, has a certain consistency of tone and characterization: he does not fade into the papier-mâché backdrop, nor does he 'peter out' to merge and disappear into his creator, as do most other Nabokovian main characters. The following remarks about the theme of art as suggested by and glimpsed through the narrative do not mean to deny the compelling presence of the realistic foreground, but point to an aspect of the novel wherein many of Humbert's aims and pronouncements converge with his desires.

. . . . . . The intricate structure of *Lolita* comprises a number of themes and metaphors, all of which are fitted into the quasi-realistic American setting and yet extend the implications of Humbert's passion for nymphets into a treatment of the thrills of a butterfly hunt, the problems of a chess game, and assorted parodies of traditional and contemporary topics.[8] Nevertheless, the theme of artistic creation deserves particular attention: an illuminating and pervasive motif throughout the book, it is reflected in the 'moral apotheosis' of H.H., the role of Lolita, and the form of the entire novel. In view of a certain aspect of Nabokov's definition of fiction and art (as the realm where the norm is 'ecstasy'), Humbert's obsession is best described as 'artistic'. The emotional intensity, coupled with the sylistic care which Humbert lavishes on his Lolita (and Nabokov on his *Lolita*), strives to attain a beauty and perfection which is closest to 'aesthetic bliss'.[9] □

A number of important points emerge in this extract that indicate both the established terrain of formalist *Lolita* criticism in the 1970s, and Bader's engagement with it. In the footnote to her opening remarks, Bader points to a number of key thematic and topical readings of the novel from the 1950s and 1960s: Lionel Trilling on troubadours, Diana Butler on butterflies, and G.D. Josipovici on parody and emotion, all appear in her list. In contrast to this kind of reading, Bader wants to offer a sustained account of Humbert Humbert's narrative of 'ecstasy', and V.N.'s narrative of artistic creation. At the same time, and in the main body of her text, Bader is careful to acknowledge the significance of the conventions of realism in the novel. She admits the 'compelling presence of the realistic foreground', but for the purposes of her own argument it must be set aside. This critical move – of acknowledging a prominent feature of the novel but claiming that it cannot be dealt with in the context of a particular reading – is reminiscent of Page Stegner's position (see chapter two of this Guide). Bader's acknowledgement of a 'realism' that is 'there' but 'not there' prefigures the powerful shift in the critical stance of the 1980s, when that 'realism' becomes impossible to set aside. Indeed, this sense of a problematic distinction between the 'realistic' and the 'aesthetic' aspects of the text will move into the critical foreground. It is also important to note Bader's insight into what she describes as a 'network of details' of which the narrator Humbert Humbert may be unaware. Again, although Bader does not take up directly this question of alternative narrative possibilities, she does anticipate later developments in the critical history of the novel. Let us now return to Bader's reading of *Lolita*, and her discussion of the creative schemings of Humbert Humbert's narrative.

■ Humbert is master of the characters within the scope of his journal. He manipulates them according to his whim – except for the character of Lolita, who obsesses him. His vision reflects the manifold recesses of literary possibility. He ironically sees himself in the pose of the creative artist: 'Humbert the Cubus schemed and dreamed – and the red sun of desire and decision (the two things that create a live world) rose higher and higher, while upon a succession of balconies a succession of libertines, sparkling glass in hand, toasted the bliss of past and future nights' (p. 67).[10] His vision is directed at the image of illusion with illusion, as his constant references to mirrors and lakes suggest. His fantasy spans the past and the future. The potentiality of perfection lures him on in his painful affair with Lolita – but her essence, which is rooted in the present, eludes him.

We cannot ascertain whether Quilty is actually following their car, or whether the 'clues' of the hotel registers were really diabolically planted by Quilty. What is important is that Humbert is driven to the edge of madness by the effort to preserve Lolita in his own image, and the guilt and shame of his irreparable tampering with her magic serve to point to his inability to attain the perfect literary 'equipoise' between her movement in everyday life and her immobile existence in the realm of art.[11] Humbert is perennially toying with shifting scenes and dialogues: the enactment of the final murder scene with Quilty is the amalgam of numerous versions of murders culled from Humbert's dreams and hallucinations. This may account for the nightmarish, unreal quality of the final scene, as if Humbert had not quite decided how the scene should take place, and is experimenting with a dummy Quilty to determine the best posture and the most suitable number of bullets.

Humbert constantly hears unsaid echoes of conversations, and this gives the impression that the unused lines which he has decided to eliminate from the final version are still lingering behind the irrevocably 'used' ones. At The Enchanted Hunters Inn, Humbert has a conversation with a still uncreated Quilty, to whom he has decided to give a voice, but not a name or a face. Even the act of 'creating' Quilty's voice is dramatized: 'The rasp of a screwing off, then a discreet gurgle, then the final note of a placid screwing on . . . His voice addressed me: "Where the devil did you get her?" "I beg your pardon?" "I said: the weather is getting better"' (p. 17). Humbert mentally adds 'stillborn babies' to a motel's otherwise innocuous list of things not to be flushed in the toilet; his description of himself fluctuates between Humbert the Wounded Spider and Humbug the Giant Killer.

He is gradually enveloped by the consequences of his desecration, at first only as a vague hint, later as a perpetual shadow. Still at the beginning of their romance, he retroactively sees himself and Lolita in a symbolic relationship: 'She was sprawling and sobbing, and pinching my caressing hand, and I was laughing happily, and the atrocious, unbelievable, unbearable, and, I suspect, eternal horror that I know now, was still but a dot of blackness in the blue sky of my bliss' (p. 154). [A certain tension appears in Bader's reading at moments like this when her attempt to describe *only* the rhetoric of Humbert's fantasy creation of Lolita comes up against the representation of events in the text. To call what takes place between Humbert and Lolita as 'their romance', and then to describe this particular scene in terms of a symbolic relationship, is to risk losing altogether the 'realistic foreground'. Lolita is 'sobbing' and 'pinching' not just because Humbert has performed another sexual 'operation', but because he has 'retracted some silly promise she has forced [him] to make in a moment of blind impatient passion'.[12]]

Perhaps Quilty serves partly to dramatize Humbert's ritualistic killing of pseudo-art, which has defiled his own passionately loved art object. It is not until Humbert decides to kill Quilty that the playwright actually begins to 'exist'. Humbert the artist sees that the plot necessitates Quilty's appearance, and 'in the methodical manner on which I have always prided myself, I had been keeping Clare Quilty's face masked in my dark dungeon, where he was waiting for me . . . I have no time right now to discuss the mnemonics of physiognomization' (pp. 264–265). Apparently Humbert does not leave himself enough time to do a thorough characterization, because he describes the about-to-be-eliminated Quilty as 'this semi-animated, subhuman trickster' (p. 269).

In sharp contrast to the half-emerging characters around her, Lolita is described in minute detail: her smell, her mannerisms, her thigh and arm measurements are given with meticulous precision. But only too late does Humbert realize that he has given her no soul, that in spite of his painstaking artistry he has failed to appreciate her wonder and mystery, and it shocks him to the border of unconsciousness to think that 'I simply did not know a thing about my darling's mind and that quite possibly behind the awful juvenile clichés, there was in her a garden and a twilight, and a palace gate' (p. 259) [This is one of the most frequently quoted passages from *Lolita*. Bader reads it as a retrospective declaration of regret, on Humbert's part, for failing to fully 'appreciate' the 'wonder and mystery' of Lolita. In the 1980s, this passage becomes one of the key starting points for thinking about what Humbert has *taken* from Lolita.]

Humbert's awareness of the peril of his artistic attempt makes him a jealous guardian of Lolita, both to protect himself and to keep her from being soiled by the 'dirty children who were her contemporaries'. After she has left him, Humbert finds that she has broken something in him: 'One essential vision in me had withered: never did I dwell now on possibilities of bliss with a little maiden, specific or synthetic . . . never did my fancy sink its fangs into Lolita's sisters, far, far away, in the coves of evoked islands' (p.235). He is still dominated by the compulsion to track down Lolita and Quilty, but he knows that he can derive no happiness from indulging in his monomania. He has given up the dream of actualizing the phantoms of the imagination, phantoms which were initially 'perfect, just because the vision was out of reach, with no possibility of attainment to spoil it by the awareness of an appended taboo; indeed it may well be that the very attraction immaturity has for me lies . . . in the security of a situation where infinite perfections fill the gap between the little given and the great promised – the great rosegray never-to-be-had' (p.241). This description corresponds to Humbert's 'pre-dolorian past', when the promise of attaining the ideal was made by Annabel. 'Since I sometimes won the race between my fancy and nature's reality, the deception was bearable. Unbearable pain began when chance entered the fray and deprived me of the smile meant for me . . . The radiant foreglimpse, the promise of reality, a promise not only to be simulated seductively but also to be nobly held – all this, chance denied me – chance and a change to smaller characters' (p.241). The terminology of drama and print ('smaller characters'), along with a hint of the omniscient author's control ('chance'), is used to express Humbert's sense of the circumscribed nature of his world and of his imaginative range.

If Humbert sees a 'succession of balconies with a succession of libertines' (the libertines being the multiple reflections of his lustful self, refracted in the process of recreation), so Nabokov sees a succession of Humberts on shifting fictional levels. Gaston, the lovable, harmless pervert, and Quilty, the witty, vulgar, commercial nympholept, dramatize extremes of Humbert's varied personality. The novel builds up and undermines its 'realistic' illusion, presenting a succession of characters on a succession of mimetic levels.[13] While Humbert frequently appears to be the sole creator of his narrative, various details, acts of McFate, flutterby insects, and the shadow extending from the Foreword point to the author who created Humbert. Within the narrative sequence of the theme of creation, Humbert, the passionate but minor author, loses control of his main character and becomes a slave to her in the act of abusing her; his lust gives way to tenderness when he realizes that affection is the mainspring of creation. (This realization, which takes place during Humbert's visit to Dolly Schiller, is foreshadowed by the school play in which Lolita acts, though the play is a parodic distortion of the 'outer' novel's action.) Whether or not we are to 'believe' Humbert's final conversion and declaration of love does not seem to me to be an issue in the novel. The element of surprise, of the contradiction and inconsistency joyfully embraced and passionately asserted, becomes metaphoric of the artist's relationship to his material. Humbert's unconventional obsession is a necessary aspect of imaginative transformation, and his acceptance of his love for the grown-up Lolita provides for his moral apotheosis into the realm of art.

Humbert to the end remains partly destructive and ludicrous (Nabokov's moral condemnation always hovers around Humbert's rhetoric), but he is allowed the saving recognition that feeling is primary and that grace springs from love lavished on illusory or alien objects. On the level of the art theme, *Lolita* deals with the complexities of a fictional world, with certain artistic problems in the portrayal of imaginative reality, a consideration which is already at least once removed from the philosophical problem of perceiving reality. The questions tackled by *Lolita* are artistic, or aesthetic, and the 'moral' dilemma is treated in aesthetic terms. Humbert's 'vice' is the inexpert artist's brutal treatment of a tantalizingly undeveloped subject, whose fragile soul Humbert has violated. The grossest violation is Quilty's, the commercial artist's, and his crime is so monstrous that it merits the greatest punishment in a novel about artistic creation: he is left deliberately half-created.

What Nabokov, living in his workshop 'among discarded limbs and unfinished torsos' (p.289), attempts to achieve is an artistic triumph related to the basic problem of fiction. Humbert observes that 'we are inclined to endow our friends with the stability of type that literary characters acquire in the reader's mind . . . Never will Emma rally, revived by the sympathetic salts in Flaubert's father's timely tear. Whatever evolutions this or that popular character has gone through between book covers, his fate is fixed in our minds . . . Any deviation in the fates we have ordained would strike us as not only anomalous but unethical' (p.242). But Humbert, weaving in and out of madness, treating Lolita with alternate cruelty and ecstasy, has no 'stability of type'. He has been deliberately created to embody the metaphoric perversion and contradictions inherent in the desire to possess and to create. The journal he writes reflects this instability, and we will never know how much of his life was coincidence, how much of it chance, how much of it the cruel machinations of a rival. Whether he is mad or not, whether he imagined the entire story of his affair with Lolita, is not answered by the book. His complexities are the embodiments of artistic problems and of the creative process. His fantasy-life is indistinguishable from his 'real' life. The characters he encounters, the conversations he records, cannot be checked against a yardstick of 'what really happened'. Nabokov, in creating Humbert, has attempted to write a book in which the characters are infinitely fluid, and the action takes place on a 'succession' of fictional planes, so that the characters cannot be finally 'stilled' or 'fixed' as being particular 'types', whose fate is sealed forever within the confines of the covers of the book.

Nabokov lightly foregoes the obligation to give us all the necessary information about the characters or the nature of the action. He has 'transcended the heritage' of the author's responsibility for providing final answers, or defining the limits of his work. Humbert's obsession is the pursuit of ecstasy through artistic creation. This quest for a pattern within his obsession is conveyed by various metaphors for the act of writing. These metaphors often assume a 'realistic' aura, at least momentarily, but eventually they fuse into the creating mind of Humbert. The despair, shame, agony, and tenderness with which Humbert fashions the figure of Lolita is the subliminal journey in the novel. It is a journey through the mind of a mad yet lucid memoirist whose tale reveals artistic as well as emotional agony. In the act of tracing this perverted quest for ecstasy, the omniscient author creates an allusive web beyond his hero's awareness. Artistry and perversion thus enact a quasi-realistic drama of verbal gaiety and emotional intensity. This heightened drama illuminates the undercurrents, both playful and agonizing, of the literary process.[14] □

In Bader's reading, an important phrase is 'no possibility of attainment to spoil it'. This is to cast the narrative structure of the novel – sexual desire for Lolita, desire to create Lolita/*Lolita* in writing – in Lacanian terms of desire as an impossible demand that can never be achieved.[15] Surprisingly (or not, given the complicated network of critical alliances and allegiances that can be traced throughout the critical history of the novel) this is to situate Bader with Josipovici (see chapter two of this Guide) in registering the move from desire to enactment as the problem on which the novel turns.

One of the most interesting and less well-known books to appear on Nabokov in the 1970s is the study (from the other side of the Atlantic) by G. M. Hyde, *Vladimir Nabokov: America's Russian Novelist* (1977). The book appeared in the Critical Appraisals Series under the general editorship of John Fletcher. The declared aim of the series is to offer fresh approaches to works that may be considered post-modern, and to 'render accessible what is challenging and often difficult'. A broad definition of post-modernism is given as 'work produced roughly since the Second World War which explores media in a more or less radical way'.[16] As a lecturer in Comparative Literature, Hyde is keen to draw attention to the ways in which Nabokov's novels reveal both his 'continuity with classic Russian literature' as well as his modernist innovations and revisions of Russian literary traditions. In regard to what he refers to as 'pat' comparisons of Nabokov with American novelists, Hyde urges caution. At the same time, and in keeping with Julian Moynahan's reading of *Lolita*, he draws attention to the links between Nabokov and Scott Fitzgerald.[17]

Hyde discusses *Lolita* in conjunction with *The Eye* (1930) and *Despair* (1936), two of Nabokov's early Russian novels, which were translated into English in the 1960s. The title of the chapter in which *Lolita* is discussed, 'Divided Selves', is an important indication of Hyde's critical framework, since it is inspired and informed by R.D. Laing's controversial book on radical psychiatry, *The Divided Self: An Existential Study in Sanity and Madness* (1960).[18] Laing's project was to attempt to make madness comprehensible, and to bring to public attention the hidden world of psychosis. Hyde's reading of *Lolita* is not a crude psychologising of author, character or event, the kind of psychological reading famously abhorred by Nabokov, for example.[19] He does not in any simple sense 'apply' Laing's theories of schizophrenia to Nabokov's protagonists. His purpose is to reveal connections between Laing's understanding of identity – its potential for disintegration and the construction of 'real' and 'false' selves – and the fictional worlds of Nabokov's characters. For Hyde, the link between Laing, *Lolita*, and Nabokov's Russian literary heritage is the idea of the 'superfluous man', a fictional hero marked by the problem of identity (or the conflict between private desires and social rules):

■ *Lolita* **expands infinitely into considerations of the interaction of Europe and America (history versus geography, 'culture' versus 'community') but is at bottom a moral tale in which a fantastic pilgrim's progress (or regress) is enacted in a world in which material objects, instead of congealing into allegorical patterns as they do in Bunyan's chronicle, lie scattered like bones in a spiritual desert awaiting the life-giving word which will cloth [*sic*] them in imaginative flesh. Entering an alien language, Nabokov (while still profoundly concerned with cultural displacement) has drawn closer to his lost hero than he ever was to Hermann: he too 'has only words to play with'. This does not mean that the novel is not concerned to organize the word-games of which it is composed into moral sense. Humbert, indeed, is represented as burdened by the desire to break out of his prison-house of language (a prison strikingly represented by Gaston and his attic portraits of great cultural inverts who lean ominously down on you).[20] His cultural baggage, which he drags with him across an uncomprehending continent and back, is at one and the same time the only world in which he feels at home (domestic America being to him as grotesque as his own sick fantasies, and inevitably hostile) and the spiritual Axel's Castle which holds him in its magnetic magic.**

Here the erotic spell is woven which turns a hoydenish American teen-ager into Helen of Troy: and more, since to Faust's lust and insatiable curiosity Humbert adds love.[21] The narrative is shaped by the time of memory and desire.

This quest is evidently one which penetrates and deforms its object. But if this makes it neurotic, it is from this, too, that it derives its mythic power. D.H. Lawrence, in his *Studies in Classic American Literature*,[22] has written of Poe (whose 'Annabel Lee' with its 'kingdom by the sea' – Humbert's riviera – its knowing boy/girl love, its envious winged seraphs – gentlemen of the jury – its necrophilia and dread of death pulses through Humbert's mind) that, concerned with the disintegration processes of his own psyche, Poe is 'more a scientist than an artist'.[23] His 'ecstasy of spiritual, nervous love' divorced from a 'real central or impulsive being in himself' drove him to murderous dissection:

> What he wants to do with Ligeia is to analyse her, till he knows all her component parts, till he has got her all in his consciousness. She is some strange chemical salt which he must analyse out in the test-tubes of his brain, and then – when he's finished the analysis – *E finita la comedia!* But she won't be quite analysed out. There is something, something he can't get ... ...[24]

Behind the synthetic brilliance of Humbert's prose lies a similar dissociation as, enacting a tragic parody of the early pioneers, he rides on his enchanted hunt through the Valley of Many-Coloured Grass (the setting of Poe's story 'Eleanora'), which Lawrence appropriately glosses as 'the valley of prismatic sensation'.[25] Poe's sensibility is that of the analytic Puritan conscience searching for an ultimate meaning in the exercise of a monstrous will, consuming itself in the face of a blank and hostile land. Humbert's experience, while containing elements of a Europe/America antithesis, is fundamentally at least as typically American as Poe's. Like Poe, he suffers from the American disease of hypertrophied consciousness; and, again like Poe, is haunted by the ghostly conflict of Good and Evil, God and the Devil battling for supremacy in his conscience. For Humbert has a conscience and he has a mind, and he is driven to madness by the mindlessness and blank functionalism he finds all about him. In the end his case is representative, which is why it seems so tragic. It refuses to be subsumed by generalizations about the materialism of the American way of life or the brilliance of Nabokov's prose style. 'Look at this tangle of thorns', he tells us at the end of the first paragraph, and indeed it does almost look like a crown.

Humbert is haunted by images of primal rose gardens as poignant as those in [T.S. Eliot's poem] 'Burnt Norton', but Nabokov, with a cultural apparatus strictly extra-territorial (his ancestral houses having all been nationalized) cannot exorcise them by referring them to a given religious and literary tradition, inexorably working back through the recreation of metaphysical concepts to the place we started from as Eliot does. [Hyde notes that 'the allusion is to T. S. Eliot's *Little Gidding*'.] Humbert's mind is heterodox, his life severed at the root. The key to *his* kingdom is what he euphemistically calls (in Chapter Five, evoking his frustrated childish sexuality) the 'sceptre of his passion'. With this deadly love he will unlock the gates of space and time and enter again his 'first world', where Annabel Lee, who never grows up, is playing still on her 'intangible island of entranced time'. The undertaking demands great art; but Humbert, like Hermann, feels that art is to madness close allied. The comprehension and evaluation of Humbert's sickness demands an even greater art: Nabokov's, which has assimilated Humbert's fantasies. We should not be misled by Humbert's virtuosity into equating the two, for behind the scenes Clare Quilty, the agent and former collaborator of one Vivian Darkbloom (an androgynous anagram of V. V. Nabokov lurking in the pages of *Who's Who in the Limelight*), (pp. 32–3), plots the abduction of Lolita with the inside information of a demon born of Humbert's ineluctable conscience. One may easily, of course, accuse the author of complicity in the tipping of the moral balance against Humbert, but then one could bring the same accusation against Tolstoy for setting at the head of Anna Karenina the words 'Vengeance is mine and I will repay' and suppressing the explanatory phrase, 'saith the Lord'.

Humbert ransacks his literary culture to provide examples of the Great Nympholepts of History, and exhausts a world of sexual experience in his quest for the archetypal nymphet; so that when, at last, McFate (Humbert's understudy for the role of Destiny) leads him to Lolita, he welcomes his damnation as a blessed release, embracing the dolorous haze of Swinburne's Lady of Pain (Dolores),[26] and reaping the whirlwind: for she is as destructive as Carmen,[27] and her 'theme tune' a song called 'Little Carmen', to the mechanical jingle of which (modelled on Belloc's nostalgically masochistic poem about Miranda and an inn, echoed at *The Enchanted Hunters*) Humbert fantasises intercourse (technically masturbation, the only 'real' sexual act in this novel). The key which will unlock Humbert's rose-garden, releasing him from the chic suburban horrors with which Charlotte has cluttered his life and giving him back the past which Charlotte has sought to destroy, is in his pocket. The parodies of Eliot (specifically 'Ash Wednesday' and 'The Waste Land', in Chapters Five and Thirty-Five) by no means lay his ghost. In the crucial Chapter Twenty-Eight (set in *The Enchanted Hunters*, a Disneyland reconstruction of the House of Usher where Humbert's quest gets snarled up with the cheapest kind of bogus frontier mythology, while Quilty writes and waits in the wings), Humbert talks of God and the Devil, of evil and sensuality, and of himself as 'Jean-Jacques Humbert' (cf. Leopold Bloom's meta-morphoses, the sad collage of his consciousness strung on a thread of basic decency). He tells us of his innocence (and his guilt) and above all of his naïvety and sorrow, and all the while he holds the key to 'the hermetic vision which I had locked in' (p. 122): a drugged nymphet. If we think of the last section of 'The Waste Land' (*What the thunder said* . . . and a thunderstorm is gathering around the inn) we discover the germ of this episode, and perhaps the main theme of the novel:

> I have heard the key
> Turn in the door once and turn once only
> We think of the key, each in his prison
> Thinking of the key, each confirms a prison
> Only at nightfall, aethereal rumours
> Revive for a moment a broken Coriolanus.[28]

Humbert is the broken Coriolanus, the shattered hero, both shattered *and* a hero, whose key, whose phallus (its tag he calls a 'dangler'), is to serve and release him from the prison of his loneliness and frustration – a release accompanied by a rush of water (the thunderstorm echoes that of Eliot's poem, and the motif is taken up parodistically in the noise of waterfalls – lavatories flushing recall the waterfall of Belloc's poem, and the sound of the sea in Poe's, and the play in 'Poe' is too childishly obvious to mention). There can be no such release; Humbert's seduction by Lolita, for whom sex is a summer camp game, forbidden by dull adults (but otherwise quite devoid of the associa-tions of sin and guilt which make it meaningful for the puritanical, cultured Humbert),[29] opens the door not to freedom but to the padded cell of gloomy lust in which the enchanted hunter becomes a hunted enchanter, a mad artist-magician trapped for ever in the web spun from his entrails. As Smurov turned himself into a literary stereotype and Hermann became a character in his own novel, so Humbert lives now in the fictional microcosm of his car, perpetual timeless motion passing through a hallucinatory Valley of Many-Coloured Grass. And even in this hermetic tomb the eye of God sees the future Cain, killer of brother Quilty: the key becomes a gun in Humbert's last desperate bid for freedom.[30] His trek across a chromium desert (with cokes, chewing-gum, and ice-creams falling from heaven like plastic manna) takes place under the all-seeing eye of a strange dehumanized con-science which conceals itself in word-games. Another great American novel comes to mind (one to which *Lolita* is evidently indebted): Fitzgerald's *The Great Gatsby*:

> But above the gray land and the spasms of bleak dust which drift
> endlessly over it, you perceive, after a moment, the eyes of Doctor
> T.J. Eckleburg. The eyes of Doctor T.J. Eckleburg are blue and
> gigantic – their retinas are one yard high. They look out of no face,
> but, instead, from a pair of enormous yellow spectacles which pass
> over a non-existent nose ... ... [31]

But if for Fitzgerald the dead god is totemic, for Humbert (as for Poe)
he is cabbalistic, a secret lurking wisdom. Humbert speaks at one
point of 'the revenge that the Gods of Semantics take against tight-
zippered Philistines' (p.148), but Quilty embodies the revenge that
the Gods of Hermeneutics take against those who only have words to
play with (cf. *Pale Fire*). [The difference between 'totemic' and 'cabbalistic' in this context is that a totem is a physical representation, usually of
a natural object, whereas cabbalistic refers to a mystical, occult interpretation. 'Semantics' is a linguistic term related to meaning, and
'hermeneutics' means the interpretation of texts.] Crossing what he
calls the 'crazy quilt' of America (Book Two, Chapter One) towards
Beardsley (how much old European corruption lurks in these innocent
American names) [A reference to the illustrator, Aubrey Beardsley
(1872–98), whose work was often charged with being grotesque and
decadent.] through 'scenic drives' parodying Dante's divine landscape,
and piled with the debris of European culture, slotting in here and
there a 'quick connection' with Lolita (the terse vulgarity underlines
Humbert's lack of all other 'connections'), he becomes the 'hunted
enchanter', the Poe-figure (Poe the Poet), dissecting living tissue in a
necrophiliac search for the quick of life:

> My only grudge against nature was that I could not turn my Lolita
> inside out and apply voracious lips to her young matrix, her
> unknown heart, her nacreous liver, the sea-grapes of her lungs, her
> comely twin kidneys. (pp.161–2)

After his abduction of Lolita, Quilty scatters the trail with clues (false
names and addresses left by him and Lolita to preserve their incognito),
as sure of hitting their mark – Humbert's superstitious fascination
with language – as Weber's magic bullets.[32]

Humbert can only enter Beardsley society by a schizophrenic split-
ting: 'I used to review the concluded day by checking my own image
as it prowled rather than passed before the mind's red eye'.[33] He
obscurely recognizes that (quite apart from the 'Annabel Lee' jingle)
he is acting out Poe's neurosis (in Chapter Sixteen he remarks that he
felt instinctively that 'toilets – as also telephones – happened to be, for
reasons unfathomable, the points where [his] destiny was liable to

catch' – the po and the P.O.); but if I have chosen not to refer to Laing's book in dealing with *Lolita* it is because art and neurosis are related in this novel differently from the way they are related in *Despair*. If Humbert's penchant for metaphor is seen as a noose into which he runs, there is at the same time a feeling (both comic and tragic) that he could not have acted otherwise, and that (in however dim and mud-dled a fashion) his possession of a mind and an (albeit deadly) capacity for love stands as a small guttering candle amid the neon and car headlights: a poor thing but his own. His self, like Hermann's is divided (and the gentleman of the jury, the envious angels, will not be); but his overburdened conscience, laid bare in the poem he pre-sents to Quilty before he shoots him (not for nothing a pastiche of [T.S. Eliot's poem] 'Ash Wednesday') (p. 292), prompts the novel itself, an extraordinary act of truth-telling. *Lolita* passes in recapitulation through madness and death and emerges with an uncanny visionary clarity. Nabokov's art would never again be so perfectly integrated.[34] □

Hyde's concern with the deadly pathos of the character of Humbert Humbert is shared by Julian Moynahan. Moynahan's useful monograph, *Vladimir Nabokov* (1971), includes a brief discussion of *Lolita* in which attention is drawn to the significance of Nabokov's relation to American culture. For Moynahan, the key term linking Nabokov with America is nostalgia. His claim is that before Nabokov's arrival in America in 1940, 'we Americans had no great modern artist in nostalgia of our own'. The purpose of Moynahan's interpretation of the novel is to show 'how the book reverberates through our specifically American historic culture'.[35] Thus, Moynahan is concerned with the location and function of American culture in the narrative, and, in particular, the ways in which this is connected to the perversely romantic character of Humbert Humbert as a displaced European. In line with the influence of compara-tive studies of literature in the 1970s, Moynahan is keen to forge links and connections between Nabokov's character Humbert Humbert, and other figures in American literary history:

■ The core element of Humbert's sexual perversity, arch-romanticism, and derangement is an attitude toward time which may remind us of other eccentric or deranged heroes of American fiction. Humbert is fix-ated on the past – on his childhood love affair with 'Annabel Lee' – and his pursuit, seduction, and enslavement of Dolores Haze are an attempt to reinstate in the present and preserve into the future what was irretrievably lost in the past. The expensiveness of indulgence in this illusion is very great: it costs no less than the wrecking of a child's life, as Humbert finally admits after abandoning his corrupt rational-izations concerning the natural depravity and sexual precocity of

American little girls. Humbert and his time problem are summed up on the final page of *The Great Gatsby*, from which I quoted at the onset of this essay, and in a number of other classic American texts. [The 'time problem' Moynahan refers to here is that of Gatsby mistaking 'the past for the future'.[36]]

But how can this vile European stand in for an archetypal American? There really is no problem, America, as a 'brand new, mad new dream world where everything [is] permissible', is Europe's dream of itself according to the romantic error that past time is retrievable. Emerson, Whitman, and Hart Crane might have approved Humbert's thought, if not his exact words and their appalling application. We are all Europeans when we dream that dangerous, beguiling, ever-so-American dream.

These speculations can be pushed a bit further under the general rubric of fate, freedom, and America. *Lolita*, because it is heavy with fate, would seem to present a situation in which the margin of freedom which interests us in fictional characters, particularly in the characters appearing in modern books, has diminished virtually to nothing. For instance, Humbert is obsessed, Lolita is enslaved, Charlotte Haze is totally duped, and a character like Quilty is the slave of his sinister vices. Add in fate as the 'synchronizing phantom' arranging happenstance and coincidence upon wholly mysterious principles and freedom disappears altogether from the book. From another angle, there is freedom in *Lolita* of a rather awful sort. Humbert is free, unencumbered with compunction before his 'conversion'. Through most of the book he has the freedom of his viciousness, as does Quilty. Humbert's actions take place at a point in history when traditional sanctions have lapsed or at least loosened, and there would be little consensus of a judgement against his deeds from the 'enlightened' sector of the community, apart from agreement that he is psychologically 'disturbed'. This in effect forgives and forgets by understanding or claiming to.

Dolores Haze also is free in a sense, in that the nature of contemporary American suburban culture ties her to nothing, asks nothing of her, presents her with nothing. What is she? A junior consumer, of comic books and bubble gum, a 'starlet' with a thirst for cheap films and Coke. There is a great vacancy in and around her, a voidness and loneliness only partly created by Humbert's machinations. This vacancy is cultural in the first instance, American.

For Europe, as first de Toqueville and then D.H. Lawrence have expounded, America has figured as the place beyond cabined and confined traditions and sanctions. It has been the place where time itself might be redeemed, where the dream of a new Eden, of a second life could be realized. Naturally, there has been a dark pathological side to this. America has been the place indubitably attractive to great mischief makers, psychopaths, men on the run, unclubbable and violent persons, con men. Humbert lives on the dark side of the American freedom I am describing. There is some truth in the statement that what drove Humbert to America was his vice and the hope of satisfying it in the land of opportunity. And there is some truth in the idea that the history of Lolita, who died in childbed in a town of the 'remotest Northwest' on her way to Alaska, the last American frontier, expresses the final decadence of that European myth which we call the American dream.[37] □

Like Julian Moynahan, Douglas Fowler is also interested in the place of America in *Lolita*. In *Reading Nabokov* (1974), Fowler links America directly with the character and consciousness of both Lolita and Humbert in fascinating ways. Fowler introduces his discussion of *Lolita* with the idea that Humbert Humbert is one of Nabokov's 'favorites' (*sic*). For Fowler, this sense of authorial favouritism is crucial to an understanding of the ways in which Humbert Humbert is literally absolved from responsibility for decisive events in the narrative. And it is precisely such absolution from certain criminal deeds that sustains the sympathetic identification with the narrator. For example, it is clear that sexual access to Lolita is dependent on the removal of her mother. Charlotte Haze must somehow be removed from the novel, otherwise the 'plot' cannot unfold. Humbert toys with the idea of killing her, but he is 'saved' from this particular murder when fate and favouritism contrive to kill her off. In this extract from Fowler's opening discussion he starts to put forward a number of tentative links between Humbert's discovery of both America and Lolita.

■ By making 'precise fate' responsible for the tragedy, Nabokov maintains Humbert's humanity if not his unequivocal innocence; and although we are going to hear a great deal about 'McFate' throughout the novel, Charlotte's death is the only important incident in the novel that occurs outside the normal boundaries of cause and effect, or of human personality expressing itself in human activity. It is by far the most important intervention in the book from outside the frame of its fictional reality. The purpose of this unlikely and singular intervention seems to be the desire on Nabokov's part to keep Humbert's appeal intact, and nothing else. [Fowler seems to overstate the argument that Charlotte's death is 'outside the normal boundaries of cause and effect'. If we look back at the plot to marry and remove Charlotte, the idea expressed by Moynahan that she is a 'dupe' also starts to look askew. H.H. drugs Charlotte Haze to avoid sexual relations with her. He wishes her dead, then translates his wishes into words by writing a diary.

Charlotte becomes curious about the secret of the locked drawer in H. H.'s room and forces an entry. What she reads in the diary is barely repressed loathing for Charlotte, and unrequited lust for her daughter Lolita. H. H. fails to convince Charlotte that the diary is simply a fiction in which only the names remain the same. What arguably kills her is the shock of belief in his written narrative, and disbelief in his defence. This seems to suggest that reading can be deadly in *Lolita*.[38]]

But not only is Humbert kept from cold-blooded murder; Nabokov saves him from the act of actually deflowering precocious Dolores Haze. Charlie Holmes, the 'coarse and surly but indefatigable' son of the headmistress of the aptly named Camp Climax, has spent 'every blessed morning' of Lo's stay there copulating by turns with her and her friend Barbara in the 'beautiful innocent forest brimming with all the emblems of youth'. By showing that Lolita's sexual corruption pre-dated Humbert's contribution to it, Nabokov once again shifts moral responsibility away from his favorite. Humbert's crime is kept within strict limits: he is no killer of innocent women and no deflowerer of innocent children. Fate creates the parental vacuum into which his love and lust proceed. Even then it turns out to be Lo's own sexual corruption that initiates their relationship: 'I am going to tell you something strange: it was she who seduced me . . . Suffice it to say that not a trace of modesty did I perceive in this beautiful hardly formed young girl whom modern co-education, juvenile mores, the campfire racket and so forth had utterly and hopelessly depraved' (p. 134–5).[39]

In moral terms, then, Humbert is not wholly responsible for his own entry into his relationship with Lolita: fate kills Charlotte, and Lolita seduces him. That Humbert's impurity contributes the lesser share to the crime is evidence to me of Nabokov's willingness to preserve the moral integrity of his favorites at the expense of almost all other factors in his work. This willingness may well be looked at as a rigid and basic given of his fiction, a prejudice that limits the plot activity in his novels.

Humbert's real crime is keeping Lolita in captivity by means of bullying and blackmail – granting that the reader, if not the legal system, puts aside as only a technicality the question of statutory rape. And here we of course condemn him. But even this unpleasant bond of coercive intimidation – and it is emphasized several times by a cackling Humbert ('I succeeded in terrorizing Lo') – is qualified by several factors that relieve Humbert of pure monstrousness and make of him something a great deal more human and sympathetic than a cardboard Svengali. For one thing, he is rendered foolish and not a little pathetic in his attempts to keep Lolita 'happy'. The essential comic leverage of the novel is provided by the slide into teen-neon-roadside America of that extraordinarily sophisticated, refined and cosmopolitan intelligence, the involvement of that sensibility in Lolita's enchanting beauty and 'eerie vulgarity' – and in America's. Whereas the novel's comedy depends on Humbert's ensnaring himself in the meretricious foolishness of Lolita and mid-century America, the novel's pathos, or tragedy, depends on Humbert's awareness of the authentic beauty of his mistress and of America, and on the contrast between the possibilities of his consciousness and the Procrustean violence to which Lolita and America subject that consciousness: 'A great user of roadside facilities, my unfastidious Lo would be charmed by toilet signs – Guys-Gals, John-Jane, Jack-Jill, and even Buck's-Doe's; while lost in an artist's dream, I would stare at the honest brightness of the gasoline paraphernalia against the splendid green of oaks, or at a distant hill scrambling out – scarred but still untamed – from the wilderness of agriculture that was trying to swallow it' (p. 155).

Although no easy equation between Humbert's two great discoveries, Lolita and America, ought to be enforced, they are obviously composed of the same cells and tissues. Humbert, composed of other stuff, necessarily offers a perspective that is outside both of them: 'On especially tropical afternoons, in the sticky closeness of the siesta, I liked the cool feel of armchair leather against my massive nakedness as I held her in my lap. There she would be, a typical kid picking her nose while engrossed in the lighter sections of a newspaper, as indifferent to my ecstasy as if it were something she had sat upon, a shoe, a doll, the handle of a tennis racket, and was too indolent to remove' (p. 167).

In this manner, Humbert's narration and perspective offer us his passion and yet an ironic qualification and placement of that passion, 'a shoe, a doll, the handle of a tennis racket', that make it more than a little ludicrous. And yet it is only through his sensibility that the beauty in Lolita and America are made available to us, for both the young girl and the New World are partially unconscious of themselves: 'Not only had Lo no eye for scenery but she furiously resented my calling her attention to this or that enchanting detail of landscape; which I myself learned to discern only after being exposed for quite a time to the delicate beauty ever present in the margin of our undeserving journey' (p. 154).[40] □

Fowler seems to point to something complicated here about the beauty and seductive charms of Lolita and America as both deeply connected and somehow unrepresentable *without* the self-conscious narration of Humbert the observer, the outsider. In one sense, this problem of representation anticipates sophisticated post-structural readings of the novel in the 1990s; of the figure of Lolita and the rhetorical presence of American culture (see Bronfen and Bowlby in chapter five of this

Guide). We will now return to Fowler's discussion of how the novel represents America and Lolita's relation to it, taking up his commentary in the section entitled 'Humbert, Lolita, and America'.

■ Does the novel really affirm the possibilities of American life? In the novel's climactic scene, Humbert finally falls in love with Mrs. Richard Schiller. But Lolita, meretricious and far less vulnerable than Humbert, dismisses Humbert's metamorphosis as irrelevant, almost silly:

> She considered me as if grasping all at once the incredible – and somehow tedious, confusing and unnecessary – fact that the distant, elegant, slender, forty-year-old valetudinarian in velvet coat sitting beside her had known and adored every pore and follicle of her pubescent body. In her washed-out gray eyes, strangely spectacled, our poor romance was for a moment reflected, pondered upon, and dismissed like a dull party, like a rainy picnic to which only the dullest bores had come, like a humdrum exercise, like a bit of dry mud caking her childhood. (p. 274)

Once more, the brainless and lobotomized triumph through sheer indifference.[41] And once more, the sensibilities of greatest subtlety, sensitivity, and vulnerability are singled out for the cruelest blows. This passage indicates no real possibilities of life in the American mode; quite the opposite. The Schillers *are* America, just as Charlotte is. [Emphasis Fowler's.] Life for the consciousness of real sensitivity is impossible in the terms the novel presents to us: to this Lolita, to this Mrs. Richard Schiller, Humbert is simply 'a bit of dry mud caking her childhood', and her ultimate triumph – a triumph she is incapable of even appreciating – is her indifference to him, her preference for Quilty over him, her choice – the proper one for her – of a Mrs. Richard Schillerdom over anything he could offer. She and Dick are going to go to Alaska and make big money; she has no use for Humbert. This extinguishes him utterly. All that he can do is to remove Quilty, a *real* monster, from the world, an act of which we of course fully approve but Lolita would not. Quilty is not a monster to her, nor is he to the society which tolerates and even rewards him.

After the murder, when Humbert is at last standing beside the enormous valley while he waits for the police to fetch him, his final vision of his crime is of a moral sensitivity completely beyond Lolita's capabilities: 'What I heard was but the melody of children at play, nothing but that . . . I knew that the hopelessly poignant thing was not Lolita's absence from my side, but the absence of her voice from that concord' (pp. 309–10).

The poignancy of this loss afflicts only Humbert. Mrs. Richard

Schiller, who finds Quilty a 'genius', who finds Humbert only some 'dry mud caking her childhood', and who is busy incubating a philistine fetus in her stretched belly, is not given this sensitivity.

The crime for which Humbert is responsible is a crime against his own ethical sense rather than against Lolita, for she is quite as indifferent to the injury he supposes he has done her as she is indifferent to his love of her. In this instance, 'crime' is a wholly subjective affair, existing only in the mind of the criminal.

Notice the light-years of difference between Lolita's consciousness and Humbert's as he leaves her for the last time:

> 'One last word', I said in my horrible careful English, 'are you quite quite sure that – well, not tomorrow, of course, and not after tomorrow, but – well – some day, any day, you will not come to live with me? I will create a brand new God and thank him with piercing cries, if you give me that microscopic hope' (to that effect).
>
> 'No', she said smiling, 'no'.
>
> 'It would have made all the difference', said Humbert Humbert.
>
> Then I pulled out my automatic – I mean, this is the kind of a fool thing a reader might suppose I did. It never even occurred to me to do it.
>
> 'Good by-aye!' she chanted, my American sweet immortal dead love; for she is dead and immortal if you are reading this. I mean, such is the formal agreement with the so-called authorities. (p. 282)

Thus, neither Lolita nor America is presented to Humbert as a real possibility. Quite the opposite: life is utterly impossible for Humbert on their terms. The exhilaration in Humbert's tone is not any simple exhilaration with the mid-century American scene. In fact, in his Afterword notes, 'On a Book Entitled *Lolita*', Nabokov indicates a certain gleeful reveling in Lolita's and America's lobotomized but lively vulgarity: 'Nothing is more exhilarating than philistine vulgarity' (p. 317).

But Humbert's delight in the 'philistine vulgarity' seems to be more complex than any simple Camp experience, any simple superiority; the stripes and patterns of that surface are, after all, the terms of his own elaborate 'deception' and 'mimicry'. The American milieu is not simply savaged for comic effect; it contains an irreplaceable, irresistible potentiality. If art is 'fantastically deceitful and complex', then the terms of seducing girl-children and keeping them in thrall in the midst of mid-century America offer to Humbert a thrilling artistic possibility, a problem that, like bullfighting or mountain-climbing, involves not only the artistry but the safety of the protagonist. The measure of his skill is his survival.[42] □

If Fowler's reading prefigures, in one sense, the idea of unrepresentability in relation to Lolita, it also bears all the signs of an overwhelming identification with Humbert Humbert as a soul of sensitivity and literary sensibility. The American/Lolita is read as the signifier of crude vulgarity, and in her pregnant state she becomes quite literally the bearer of an American philistine future. A number of things need to be noted here. First of all, Fowler overlooks the unborn child who dies with Lolita. Secondly, this commitment to Humbert's narrative risks a reading that is in itself peculiarly literal. In other words, in his reading of a novel that by the 1970s is famous for its unreliable narrator and dazzlingly fluid narration, Fowler is only too willing to fix Humbert as the plausible, vulnerable figure of sensitive integrity at the mercy of the insensitive and undeserving Lolita. This sympathetic identification with the narrator becomes even more paradoxical in the following extract from Fowler, since he amply demonstrates the presence of literary and linguistic devices and conventions that make his own identification possible. Let us now return to the conclusion of Fowler's discussion of *Lolita* at the point at which he addresses the questions of fantasy and desire in the novel.

■ Humbert's fantasy, his superimposition of his magical and private vision on the world around him, transforms everything. Humbert is not recording America but transforming it for us through the tinted lenses of his magical perversion. This sense of the objective surface made magical by the subjective imagination not only illuminates things outside Humbert; it also shows how Humbert sees himself flawlessly acting out his role of American daddy while deep in enemy territory. The possibilities that Humbert senses do not really reside in America or America's roles but behind the façade. These possibilities, not its own intrinsic merit, are what makes the façade interesting or amusing. By telling the story from Humbert's vantage, Nabokov allows all the facts to become tinted with Humbert's subjective magic. If the story had been narrated omnisciently, the pathetic irony in the contrast between the world's fact and Humbert's fantasy would have been a great deal more difficult to deal with, for the omniscient voice would necessarily alert us to Humbert as pitiable object, and his fantasy would become as obtrusive as the chill drabness of the life it transforms.

. . . First-person narration by a fantasist can have, of course, a pathos that is real enough; but the madman's voice need never express it *directly*, and this phenomenon necessarily alters our reaction to the fiction.

Humbert is a great deal more sane than Kinbote [*Pale Fire*], but Nabokov has taken pains to touch Humbert's voice with an obsession and an illegitimate ecstasy that give a crazy zest and bumptiousness to his presentation of America. Humbert's sense of himself as alien and

impostor lends an ironic verve to his extended impersonation of a gen-
teel American daddy; the more 'innocent' the milieu, the more suitable
he finds it as a setting for his erotic fantasies, because the sensual
thrills he can derive only from girl children are partially an escape
from time, and the trappings of innocence are, of course, inevitably the
trappings of the young. Some of Humbert's most thrilling moments are
imaginatively connected with Lolita as a schoolgirl:

> At one of [the desks], my Lolita was reading the chapter on
> 'Dialogue' in Baker's *Dramatic Technique*, and all was very quiet, and
> there was another girl with a very naked, porcelain-white neck and
> wonderful platinum hair, who sat in front reading too, absolutely
> lost to the world and interminably winding a soft curl around one
> finger, and I sat beside Dolly just behind that neck and that hair,
> and unbuttoned my overcoat and for sixty-five cents plus the per-
> mission to participate in the school play, had Dolly put her inky,
> chalky, red-knuckled hand under the desk. Oh, stupid and reckless
> of me, no doubt, but after the torture I had been subjected to, I
> simply had to take advantage of a combination that I knew would
> never occur again. (p. 200)

The novel is a *tour de force* for Humbert's voice, which of course
expresses Humbert's sexuality, Humbert's flight from time and death,
Humbert's mimicry, Humbert's moral metamorphosis. The monstrosity
of the narrator Humbert and his solipsism, unlike Kinbote's, are not
disconnected from the real world – they triumphantly transform that
world and its commonplaces into a stage-set fraught with erotic potent-
ialities and thrilling dangers, engaging Humbert himself and through
him the reader in the narrative.[43] □

Is Fowler finally convinced that Humbert Humbert is monstrous?
Perhaps not. If there is a blindness to be identified in Fowler's reading, it
is in the refusal to acknowledge that Humbert's version of Lolita is precisely that – Humbert's version. As critics before and after Fowler have
shown, that version is complicated and contradictory, and at times
beyond reason. For modern readers, the deeply snobbish and misogynistic rhetoric of Fowler's interpretation of *Lolita*, which connects class and
self-conscious integrity with a crude sexual difference, appears to be
shockingly unmitigated by any attempt to represent the American girl
with justice. Furthermore, there is clearly something troubling about the
evocation of Hemingwayesque notions of masculine pursuits and challenges that, in linking the desire for Lolita with bullfighting and
mountain-climbing, seems to offer up paedophilia as a 'sporting pas-
time'. Fowler is attracted to H. H.'s narrative because of the way in which

it marks the culmination of a particular mode of criticism. At the very onset of the 1980s, a significant shift takes place in *Lolita* criticism that will reveal the ethical implications of such blatant critical identification with Humbert's desires. From now on, there is no getting away from the fact that the cost of that identification is the figure of the girl – Lolita.

CHAPTER FOUR

Nabokov's 'Monster of Incuriosity': Kindness, Cruelty, and the Ethics of Reading *Lolita* in the 1980s

IT IS tempting to mark Ellen Pifer's reading of *Lolita* in 1980 as a defining moment in the critical history of the novel. After the death of Vladimir Nabokov in 1977, Pifer is one of a number of critics to argue for a re-examination of the author's reputation as 'an aesthete indifferent to humanity'. This is to be done through a reconsideration of the plotting of the novel and its ethical effects. Concerned specifically with the question of what happens to Lolita at the hands of Humbert Humbert, Pifer suggests that the problem of reading Nabokov turns on the distinction between the 'cleverness of his charming villains' and the 'reality of their deeds'.[1] Turning her attention to Humbert Humbert's narrative, she urges readers to resist the seductions of the beautiful language and the cleverness in order to look at the real effects of what Humbert *does* to Lolita. Beautiful language and vile deeds, formal aesthetics and 'real' content, such distinctions and appeals are not unfamiliar in regard to the history of this particular novel. In a slightly different form they repeat and restate the terms on which debates about *Lolita* have been conducted since the beginning of its life. It is Ellen Pifer's contention that, in the past, too much of the wrong sort of attention has been paid to Humbert's narrative. Distracted and seduced by the abstractions of beautiful language, readers have turned away from the fact that Nabokov's 'poor Lolita is having a rough time'.[2] Pifer's critical project to restore Nabokov's reputation as an ethical writer is inseparable from the effort to recover a narrative for Lolita. As readers, we are called upon to 'see through' Humbert's narrative and the story he tells about Lolita. According to Pifer, that story has held sway, not just because of the power of Humbert's narrative, and the author's writerly talent, but because of the way the narration appeared to harmonise with Nabokov's pronouncements on art and aesthetics. And yet, as Richard Rorty's reading makes clear, Nabokov emphasised repeatedly that the sympathies of the novel come to rest with Lolita.

What is defining about Pifer? In acknowledging the persuasions and the aesthetic attractions of Humbert's narrative, Pifer argues that his crime is to force his private fantasies on to Lolita, to intrude on her internal world. It is through the invasion of 'Lolita's private kingdom' that 'Humbert usurps her rightful claim to an independent existence'. And it is in recognising the enormity of this intrusion that readers acknowledge the crime. But readers must also acknowledge that Humbert recognises it too. For Pifer, it is only this double recognition of the criminality of Humbert, *and* his remorse, that will allow us to keep the 'beauty of the language' and the 'depth and poignancy of the narration'.[3]

■ . . . Like an author dreaming up a character, Humbert despotically transforms the twelve-year-old American kid into an aesthetic mirage: 'Lolita had been safely solipsized . . . I was above the tribulations of ridicule, beyond the possibilities of retribution. In my self-made seraglio, I was a radiant and robust Turk, deliberately, in the full consciousness of his freedom, postponing the moment of actually enjoying the youngest and frailest of his slaves' (p. 62).[4] Through the play of inspired imagination, Humbert invents a Lolita who, most conveniently, possesses 'no will, no consciousness – indeed, no life of her own' (p. 64). In the end, Humbert's mental usurpation of Lolita's identity has very real and destructive consequences. As her sole guardian, Humbert uses all the resources at his disposal to control Lolita and hamper her freedom. When bribes and threats fail, Humbert resorts to clandestine raids on Lolita's meager savings, which she attempts to hide from him. He even burgles 'eight one-dollar notes', which he finds stashed away in a book, because he fears that otherwise she 'might accumulate sufficient cash to run away' (pp. 186–7).

After Lolita succeeds in escaping from Humbert, he reviews their life together; gradually he comes to recognize that during those years he 'simply did not know a thing about [Lolita's] mind and that quite possibly behind the awful juvenile clichés, there was in her a garden and a twilight, and a palace gate – dim and adorable regions which happened to be lucidly and absolutely forbidden' to him (p. 286). This remote and walled garden is the private landscape that every individual shelters within his internal life. It is that private kingdom where each of us is, like the artist, a sovereign power. Humbert ultimately recognizes that he has invaded Lolita's private kingdom and usurped her rightful claim to an independent existence. Because of this physical and psychic invasion of Lolita's privacy, Humbert understands, 'something within her' has been 'broken' by him (p. 34). He perceives the devastating effects that his solipsistic ardor has had on Lolita's life, and it is this understanding that lends such depth and poignancy to his narration. [It is essential to the terms of Pifer's argument that we read Humbert's recognition as something like remorse. This is where the ethics of *Lolita* are to be found. David Rampton's reading of the novel in chapter five of this Guide, however, casts doubt on the good faith of Humbert's narrative of understanding.]

Humbert's recognition of his culpability is, after all, what makes him so much more sympathetic a character to us than Axel Rex; yet at times Humbert confuses his creative gifts of perception, his artistic sensibility, with moral virtue. He even declares himself more poet than pervert when describing the tender love of 'unhappy, mild, dog-eyed gentlemen' for their nymphets: 'We are not sex fiends! We do not rape as good soldiers do . . . Emphatically, no killers are we. Poets never kill' (p. 90).[5] By elevating himself to the status of 'pure' poet, Humbert understandably desires to remove his actions from the ethical sphere of life and consider them only as art. But these attempts prove futile; guilty Humbert must ultimately confront the violence he has wrought upon Lolita. The 'simple human fact', which inhuman art cannot disguise, remains: 'Dolores Haze had been deprived of her childhood by a maniac' (p. 285). Humbert's eloquent self-revelation serves to enlighten the reader as well. He may not have murdered Charlotte Haze, but in some ways Humbert has butchered Lolita's life. By the novel's end, poet or no poet, Humbert perceives his hands to be those of a mangler and a 'sex fiend'. Gazing at Dolly Schiller's proletarian husband, elegant and aesthetic Humbert recognizes his moral inferiority to this simple man. He writes, 'His fingernails were black and broken, but the phalanges, the whole carpus, the strong shapely wrist were far finer than mine: I have hurt too much too many bodies with my twisted poor hands to be proud of them' (p. 276).

The power and passion of the imagination do not grant the ardent dreamer any ultimate authority over his fellow man, who has an unquestionable claim to his own dreams and desires. Paradoxically, Humbert is able to grant to Lolita, within 'the refuge of art', what he denies her during their brief life together: the grace of absolute freedom. Having solipsistically denied his nymphet any 'will', 'consciousness', or 'life of her own', Humbert is nevertheless able, in retrospect and with the detachment of the artist, to summon an image of Lolita's essential and unfettered self:

> The exquisite clarity of all her movements had its auditory counterpart in the pure ringing sound of her every stroke. The ball when it entered her aura of control became somehow whiter, its resilience somehow richer, and the instrument of precision she used upon it

seemed inordinately prehensile and deliberate at the moment of clinging contact . . . My Lolita had a way of raising her bent left knee at the ample and springy start of the service cycle when there would develop and hang in the sun for a second a vital web of balance between toed foot, pristine armpit, burnished arm and far back-flung racket, as she smiled with gleaming teeth at the small globe suspended so high in the zenith of the powerful and graceful cosmos she had created for the express purpose of falling upon it with a clean resounding crack of her golden whip. (pp. 223–4)

Humbert's use of the possessive epithet – 'my Lolita' – here expresses tender affection rather than solipsistic desire. This image of Lolita, which he evokes near the end of the novel, is of a human being most perfect in her freedom. Poised in time, or eternity, commanding the space that surrounds her, Lolita reigns – 'golden whip' in hand – like a figure of antique statuary.

Contemplating the exquisite clarity and grace of Lolita's movements and the 'classical purity of trajectory' in her tennis serve, Humbert acknowledges both the perfection and the essential inutility of her tennis form: 'Her form was, indeed, an absolutely perfect imitation of absolutely top-notch tennis – without any utilitarian results'. Any 'second-rate but determined player, no matter how uncouth and incompetent', could 'poke and cut his way to victory' over Lolita's elegant but inefficient strokes. Lolita's tennis, adds Humbert, 'was the highest point to which I can imagine a young creature bringing the art of make-believe, although I daresay, for her it was the very geometry of basic reality' (pp. 233–4). We may fruitfully apply Humbert's descriptive terms to a consideration of Nabokov's enterprise as a novelist. For in his dedication to 'the art of make-believe', to self-conscious artifice that carries no useful social messages and claims no extra-literary function, Nabokov presents us, nonetheless, with 'the very geometry of basic reality'. Nabokov's art celebrates human consciousness, 'the only real thing in the world', and delineates its laws. These laws are not, as we have seen, identical with Nature's; they are, to repeat Charles Kinbote's phrase, 'anti-Darwinian' [*Pale Fire*]. In the realm of Nabokov's fiction, which may rival Nature but never pretends to be her *creation*, the very notion of 'survival of the fittest' proves an inadequate perception of human life. Celebrating the 'anti-Darwinian' laws of consciousness, Nabokov's artifice reveals, instead, that the despot is his own puppet, the murderer his own victim.

The patterns of self-conscious artifice illuminate the 'geometry' of consciousness and its reality. Human consciousness is unique in the world, something fragile and at the same time infinitely powerful. And man's creations, his works of art, are shown to be as fragile and as

powerful as the consciousness of which art is a supreme manifesta-
tion. Art derives its power from the elusive play of infinite
consciousness in the face of death's inevitable triumph. Like Lolita's
tennis form, art is, in Nabokov's words, both 'futile' and 'organic', not
useful and mechanical.[6] Only in unique, independent, and essentially
nonutilitarian forms, then, does art embody the true nature of man,
who may not justifiably be subverted to serve any individual or collective will. Only by art's freedom from function will it truly 'serve' us.

Through the presentation of his worlds as invented ones, his characters as 'galley slaves', and himself as an author impersonating an
anthropomorphic deity, Nabokov reminds us that the only power
available to the artist is to create the very best, the most unique and
'inhuman', art that he can. But the artist's god-like authority extends
no further than the flat frame of the canvas. As he refrained from
claiming greatness, or even goodness, for some of his most talented
artists, from Axel Rex to Van Veen, so Nabokov disdained the aesthete's suggestion that the values of art may substitute for, or eliminate, the moral imperative of human existence. The distortive mirror
of art may only reflect life in its own way – the processes of imagination being both absolute and strictly limited. Nabokov demands from
his readers the same rigorous detachment with which he, as an author,
contemplated the special privileges of artistic creation. We are not to
be so taken with the cleverness of his charming villains, nor with the
beauty of their language, that we dismiss the reality of their deeds.
With regard to the prerogatives of art, Nabokov was a more rigorous
moralist than many of his own interpreters. To Humbert Humbert, his
aspiring artist, Nabokov blatantly denied any moral sympathy.
Despite his character's talent, imagination, and capacity for aesthetic
bliss, Nabokov called Humbert 'a vain and cruel wretch who manages
to appear "touching". That epithet, in its true, tear-iridized sense, can
only apply to my poor little girl [Lolita].'[7] With her bad manners and
juvenile clichés, the real Lolita offends Humbert's good taste and con-
tinental elegance. But for this Lolita Nabokov reserved his tenderness
and moral sympathy. If Lolita is the victim of American pop culture
she is even more cruelly the victim of Humbert's aesthetic proclivities.
Against the powerful force of his animated imagination, Lolita wields
her trite toughness like a weapon. It is the shield she raises, with
small success, to defend that besieged kingdom – her personal identity.

Nabokov's expressed tenderness for his 'poor little girl' makes
obvious what should be apparent to his readers in any case. Despite
the author's subjugation of his 'galley slaves' within the world of artifice, Nabokov was far from indifferent to his characters or hostile to
the real human beings they so convincingly resemble. And despite the
many differences between Nabokov's early Russian and later English

novels, a synoptic view of these works reveals how unswerving was his commitment to certain moral as well as aesthetic principles. ['Synoptic' means 'taking a comprehensive mental view'.] Keenly aware of the transgressions all human beings commit against each other as they pursue, and try to realize, their solipsistic dreams and desires, Nabokov himself was no solipsist. The very form of his fiction illustrates that the artist's private world is not coterminous with ours; he does not seek to extend his personal dominion beyond the printed page. In a recorded interview, Nabokov took the opportunity, moreover, to address the tendency of so many of his critics to label him as an aesthete indifferent to humanity. He invited such critics to reassess their appraisals, confronting them with a characteristically flamboyant, albeit serious, challenge: 'In fact I believe that one day a reappraiser will come and declare that, far from having been a frivolous firebird, I was a rigid moralist kicking sin, cuffing stupidity, ridiculing the vulgar and cruel – and assigning sovereign power to tenderness, talent, and pride'.[8] What Nabokov does *not* say here, but explicitly demonstrates throughout his fiction, is that the artist's own talent and pride have, on more than one occasion, come under the fire of his attack. Some of Nabokov's most talented and proud artists – Axel Rex, Humbert Humbert, and Van Veen – are exposed, in their cruelty, for seeking to extend their sovereign power beyond the domain of art. Unlike their author, they do not perceive a distinction between the natural condition of human freedom and the inhuman privileges of art. Such failure of insight constitutes, for this celebrated champion of aesthetic bliss, the most lethal form of vulgarity. Misconstruing Nabokov's dedication as an artist to aesthetic bliss – failing to recognize the enduring humanistic values that inform his perception of reality – makes us liable to the same criticism.[9] □

Richard Rorty takes up some of Pifer's artistic and ethical concerns through a philosophical discussion of the idea of cruelty in the novel. Drawing on Nabokov's famous Afterword to *Lolita*, Rorty uses this private vision of artistic experience to produce a kind of reading template for the novel. Nabokov's notion of a sequential movement that starts with curiosity and culminates in aesthetic bliss is taken up as the key to an ethical search of the text. Rorty's reading of *Lolita* is to be understood in the context of his broader project in *Contingency, Irony, and Solidarity* (1989). Rorty's enterprise is to look at where particular authors and texts might be positioned in relation to the idea of cruelty. In asking how books might help us to be less cruel, Rorty distinguishes between two types of books. The first type helps to reveal 'how social practices [for example, slavery, poverty, and prejudices] which we have taken for granted have made us cruel'.[10] Included in this category of writing about cruelty is, for example, Harriet Beecher Stowe's *Uncle Tom's Cabin* and Richard Wright's *Native Son*. The second type 'is about the ways in which particular sorts of people are cruel to other particular sorts of people'.[11] For Rorty, Nabokov's novels *Lolita* and *Pale Fire* are exemplary of the sort of book that dramatises 'the blindness of a certain kind of person to the pain of another kind of person'.[12] Rorty is careful to note that this is only a 'rough' distinction for the purpose of his argument. Indeed, the chapter on George Orwell (in which he is compared to Nabokov as an author who writes from the inside of cruelty) demonstrates the extent to which the categories are not fixed. In regard to his analysis of *Lolita*, Rorty maintains that in the world of Nabokov's writing, the greatest crime is the failure to notice and the failure to respond to the suffering of others. Thus, *Lolita* is valued as a book that 'helps us avoid cruelty, not by warning us against social injustice but by warning us against the tendencies to cruelty inherent in searches for autonomy'.[13]

In regard to the related notions of cruelty and incuriosity, something like this has been noted before. We might recall, for example, Kingsley Amis's critical response to the novel in the 1950s (see chapter one of this Guide), and his rather prescient conclusion that Lolita is always 'the object of desire but never curiosity'.[14] The important difference between Amis's reading on the one hand, and the readings of Pifer and Rorty on the other, is that, having acknowledged the worst of Humbert's deeds, Amis has no desire to save the book for 'literature'. Rorty's main examples of cruelty and incuriosity in *Lolita* are not primarily related to the larger question of what Humbert does to Lolita, or his failure to desist when he notices the effect.[15] Rorty's interest is in the fine detail of the text that has been overlooked, not only by Humbert, but by other readers. As the following extract demonstrates, Rorty's reading is both persuasive and suggestive in its approach to the structures of cruelty in the text. At the same time it confidently maintains the idea of literary value, and shores up the reputation of *Lolita* as an exemplary twentieth-century fiction.

■ **Nabokov's greatest creations are obsessives – Kinbote, Humbert Humbert, Van Veen – who, *although they write as well as their creator at his best,* are people whom Nabokov himself loathes – loathes as much as Dickens loathed Skimpole.** [Harold Skimpole is a character in Dickens's *Bleak House* (1852–3), a novel that Nabokov both taught and wrote about. Rorty draws extensively on Nabokov's *Lectures on Literature* (1980) in his discussion of *Lolita*.] **Humbert is, as Nabokov said, 'a vain and cruel wretch who manages to appear "touching"' – manages it because he can write as well as Nabokov can.**[16] **Both Kinbote and Humbert are exquisitely sensitive to everything which affects or provides expression for their own obsession, and entirely incurious about anything that affects anyone else. These characters dramatize, as it has never** before been dramatized, the particular form of cruelty about which Nabokov worried most – incuriosity.

Before giving examples from the novels of this cruel incuriosity, let me offer another sort of evidence to back up the claim I have just made. Remember Nabokov's rapid parenthetical definition of the term 'art' in the passage about 'aesthetic bliss' cited early in this chapter. Writing what he knew would be the most discussed passage of what he knew would become his most widely read manifesto, the Afterword to *Lolita*, he identifies art with the co-presence of 'curiosity, tenderness, kindness, and ecstasy.' Notice that curiosity comes first.[17]

Nabokov is, I think, trying to jam an *ad hoc* and implausible moral philosophy into this parenthesis, just as he is trying to jam metaphysical immortality into the phrase 'other states of being', which he uses to define 'aesthetic bliss'. If curiosity and tenderness are the marks of the artist, if both are inseparable from ecstasy – so that where they are absent no bliss is possible – then there is, after all, no distinction between the aesthetic and the moral. The dilemma of the liberal aesthete is resolved. All that is required to act well is to do what artists are good at – noticing things that most other people do not notice, being curious about what others take for granted, seeing the momentary iridescence and not just the underlying formal structure. The curious sensitive artist will be the paradigm of morality because he is the only one who always notices everything.

This view is, once again, an inverted Platonism: Plato was right that to know the good is to do it, but he gave exactly the wrong reason. Plato thought that 'knowing the good' was a matter of grasping a general idea, but actually knowing the good is just sensing what matters to other people, what their image of the good is – noticing whether they think of it as something round and creamy and flushed, or perhaps as something prism-shaped, jewel-like, and glistening. The tender, curious artist would be the one who, like Shade and unlike Skimpole or Kinbote, has time for other people's fantasies, not just his own. He would be a nonobsessed poet, but nonetheless one whose poems could produce ecstasy.[18]

But Nabokov knew quite well that ecstasy and tenderness not only are separable but tend to preclude each other – that most nonobsessed poets are, like Shade, second rate. This is the 'moral' knowledge that his novels help us acquire, and to which his aestheticist rhetoric is irrelevant. He knows quite well that the pursuit of autonomy is at odds with feelings of solidarity. His parenthetical moral philosophy would be sound only if it were true that, as Humbert says, 'poets never kill'. But, of course, Humbert does kill – and like Kinbote, Humbert is exactly as good a writer, exactly as much of an artist, capable of creating exactly as much iridescent ecstasy, as Nabokov himself.[19] Nabokov

would like the four characteristics which make up art to be inseparable, but he has to face up to the unpleasant fact that writers can obtain
and produce ecstasy while failing to notice suffering, while being
incurious about the people whose lives provide their material. He
would like to see all the evil in the world – all the failures in tenderness and kindness – as produced by nonpoets, by generalizing,
incurious vulgarians like Paduk and Gradus.[20] But he knows this is
not the case.[21] Nabokov would desperately like artistic gifts to be sufficient for moral virtue, but he knows that there is no connection
between the contingent and selective curiosity of the autonomous
artist and his father's political project – the creation of a world in
which tenderness and kindness are the human norm. So he creates
characters who are both ecstatic and cruel, noticing and heartless,
poets who are only selectively curious, obsessives who are as sensitive
as they are callous.[22] What he fears most is that one cannot have it both
ways – that there is no synthesis of ecstasy and kindness.

The two novels of his acme spell out this fear.[23] The remarkable
thing about both novels is the sheer originality of the two central characters – Humbert and Kinbote. No one before had thought of asking
what it would be like to be a Skimpole who was also a genius – one
who did not simply toss the word 'poetry' about but who actually
knew what poetry was. This particular sort of genius-monster – the
monster of incuriosity – is Nabokov's contribution to our knowledge
of human possibilities. I suspect that only someone who feared that he
was executing a partial self-portrait could have made that particular
contribution.[24]

Let me offer some further evidence for this interpretation of the two
novels by citing another remark from the Afterword to *Lolita*. Nabokov
is listing 'the nerves of the novel . . . the secret points, the subliminal
co-ordinate by means of which the book is plotted' (p. 315).[25] Among
those secret points, he tells us, is 'the Kasbeam barber (who cost me a
month of work).'[26] This barber appears in only one sentence:

> In Kasbeam a very old barber gave me a very mediocre haircut: he
> babbled of a baseball-playing son of his, and, at every explodent,
> spat into my neck, and every now and then wiped his glasses on
> my sheet-wrap, or interrupted his tremulous scissor work to pro-
> duce faded newspaper clippings, and so inattentive was I that it
> came as a shock to realize as he pointed to an easelled photograph
> among the ancient gray lotions, that the moustached young ball
> player had been dead for the last thirty years. (p. 211)

This sentence epitomizes Humbert's lack of curiosity – his inattentive-
ness to anything irrelevant to his own obsession – and his consequent

inability to attain a state of being in which 'art', as Nabokov has defined it, is the norm. This failure parallels a failure described earlier in the book, one which occurs when Humbert transcribes from memory the letter in which Charlotte proposes marriage to him, and adds that he has left out at least half of it including 'a lyrical passage which I more or less skipped at the time, concerning Lolita's brother who died at two when she was four, and how much I would have liked him' (p.68).

This is one of only two passages in the book in which Lolita's dead brother is referred to. The other is one in which Humbert complains that Charlotte rarely talks about her daughter – the only subject of interest to him – and in particular that she refers to the dead boy more frequently than to the living girl (p.80). Humbert mourns that Lolita herself never referred to her pre-Humbertian existence in Humbert's presence. But he did once overhear her talking to a girlfriend, and what she said was: 'You know what's so dreadful about dying is that you are completely on your own' (p.282). This leads Humbert to reflect that 'I simply did not know a thing about my darling's mind' and 'that quite possibly, behind the awful juvenile clichés, there was in her a garden and a twilight, and a palace gate – dim and adorable regions which happened to be lucidly and absolutely forbidden to me, in my polluted rags and miserable convulsions'.

Continuing this meditation on possibilities which had not previously occurred to him, Humbert remembers an occasion on which Lolita may have realized that another of her girlfriends had 'such a wonderful fat pink dad and a small chubby brother, and a brand-new baby sister, and a home, and two grinning dogs, and Lolita had nothing' (p.285). It is left to the reader to make the connection – to put together Lolita's remark about death with the fact that she once had a small, chubby brother who died. This, and the further fact that Humbert does not make the connection himself, is exactly the sort of thing Nabokov expects his ideal readers – the people whom he calls 'a lot of little Nabokovs' – to notice. But, ruefully and contemptuously aware that most of his readers will fall short, he tells us in his Afterword what we have missed.

Consider the impact of being told this on the reader who only then remembers that the death of a child is Nabokov's standard example of ultimate pain – the occasion for John Shade's poem 'Pale Fire' as well as the central event in *Bend Sinister*. It dawns on this reader that he himself was just as inattentive to that month-long sentence, and to that dead moustached son, as Nabokov suspected he had been. The reader, suddenly revealed to himself as, if not hypocritical, at least cruelly incurious, recognizes his *semblable*, his brother, in Humbert and Kinbote. ['Semblable' means 'a counterpart or equal'.] Suddenly *Lolita* does have a 'moral in tow'.[27] But the moral is not to keep one's hands off little girls but to notice what one is doing, and in particular to notice what people are saying. For it might turn out, it very often does turn out, that people are trying to tell you that they are suffering. Just insofar as one is preoccupied with building up to one's private kind of sexual bliss, like Humbert, or one's private aesthetic bliss, like the reader of *Lolita* who missed that sentence about the barber the first time around, people are likely to suffer still more.[28] □

Unlike Rorty, the critic Elizabeth Dipple cannot easily dismiss the relation of the literary text to the widespread incidence of child sexual abuse. Dipple's reading of *Lolita* appears as part of a chapter on Nabokov in her study of contemporary fiction, *The Unresolvable Plot* (1988). Although Dipple's discussion is focused primarily on the 'aesthetic excellence' of the novel and its exemplary status in post-modern fiction, she is troubled by the 'moral' questions raised by the text. The insight of this reading is that the narrative of *Lolita* continues to be problematic because it seems to offer no ethical direction for readers who are unsure about what to make of it. In the following extract, Dipple takes up Nabokov's famously challenging statement in the Afterword to the novel, that '*Lolita* has no moral in tow'.

■ Nabokov's insistence that he has no moral in tow raises a serious question about *Lolita*, his greatest book and most enduring success. As part of the frame of the novel, Nabokov creates a primitively moral psychoanalytical literary critic, John Ray Jr, as a satirical example of the shortcomings of his genre. In Ray's *Foreword* to the first-person book written by the imprisoned Humbert Humbert, he parodies the foolishness of the sociological-critical-psychoanalytic-ethical-literary (remember Polonius) mind that only foggily perceives the nature of a literary text:

This commentator may be excused for repeating what he has frequently stressed in his own books and lectures, namely that 'offensive' is frequently but a synonym for 'unusual'; and a great work of art is of course always original, and thus by its very nature should come as a more or less shocking surprise. I have no intention to glorify 'HH'. No doubt, he is horrible, he is abject, he is a shining example of moral leprosy, a mixture of ferocity and jocularity that betrays supreme misery perhaps, but is not conducive to attractiveness. He is ponderously capricious. Many of his casual opinions on the people and scenery of this country are ludicrous. A desperate honesty that throbs through his confession does not absolve him from sins of diabolical cunning. He is abnormal. He is not a gentleman. But how magically his singing violin can conjure up a tendresse, a compassion for Lolita that makes us entranced with the book while abhorring its author! (p. 5)[29]

Ray possesses the marginal quantity of aesthetic sense Nabokov is willing to allow to the critic/psychoanalyst, enough to know that the 'tendresse' of a writer's 'singing violin' can keep the reader entranced. But Ray's aesthetics are fogged over by moral intrusion, by his next statement that *Lolita* will be fascinating for psychoanalysts, and by an earlier claim in the *Foreword* that the book is 'the development of a tragic tale tending unswervingly to nothing less than a moral apotheosis'. In fact, the satire against the moralistic reader/critic that Nabokov believed would be obvious and amusing has been a marring problem for many readers, and one to which attention must be paid.

There are two reasons for this momentarily crippling moral difficulty: first is the response of ethical readers who at first gasp cannot perceive the ascendancy of the literary aestheticism that *Lolita* dominantly embodies. Second is what must be called Nabokov's naivety in assuming riskily that no large moral anger would be called forth by the particular sexual tastes of his anti-hero, Humbert Humbert; indeed his cavalier callousness about sexual practices is seen too in another way in his belittling attack on homosexuality in *Pale Fire*. Although all his fiction shows a notable interest in eroticism, Nabokov seems to underestimate the sexual abuse of children, or rather his interest in literary possibility is so large that he fails to perceive another dimension. In the late 1980s when the misuse of children is so much before us, the plot of *Lolita* causes uneasiness and many readers stubbornly deny its higher forum of aesthetic excellence. In other words, Nabokov *should* perhaps, at least on one level, have a more exacting moral in tow.

On the other hand, and for dramatically important reasons, he cannot. I can think of no fictional text in which major incontrovertible forces battle each other more troublingly than in *Lolita*, but I must also agree with the aesthetic-narcissist school (see for example Genet and the late pornographic works of Robbe-Grillet) that unmonitored sexuality has vital uses within the aesthetic program of literature. But John Ray Jr is, from the point of view of most readers, right in saying that *Lolita* builds to a moral apotheosis, and indeed it is the apparent ethical reversal of Humbert Humbert's solipsism that forms the secondary theme of this great novel, making it not merely a product of narrow aestheticism but one of the more profound literary achievements of our century. Nabokov may be serious in claiming that a moral reading injures the text: certainly it separates a few scenes near the end of the book from the unbroken parodic play of the work as a whole. On the other hand, the affective power in these scenes is stronger than the coolness required of parody.

Nabokov clearly has a program for the novel, and although he feels it is not the reader's business to intrude with an interpretation of its larger intentions, readers are instantly forced to see more than such elegant details as the splendid prose snapshots of Lolita playing tennis or one of the dozens of colors in Nabokov's sunsets. Beyond aestheticism, the reader's first large apprehension of *Lolita* must be that it is a celebration and continuation of the western literary tradition of love poetry. As such, it is played off parodically against a long string of antecedents that established the trope of the immortality of the beloved through the literary genius of the lover ... ...[30] □

If Dipple suggests that the problem of Humbert's sexual taste is impossible to ignore, she also suspends the problem by seeming to return to an earlier moment in the critical history of the novel, when the difficult question of sex and sexuality was displaced onto the idea of love. As we noted in the first chapter of this Guide, Lionel Trilling avoided the problem of addressing sex in *Lolita* by redescribing the novel as a love story. However, as Dipple intimates, the question of sexual representation in literature presents itself in different forms in the 1980s. If the earlier distinctions between love and sex are tied to literary efforts to keep *Lolita* free from charges of obscenity and pornography, concerns in the 1980s are more closely related to contemporary debates about child sexual abuse, and sexual violence against girls and women. It is perhaps surprising to find that, in his third literary biography of Nabokov (1987), Andrew Field can assert with breezy confidence that *Lolita* is not about sex at all.

■ There is not, when you think of it, a single actual 'sexual' scene in all of Nabokov, except for the one in 'Lilith', though there are ever so many pages of sensual deep breathing mingled with muffled ventriloquial snorts of derisive laughter.[31] □

The ironising of 'sexual' in this passage seems to assume a consensual interpretation of the meaning of the word in relation to Nabokov's literary oeuvre. As far is Field is concerned, when we talk about *Lolita*, we are not talking about sex. Although Field is overtly dismissive of interpretations of the novel that dwell on the sexual content, he does raise the vexed question of what constitutes sex in literature. As the critical history of *Lolita* demonstrates, that question continues to provoke new responses to the problematic relation between literary representation and lived experience – art and life.

Contrary to Field, many readers and critics have interpreted scenes in the novel as sexual. Furthermore, it is argued that Nabokov's literary (sexual) encounters between adult men and girl children cannot be disconnected from the expression and criminal enactment of such desires in society. The problem of how to respond to the endlessly difficult relation between literature and other forms of cultural reality is at the heart of the various approaches to the novel in the 1980s. Gladys Clifton forcefully addresses this relation in her article 'Humbert Humbert and the Limits of Artistic Licence' (1982). In common with the majority of critical interpretations in the 1980s, albeit from different perspectives and positions, Clifton wants to argue that readers have 'overvalued Humbert's perspective and undervalued Lolita's'.[32] In other words, Humbert has been getting away with murder. Like Pifer, then, Clifton is appealing to readers to refuse the distractions of Humbert's 'fancy prose'.

■ Humbert Humbert frequently insists on his status as a poet, especially in the first part of *Lolita*. While this can be taken as a bit of seductiveness toward the readers (the 'ladies and gentlemen of the jury', to whom he addresses his self-justification),[33] he soon abandons the originally stated purpose for writing his story, which was to produce a document that might be used in his defense at his trial for the murder of Quilty; instead, he becomes caught up in re-creating the past he has shared with Lolita, and with the attempt to get the reader to view it – statutory rape notwithstanding – in the same tragic and romantic light as he does. Distracted by his charm, his wit, his intelligence, and – yes – his murderer's fancy prose style, we may momentarily forget that he is indeed the monster he says he is.

But whenever Humbert begins to describe the actual details of his life under 'the perilous magic of nymphets', a grotesque gap appears between his fantasy of 'bliss' and his life with a flesh-and-blood American teen angel . . . . . .[34] □

Clifton's concern with the 'grotesque gap' between Humbert's fantasy of 'bliss' and its cruel enactment on the 'flesh-and-blood' body of Lolita is shared by the feminist critic Linda Kauffman. Kauffman's reading of the novel, 'Framing *Lolita*: Is There a Woman in the Text?' (1989), is contained in a collection of essays entitled *Refiguring the Father: New Feminist Readings of Patriarchy*, and is explicitly informed by late-1980s feminist debates about child sexual abuse and incest. To this extent, the reading is fervently committed to exposing the sexual politics of representation in the narrative itself, and in the critical history of the novel. In contrast to Dipple's tentative anxieties about the boundaries between life and art – sexual violence and literary expression – Linda Kauffman's reading offers a sustained feminist attack on the critical history of the novel. For Kauffman, the issue of child sexual abuse cannot be displaced by questions of aesthetic appreciation. Kauffman is at pains to demonstrate some of the crude sexist assumptions at work in influential (male) readings of the novel, and she does this by confronting the rhetoric of literature with the literal language of feminist sexual politics.

Trilling's influential reading of the novel as a narrative of love is one of Kauffman's major targets, but her critical attack on what she sees as romantic misreading and critical misrecognition of Nabokov's artistic project would include Field. Kauffman, like Richard Rorty, is also interested in Nabokov's lecture notes on Dickens's *Bleak House*. She sees Nabokov's reading of Dickens as evidence of Nabokov's sympathetic identifications with Lolita and, importantly, with the idea of child abuse in all its forms. For Kauffman, *Lolita* must be read as a critique of (to borrow Dipple's phrase) 'the misuse of children'.

■ Trilling is right to notice the overt erotic activity on every page, but wrong to conclude that the novel is about love, not sex. *Lolita* is not about love, but about incest, which is a betrayal of trust, a violation of love. How have critics managed so consistently to confuse love with incest in the novel?[35] □

It is worth noting here the way in which Kauffman's argument reflects and reproduces the confrontation of languages between Lolita and Humbert within the narrative of *Lolita*. We might recall, for example, that Lolita uses the terms 'rape' and 'incest' to describe what Humbert has done to her: terms that are in collision with the literary flourishes of Humbert's 'artistry'. Further to this uneasy relation between the literal and the literary, Kauffman's reading is particularly insightful in revealing what she views as mistaken sympathetic identifications that critics have made with the character of Humbert. Informed by feminist approaches to literature, semiotics, psychoanalysis and anthropology, Kauffman's analysis draws attention to the relation between the representation of the girl in the text and the way the text (and the girl) have circulated between male critics. As we can see in the following substantial extract, Kauffman argues that male critics have been seduced by the narrative of *Lolita*. Her urgent appeal is that readers and critics must resist such persuasions and identifications, in order to 'reinscribe' the literal child into the literary text.

■ The challenge for feminist criticism is thus to read against the text by resisting the father's seductions. Is it possible in a double movement to analyze the horror of incest by reinscribing the material body of the child Lolita in the text and simultaneously to undermine the representational fallacy by situating the text dialogically in relation to other texts? ['Fallacy' in this context refers to 'a mistaken belief' in the representations of the text, namely Humbert and Lolita; 'dialogically' means to bring texts together, to place them 'in dialogue' with each

other.] It is in the interest of feminist criticism to expose the representational fallacy, since the most sexist critical statements come from
critics who take the novel as a representation of real life.

Trilling, for instance, paradoxically begins by citing Humbert's
'ferocity . . . his open brutality to women'. Yet, Trilling continues:
'Perhaps [Humbert's] depravity is the easier to accept when we learn
that he deals with a Lolita who is not innocent, and who seems to have
very few emotions to be violated; and I suppose we *naturally* incline to
be lenient towards a rapist – legally and by intention H.H. is that –
who eventually feels a deathless devotion to his victim!' (p. 14).

Trilling does not find rape and incest shocking; what shocks him is
how few contemporary novels are about love, but *Lolita* is one of them,
despite the fact that Humbert's greed is, as Trilling notes, 'ape-like'.

One might expect that critics who read the novel as a representation of real life would pay more attention to Lolita, but few have
imagined what her victimization is like. Instead they identify with the
sensations Humbert records about his body by uncritically adopting
his viewpoint. Thomas Molnar is representative:

> The central question the reader ought to ask of himself is whether he
> feels pity for the girl. Our ethical ideal would require that we look
> at Lolita as a sacrificial lamb, that we become in imagination, her
> knight-protector. Yet this is impossible for two reasons. One is very
> simple: before yielding to Humbert, the girl has had a nasty little
> affair with a nasty little thirteen-year-old. . . . Besides, she is a
> spoiled sub-teenager with a foul mouth, a self-offered target for lech-
> ers. . . . throughout, she remains an object perhaps even to herself.[36]

Molnar indicts Lolita for being a tease who 'asks for it', and who
deserves what she gets since she is spoiled, foul, 'damaged goods'.
Both Trilling and Molnar castigate Lolita for being unknowable.
Despite his will to power, it is Humbert who never knows Lolita; he
even confesses that there are depths in her inaccessible to him
(p. 259).[37] Humbert is, moreover, a notoriously unreliable narrator
who lies to psychiatrists, deceives two wives, and otherwise takes
elaborate precautions to avoid detection. In view of his unreliability,
it is doubtful [that] his claim that Lolita seduced him is true; more
importantly, it is unverifiable, and credulous critics who read the
novel as a reflection of life thus end up merely reifying codes that can
be traced directly from literature, codes that – from the courtly love
tradition to *Clarissa* [Samuel Richardson, 1747–8] and modern cinema –
first idealize and then degrade the female by blaming her for her own
victimization. ['Reify' means to convert a person or an abstract idea into
a thing.]

The opposite approach to the novel as self-referential artifice is, however, no more enlightened. Take Alfred Appel, who describes the novel as a 'springboard for parody', adding: 'Humbert's terrible demands *notwithstanding*, Lolita is as insensitive as children are to their *actual* parents; *sexuality aside*, she demands anxious parental placation in a too typically American way, and affords Nabokov an ideal opportunity to comment on the Teen and Subteen Tyranny'.[38]

Such passages are ruptures in the critical stance that self-referentiality demands; when it comes to women, such critics seem to forget that their main point is that the novel is *not* realistic! In a now famous statement, Appel goes on to assert: 'By creating a reality which is a fiction, but a fiction that is able to mock the reader, the author has demonstrated the fiction of "reality", and the reader who accepts these implications may even have experienced a change in consciousness' (p. 120).

But before one can analyze a fiction that mocks the reader, or results in a change in consciousness, one needs to examine the kind of reader one has in mind. Humbert is not only an avid writer, he is an avid reader: of motel registers, class rolls, road signs, comics, even movie posters. His reading of Lolita is the model on which male critics rely – whether they read self-referentially or mimetically. And that is the source of their blindness: they fail to notice that Humbert is not only a notoriously unreliable narrator but that he is an unreliable reader too. If he were not, he would have solved the mystery of Quilty's identity. As it happens, he never does solve it; Lolita has to tell him. Like his heart, his powers of perception and his eyes are 'hysterical, unreliable organ[s]'. A voyeur, he wants to see but not be seen.

Despite his unreliability, feminist readers have the choice of either participating in their own 'immasculation' by endorsing aesthetic bliss, or of demonstrating their humorlessness and frigidity. Judith Fetterly defines 'immasculation' as the process by which 'the female reader is co-opted into participation in an experience from which she is explicitly excluded; . . . she is required to identify against herself'.[39] Consider the famous scene of Lolita on the couch with Humbert while he surreptitiously masturbates and enjoins the reader to respond:

> I want my learned readers to participate in the scene I am about to replay: I want them to examine its every detail and see for themselves how . . . chaste, the whole wine-sweet event is. . . . What had begun as a delicious distension of my innermost roots became a glowing tingle . . . not found elsewhere in conscious life. . . . Lolita had been safely solipsized. Suspended on the brink of that voluptuous abyss (a nicety of physiological equipoise comparable to certain techniques in the arts). . . . I crushed out against her left

buttock the last throb of the longest ecstasy man or monster had ever known. (pp. 57–8)

This is a scene where the father's body is the site and the source of not only aesthetic bliss but literal orgasm; both come at the same time – if, that is, the reader is male. Lolita, however, is not just 'solipsized' but annihilated, as Humbert reveals while congratulating himself in the next scene:

What I had madly possessed was not she, but *my own creation*, another fanciful Lolita – *perhaps, more real* than Lolita; overlapping, encasing her; floating between me and her, and having no will, no consciousness – indeed no life of her own. The child knew nothing. I had done nothing to her. And nothing prevented me from repeating a performance that affected her as little as if she were a photographical image rippling upon a screen and I a humble hunchback abusing myself in the dark. (p. 59, emphasis added)

Thus physical as well as aesthetic jouissance for Humbert requires psychic anesthesia or annihilation for Lolita. 'Reader! Bruder!' Humbert exclaims, 'I shall not exist if you do not imagine me' (p. 119). ['Jouissance' is a French term for something like 'extreme pleasure', introduced into literary criticism through the work of French literary theorist and philosopher Roland Barthes. There is no adequate translation of the term in the English language.[40]]

What the text mimes, then, is a bundle of relations between men, as clarified not only in the passage above but in the responses of critics like Trilling and Molnar. The incest taboo, as Lévi-Strauss reveals, has nothing to do with protecting the girl, and everything to do with ensuring that she functions as an object of exchange between men: 'it is the supreme rule of the gift . . . which allows [the incest taboo's] nature to be understood.'[41] The scene in which Humbert masturbates with Lolita on his lap is a good example of how the text makes what is male seem universal. As Patrocinio Schweickart explains in discussing the implied authorial contract:

For the male reader, the text serves as the meeting ground of the personal and the universal . . . the male reader is invited to feel his *difference* (concretely, from the *girl*) and to equate that with the universal. Relevant here is Lévi-Strauss's theory that woman functions as currency exchanged between men. The woman in the text converts the text into a woman, and the circulation of this text/woman becomes the central ritual that establishes the bond between the author and his male readers.[42]

The bond and that identification with the male body help to explain further how incest can be mistaken for love. From the opening words, Humbert's body is a palpable presence: 'Lolita, light of my life, fire of my loins. My sin, my soul. Lo-lee-ta: the tip of the tongue taking a trip of three steps down the palate to tap, at three, on the teeth' (p. 11). 'Lolita' is a word; Humbert is flesh: loins, tongue, palate, teeth. Humbert's obsession with his body is infantile; it is he who is marked by a preoedipal fascination with his own bowels, his digestion, his heartburn, his headaches, his blood pressure – and of course, his penis – that 'pentapod monster' that feels like a 'thousand eyes wide open in my eyed blood' (p. 41). As he masturbates, he 'entered a plane of being where nothing mattered, save the infusion of joy brewed within my body' (p. 57). Thus, while exploiting his role as legal guardian to enforce the law of the father, Humbert also reverses it. He turns oedipalization inside out, just as his 'only grudge against nature was that I could not turn my Lolita inside out and apply voracious lips to her matrix, her unknown heart, her nacreous liver, the seagrapes of her lungs, her comely twin kidneys' (p. 151). [Pre-oedipal is an elusive term that refers both to a particular stage in the psycho-sexual *development* of the infant subject (usually prior to the oedipal phase of three to five years), and an unconscious psycho-sexual *structure* in which the infant's primary relation is with the body of the mother (prior to the intervention of the 'law of the father'). Kauffman is using the term to draw attention to the ways in which the narrative represents Humbert's desire as being in two places at once. He is shown to be obsessed with his own body and with the body of Lolita. As Lolita's guardian, perversely, he is in a position to enforce his sexual obsessions.] **She is the *femme morcélée* par excellence.** [Kauffman is emphasising here the ritualistic significance of Humbert's fantasy of consuming the girl's vital organs.] **The incestuous father-as-his-own child: he feasts on the female body, sucking Lolita's flat breasts and 'brown rose.'** In Lacanian terms, 'Lolita' is little more than a signifier in Humbert's image-repertoire, and Humbert's revealing allusion to her heart being 'unknown' highlights how illusory his project (and his projections) are.[43] Her sole functions are in [*sic*] reflect and satisfy the body of the father. Initially, she has no reality for him except as the incarnation of his childhood love, Annabel Leigh; Lolita is little more than a replication of a photographic still. He wishes he had filmed her; he longs to have a frozen moment permanently on celluoid [*sic*] since he could not hold her still in life. She is thus the object of his appropriation, and he not only appropriates her, but projects onto her his desire and his neuroses. Significantly, she only serves as a simulacrum when her nicknames – Lolita, Lo, Lola, Dolly – are used, for her legal name, Dolores, points too directly toward another representation – Our Lady of Sorrows –

and thus to a higher law than man's. An abyss lies between the 'Lolita' who is a purely imaginary project of Humbert's desire, and the 'Dolores' whose legal guardian is the source of her suffering.

Nabokov's Authors [Kauffman's section title]

John Ray's foreword and Nabokov's afterword are diametrically opposed monologic readings. By exposing the weaknesses in such readings, one discovers what feminist criticism stands to gain by dismantling the representational fallacy. I should like to propose a dialogic reading, one that is both feminist and intertextual; one that releases the female body both from its anesthesia and from Humbert's solipsism while simultaneously highlighting textual artifice. Nabokov, I would argue, is not writing in either the one mode or the other: he is writing a book that elides the female by framing the narrative through Humbert's angle of vision. He then comments indirectly on that framing device by references not to 'real life' but to other literary texts. That the novel is an exercise in intertextuality, however, does not mitigate the horror of Lolita's treatment. [Introduced into literary theory through the work of French critic and analyst Julia Kristeva, the term 'intertextuality' is used to show the ways in which any literary text is made up of other texts, by means of citation, repetition, allusion and convention.] Instead, it reinforces it. Among the multiple levels of intertextuality operating in the novel, four in particular deserve mention because they suggest the myriad ways in which the novel allegorizes woman: the major poems in the courtly love tradition; certain stories and poems of Edgar Allan Poe; Henry James's *The Turn of the Screw* [1898]; and Charles Dickens's *Bleak House*. ['Allegory' has a long history in Western literature, encompassing a variety of genres from fable to parable. At its simplest, an allegory is a narrative with a coherent 'literal' meaning which also signifies a second order of meaning.]

Lolita is, among other things, a compendium of definitions of woman, in texts ranging from *Know Your Own Daughter* and *The Little Mermaid* to *Carmen* and *Le roman de la rose*. As in the courtly love tradition, Humbert moves from adoration to disillusionment when the beloved fails to measure up to his code of perfection. Like the knights who celebrated the chastity of the lady and the difficulty of their endeavors, Humbert boasts of his difficulties when he masturbates with Lolita on his lap. In contrast to his idealized 'lady', 'real' women are miserly, envious, fickle, loudmouthed, drunkards (like Rita, the drunk with whom Humbert lives after Lolita flees), or slaves to their bellies (like Valeria, the 'brainless baba' who is Humbert's first wife). As he reveals when he insists that Lolita has no will or life of her own, Humbert denies not just what is womanly in Lolita – he denies what is human.[44] That is why he must insist that nymphets are demonic, and it is the myth of demonic children that ties the novel to James's *Turn of the Screw*.

Nabokov confesses, 'My feelings towards James are rather complicated. I really dislike him intensely but now and then the figure in the phrase, the *turn* of the epithet, the *screw* of an absurd adverb, cause me a kind of electric tingle, as if some current of his was also passing through my own blood'.[45] James said that he devised the tale as a trap to catch the 'jaded, the disillusioned, the fastidious' reader – in other words the reader who is beyond sentimentality.[46] Similarly, sophisticated readers of *Lolita*, avid to align themselves with 'aesthetic bliss', fall into precisely the same trap by ignoring the pathos of Lolita's predicament. James said his subject was 'the helpless plasticity of childhood: that *was* my little tragedy'.[47] For Nabokov as for James, 'plasticity' is the medium that creates aesthetic bliss. But plasticity has other connotations: to mold, to form, to freeze, to fix. The governess in *The Turn of the Screw* tries to arrest the children's development; the desire to fix things indeed is one of her motives for writing her retrospective narrative. She wants to frame time itself, just as Humbert desires 'to fix the perilous magic of nymphets'. In both texts – indeed throughout Poe and Dickens as well as James – how and what you see depends on the frame: James's governess and Humbert Humbert both resort to fancy prose styles to frame a murder.[48] 'Aesthetic bliss' is a frameup. In both the governess's narrative and in Humbert's, silence, exile, and cunning lie in that gap between past and present, and determine what inflection will be given to the murder of childhood. As Poe asks in *Lenore*, 'How *shall* the ritual then be read? – the requiem how be sung/by you – by yours, the evil eye – by yours the slanderous tongue/That did to death the innocence that died and died so young?'[49]

To recognize that violence, one must first defuse the charge that any lament for the murder of Lolita's childhood is sheer sentimentality, a willful misreading of a novel meant to parody such attitudes. Lecturing at Cornell, Nabokov himself defused the charge, noting that Dickens's *Bleak House* deals 'mainly with the misery of little ones, with the pathos of childhood – and Dickens is at his best in these matters.'[50] Nabokov emphasises the astonishing number of children in the novel – he counts over thirty – and says that 'one of the novel's most striking themes' is 'their troubles, insecurity, humble joys . . . but mainly their misery' (p.65). Their parents are either 'frauds or freaks' (p.69). And then he says something that will surprise contemporary readers:

> I should not like to hear the charge of sentimentality made against this strain that runs through *Bleak House*. I want to submit that people who denounce the sentimental are generally unaware of

> what sentiment is . . . Dickens's great art should not be mistaken
> for a cockney version of the seat of emotion – it is the real thing,
> keen, subtle, specialized compassion, with a grading and merging
> of melting shades, with the very accent of profound pity in the
> words uttered, and with an artist's choice of the most visible, most
> audible, most tangible epithets. (pp. 86–7)

His allusion to 'grading and merging of melting shades, with the very
accent of profound pity', echo a poignant and revealing sentence about
Lolita's temperament to which critics like Trilling and Molnar claim
no reader has access. After he overhears Lolita commenting that 'what
is so dreadful about dying is that you are completely on your own',
Humbert realizes that 'Behind the awful juvenile clichés, there was in
her a garden and a twilight, and a palace gate – dim and adorable
regions which happened to be lucidly and absolutely forbidden to me,
in my polluted rags and miserable convulsions . . . living as we did,
she and I, in a world of total evil' (p. 259).

In his lecture on *Bleak House*, Nabokov goes on to contrast
Skimpole, who represents a child, with the real children in the novel
who are overburdened with adult cares and duties, like Charley – the
little girl who supports all her little brothers and sisters. Dickens
writes: 'She might have been a child, playing at washing, and imitat-
ing a poor workingwoman'. And Nabokov observes, 'Skimpole is a
vile parody of a child, whereas this little girl is a pathetic imitator of an
adult woman' (p. 86). The same is true of Humbert; like Skimpole, he
imitates a child. It is Humbert, after all, who wants to play forever in
his 'pubescent park, in my mossy garden. Let them play around me
forever. Never grow up' (p. 22). It is Humbert who talks baby talk to
Lolita – never she to him.[51]

Lolita, conversely, is forced to imitate adult womanhood by per-
forming 'wifely' duties before she gets her coffee. In the very act of
trying to fix her forever in childhood, Humbert not only stunts her
growth but makes her old before her time. Her fate is presaged by
Humbert's transactions with the whore Monique; he is briefly attracted
to her nymphet qualities, but she grows less juvenile, more womanly
overnight: only for a minute does 'a delinquent nymphet [shine]
through the matter-of-fact young whore' (p. 24). From the moment he
first masturbates on the couch, Humbert proceeds to turn Lolita into a
whore, calling her vagina a 'new white purse', and priding himself
upon having left it 'intact'. By the time they reach the Enchanted
Hunters Motel, he has begun paying her with pennies and dimes.

Father–daughter incest, as Judith Lewis Herman points out, is a
relationship of prostitution: 'The father, in effect, forces the daughter
to pay with her body for affection and care which should be freely

given. In so doing, he destroys the protective bond between parent and child and initiates his daughter into prostitution. This is the reality of incest from the point of view of the victim'.[52] The victim's viewpoint in *Lolita* is elided, for eventually Humbert bribes her to perform, reporting the fact as a 'definite drop in Lolita's morals' (p. 167). The fact that she ups the ante from fifteen cents to four dollars has been seen by misogynistic critics as a sign that she was a whore all along. Humbert once again reveals his obsession with his own body and once again astutely sizes up readers' allegiances when he exclaims: 'O Reader . . . imagine me, on the very rack of joy noisily emitting dimes and great big silver dollars like some sonorous, jingly and wholly demented machine vomiting riches; and in the margin of that leaping epilepsy she would firmly clutch a handful of coins in her little fist' (p. 168).

Humbert implicitly assumes that his [male?] readers will identify solely with his sexuality and sensibility. Since he presents himself as a schlemiel, the comic urge to identify with him is an almost irresistible temptation. The hilarity, however, is considerably undercut when we realize that Lolita is trying to accumulate enough money to run away – an escape Humbert thwarts by periodically ransacking her room and robbing her.

Materialist critiques of the novel could focus on the rampant consumerism of American society in 1955, since Lolita is the ideal consumer: naive, spoiled, totally hooked on the gadgets of modern life, a true believer in the promise of Madison Avenue. Yet a materialist–*feminist* perspective enables one to see something that has not been noted before: Lolita is as much the object consumed by Humbert as she is the product of her culture. And if she is 'hooked', he is the one who turns her into a hooker. She is the object of both his conspicuous consumption and concupiscence, as his voracious desire to devour her heart, liver, lungs, and kidneys demonstrates. When he sees a dismembered mannikin in a department store, Humbert comments that 'it's a good symbol for something', and 'Dolly Haze' (one of Lolita's many nicknames) comes more and more to resemble those mute, inanimate dolls on whose bodies consumer wares are hung. By the time of their final reunion in Gray Star, she has been so thoroughly prostituted that she assumes Humbert will only give her her own inheritence if she accompanies him to a motel.

What is most stunning about Ray's preface is that, despite his interest in 'reality', he says none of these things. He never once names incest; instead he refers to it as that 'special experience', and insists that '"offensive" is frequently but a synonym for "unusual"' (p. 7). The statement has disturbing implications, for it reveals an utter disregard for Lolita's suffering. Ray effaces her entirely; 'Lolita' is merely the title of a narrative by which he is 'entranced'. By thus focusing solely on Humbert's 'supreme misery', Ray becomes Humbert's dupe. In charting Humbert's quest, he replicates his crime. Is Lolita to be found in the text?[53] □

As we have seen, the 1980s ushered in a sweeping and immensely varied recognition that there is an ethical price to pay for the primacy of aesthetics in formalist readings of the text. We have already noted that the beginning of the 1980s witnessed a significant shift in relation to the literary persuasions of H.H.'s narrative. The general feeling was that enough attention had been paid to H.H.'s version of Lolita, and that the time had come to interrupt the enchantments and entrancing pleasures of literary interpretation with more material and worldly readings of the narrative (and all the elaborate plots and schemes). But this is not to suggest that concerns with the fine detail of the text disappear. If anything, far more attention will be paid in the future to the rhetoric of the novel, and to the structures of desire that have proved so compelling. As we move into the 1990s, therefore, readings of *Lolita* become increasingly complex as the full weight of post-structuralist critical knowledge and understanding is brought to bear – both on the text and on its substantial critical history. One of the challenges in the 1990s and beyond is to 'recover' a different version of Lolita. In addition to Kauffman's decisive question – is there a girl in this text? – we can also perhaps ask – why has it taken so long to find her?

CHAPTER FIVE

'The Rediscovered Girl': Rereading *Lolita* in the 1990s

THE DECISIVE question posed by Linda Kauffman in the previous chapter – 'Is Lolita to be found in the text? – could be seen as a guiding proposition for the paths taken in *Lolita* criticism of the 1990s. From various perspectives, the readings we will be looking at in this chapter are concerned in different ways with Lolita as both an effect of language – a figure of H. H.'s imagination – and Lolita as a 'real' girl who is pivotal to the plot. In one sense, there is nothing new about this seemingly paradoxical proposition, and looking back to earlier chapters it is clear that numerous critics have pondered this question. However, from the 1980s this proposition begins to receive *sustained* critical attention, brought about by a shift in perspective throughout the critical spectrum. In part this is due to the influence of feminist theories of literature and representation. What is important is the prevailing sense that the subject of Lolita has not been properly addressed. Who is Lolita? What happens *to* Lolita? How do we *read* Lolita through Humbert's obsessional narrative?

British critic Michael Wood has dramatically characterised the critical history of *Lolita* as 'after the outrage, the lazy tolerance – and after that, the vigilantes again'.[1] Seeing himself as something of a vigilante, but leaving behind any hint of moralism, Wood's ambitious reading of the novel examines and challenges many of the critical assumptions regarding the plausibility of H. H.'s narrative, in particular the question of his 'repentance'. At the same time, Wood offers a wonderfully sustained and impressive reading of *Lolita*, and the significance of her 'creation' in the narrative. With a glancing blow at the 'lazy tolerance' of 'second generation' critics of Lolita (names are withheld), Wood insists that any charge of immoderation should be addressed to the insistent narrative demand that readers 'trust Humbert's obsession even as we are repelled by it'.[2] In order to take the measure of this impossible demand, and the crime it entails in the text, we need to be more sceptical readers. Wood's reading

115

appears as a chapter entitled 'The Language of *Lolita*' in a book-length study of Nabokov, *The Magician's Doubts* (1994). This is one of the key readings of the 1990s for several reasons, some of which are sketched out above. In addition, it offers a way of thinking about the implications of the practice of reading *Lolita*, a text that, more than most, prevails upon its readers to endure the extremes of seduction. Let us now turn to the first extract from this compelling reading, in which Wood introduces the essay and sets out the terms of his argument.

■ *Lolita*, like countless detective and horror stories, presents itself as a textual game, insists not only on its verbal but on its written quality. It is a novel pretending to be a memoir with a foreword; as *Pale Fire* is a novel pretending to be a critical edition of a poem; as many novels pretend to be biographies. The text of *Lolita* is itself full of reproduced or simulated texts: letters, poems, a class list, pages from magazines and reference books, shop signs, road signs, motel signs, excerpts from motel registers, fragments of a diary. A disturbance of Humbert's mind is pictured as an unsettling of print, where thoughts turn physically into words and are mirrored in something like water, or silk or parchment: 'A breeze from wonderland had begun to affect my thoughts, and now they seemed couched in italics, as if the surface reflecting them were wrinkled by the phantasm of that breeze' (p. 131).[3]

Games are caught up in other games. Humbert Humbert offers us (or his imagined jury) a pocket diary for 1947 as 'Exhibit Number Two' (Number One was Humbert's experience of what the angels envied in Poe's poem 'Annabel Lee'). He then tells us the diary was destroyed five years ago, so that what we are reading is a reconstruction, albeit an accurate one, 'by courtesy of a photographic memory'. We sniff sceptically, but maybe our scepticism is premature:

> I remember the thing so exactly because I wrote it really twice. First I jotted down each entry in pencil (with many erasures and corrections) . . . then, I copied it out with obvious abbreviations in my smallest, most satanic hand . . .[4]

Humbert gives us every reason to distrust this text, but we end up, I think, weirdly trusting it – the more so because he tells us when he feels the afterthoughts have crowded too thickly upon him: 'Beginning perhaps amended'; 'all this amended, perhaps'.

The same odd oscillation between trust and distrust occurs with Charlotte Haze's lamentable letter to her uninterested lodger:

> You see, there is no alternative. I have loved you from the minute I saw you. I am a passionate and lonely woman and you are the love

of my life . . . Let me rave and ramble on for a teeny while more, my dearest, since I know this letter has been by now torn by you, and its pieces (illegible) in the vortex of the toilet. My dearest, *mon très, très cher*, what a world of love I have built up for you during this miraculous June![5]

There is, sadly, a genuine passion trying to speak through this drivel, but, as the American critic F. W. Dupee notes, poor Charlotte is 'whatever it is that spoils the party and dampens the honeymoon all across America'.[6] The letter these phrases come from occupies more than a page of print, and seems to be complete. It isn't: we have read only what Humbert remembers of it, although in a wonderful acrobatic twist on an already dizzying logic, what he remembers he remembers *verbatim*. 'It was at least twice longer. I left out a lyrical passage which I more or less skipped at the time, concerning Lolita's brother who died at two when she was four, and how much I would have liked him'. The text is correct, then, but abridged. But is it correct? 'There is just a chance that "the vortex of the toilet" (where the letter did go) is my own matter-of-fact contribution. She probably begged me to make a special fire to consume it'. The text of the letter now seems uncertain, but the toilet acquires a positively Tolstoyan solidity, and on inspection we begin to see shifts and interferences in the style, Humbert's sardonic eloquence invading Charlotte's raving and rambling. How could we have thought 'vortex' was Charlotte's word? And doesn't 'been by now torn by you' have a faintly Humbertian cadence?

The point of textual pretences in their simpler form must be plausibility, something verging on the actual deception of the reader, and Nabokov, as we have seen, gets something of that effect, albeit through a seemingly perverse double bluff. The larger effect of the games in *Lolita* is to make the text, or anything resembling a text, into a metaphor, an image for what is readable and misreadable in the world. Nabokov himself, in an essay on *Lolita* which is now included in most editions of the novel, fears that he must appear textually 'as an impersonation of Vladimir Nabokov talking about his own book'. Nabokov was presumably pretty sure as he wrote that he *was* Nabokov and not an impersonator. But the joke tells the literal truth of the textual game. Nabokov on the page, joined to the text of his novel, writing 'I', signing and dating his work, is no less ghostly than his characters or than any other author. The difference is that authors have flesh-and-blood histories, documentable lives which precede the traces they leave in words, and fictional characters don't. But the difference between a trace with a past and a trace without one is rather more interesting, less wide and less obvious, than the supposedly simple difference between fiction and fact.

We don't need to confuse the imagined Humbert with the unimagined Nabokov, or rush into the notion that everything is fiction. We do need to see that the important differences between these figures are going to be textual (unless we happen to be friends of Nabokov or victims of Humbert), matters of reading. Humbert points for example to what seems to be the rigidity of textual characters, their hopeless inability to change their tune:

> No matter how many times we reopen 'King Lear', never shall we find the good king banging his tankard in high revelry, all woes forgotten, at a jolly reunion, with all three daughters and their lapdogs. Never will Emma rally, revived by the sympathetic salts in Flaubert's father's timely tear.[7]

Humbert is echoing a very ancient complaint, and it is interesting that he should write of reopening *King Lear*, rather than of seeing the play again. 'Writing, you know', Socrates says to Phaedrus,

> has this strange quality about it, which makes it really like painting: the painter's products stand before us quite as though they were alive; but if you question them, they maintain a solemn silence. So, too, with written words: you might think they spoke as though they made sense, but if you ask them anything about what they are saying, if you wish for an explanation, they go on telling you the same thing, over and over forever. Once a thing is put in writing, it rolls about all over the place, falling into the hands of those who have no concern with it just as easily as under the notice of those who comprehend; it has no notion of whom to address or whom to avoid. And when it is ill-treated or abused as illegitimate, it always needs its father to help it, being quite unable to protect or help itself.[8]

Socrates seems to be saying that texts are both too fixed and too easily unfixed. Less luridly, we might say a text cannot do without interpretation, which may be secure or shaky, decent or disreputable, but will always be work (or play), cannot simply be *given*. [Emphasis Wood's.] Nabokov confirms Socrates' case with comic excess (and partly, like Plato giving us such an emphatic written Socrates, refutes the case in the way he makes it). He also anticipates and varies Derrida's famous claim that there is nothing outside the text, *il n'y a pas de hors-texte*.[9] There is plenty outside the text, Nabokov would say, but the text is usually what we've got, and pretty much all we've got. Outside the text is silence. Or noise, but in any case not language. If King Lear could escape from his tragedy, he would only, in Humbert's scenario, find himself turned into Old King Cole. Not everything is a text, but a text is a good image for much of what we know – for everything we know that is beyond the reach of our own immediate experience, and for most of what we imagine is our immediate experience too. Literature is practice for, the practice of such knowledge.[10] □

Wood then develops a systematic and rigorous analysis of the devious linguistic strategies of the novel, from the Foreword ('which allows us to believe we haven't started the novel when we have'), through the journey across America, to the final scene. In common with Ellen Pifer's revisionary reading of Nabokov's moral position in the 1980s (see chapter four of this Guide), Michael Wood insists on the connection between the vibrant representation of Lolita and the particularity of Humbert's crime. 'She is, in short, an entirely ordinary child, unbearable, lovable, funny, moody and soon trapped in the circle of Humbert's obsession. His crime is not to ruin or abduct a genius, or a paragon of manners and culture. It is to lock this girl out of her history, to shut this lively but not exceptional person away from her time and her place and her peers.'[11] Many of the interpretations of the novel from the 1980s onwards refer explicitly both to the vibrancy of the representation of Lolita, and the stealing away of her ordinary childhood. Either she is taken away from it, or it is taken away from her; in the event this is noted as a cruel loss. This did not go unnoticed in the past; we need look no further than the sophisticated and insightful commentaries of Amis and Dupee in the 1950s (see chapter one of this Guide), both of whom make the point, albeit in different terms. The difference now is an attentiveness to the implications of this representation, both within the narrative structure and for the reader's relation to the novel and its potential outcome. For Wood, the implications are far-reaching, and in this brief but extremely pertinent extract, he brings together the idea of Lolita as both an effect of language and a 'significant reality' (to borrow Appel's phrase).

■ . . . Lolita is Humbert's obsession and what escapes it, she is its name and its boundary. The 'actual' Lolita is the person we see Humbert can't see, or can only see spasmodically. In this sense she is a product of reading, not because the reader makes her up or because she is just 'there' in the words, but because she is what a reading finds, and I would say needs to find, in order to see the range of what the book can do. She needs to be 'there', that is, and she needs to be found. This surely is what reading is: a modest mode of creation, a collaboration with other minds and pictured worlds.[12] □

This is important in offering a way out of an impasse in interpretations around the question Kauffman poses about the girl in the text. For

Wood, then, there is no question that to read this book for all it is worth, in a sense to extract its full literary value, there simply has to be a sense of a 'real' girl in the text. Lolita 'must' exist for readers. Let us now return to the concluding part of Wood's reading in which he examines the troubling final meeting between Humbert and Lolita.

■ . . . One of the things we shall most remember in *Lolita* is Humbert's desolate and draining last encounter with the rediscovered girl. Nabokov either triumphs here or makes a brilliant near-miss; either does or does not transcend the fastidious cleverness which is his besetting limit. I think he triumphs, but the case is worth arguing, since it is an extremely close thing.

Lolita has abandoned Humbert for Clare Quilty, has refused the latter's more freakish sexual demands and been thrown out by him. She has drifted for almost two years, making a living by washing dishes, and has married Dick Schiller, a youthful war veteran. She is pregnant, looks worn and helpless and hollow-cheeked. She seems calm and kindly, weirdly resigned to her peculiar past and shabby present. She and Dick live in an urban American waste land some eight hundred miles from New York, their clapboard shack surrounded by 'withered weeds', lost in a region of 'dump and ditch, and wormy vegetable garden . . . and grey drizzle, and red mud, and several smoking stacks in the distance'. The drizzle is presumably laid on by the pathetic fallacy, but the rest must be there in all weathers. ['Pathetic fallacy' is a phrase introduced by the British art critic John Ruskin in 1856. It is used to describe 'the attribution of human feelings and responses to inanimate things, especially in art and literature'. In the context of Wood's citation from *Lolita*, it presumably refers to the way in which the weather, and the depressing scene, seem to evoke *and* represent H.H.'s memory of his own misery and depression.] She still thinks of the obscene Quilty as 'a great guy', and grants that Humbert was 'a good father', as if that was all he had been. This dazed tolerance is more terrible than resentment or rage because it belongs to a person who is past surprise, who has lived with more human strangeness – Humbert's obsession, Quilty's pranks and kinks – than anyone should have to. 'Yes', Humbert reports her as wearily saying, 'this world was just one gag after another'. She is still only seventeen, and the reader knows, as no one in the story does, that she will be dead in just over three months.

Much of the power of this chapter of the novel rests not on the depth or complexity of Lolita's character, or on her having acquired such a character, as David Rampton attractively argues, but on her sheer ruined ordinariness, her old lost ordinariness found again only as a ruin.[13] Life with Humbert was a cage, a travelling prison, a dreary round of sexual duty. Quilty looked like glamour and romance and freedom, but turned out to be only quirky Sadeian games. Even so Lolita regards Quilty as 'full of fun', and Humbert as a remote, hardly remembered nuisance:

> She considered me as if grasping all at once the incredible – and somehow tedious, confusing and unnecessary – fact that the distant, elegant, slender, forty-year-old valetudinarian in velvet coat sitting beside her had known and adored every pore and follicle of her pubescent body. In her washed-out grey eyes, strangely spectacled, our poor romance was for a moment reflected, pondered upon, and dismissed like a dull party, like a rainy picnic to which only the dullest bores had come, like a humdrum exercise, like a bit of dry mud caking her childhood.[14]

Our poor romance is his poor romance, no romance at all for her. The sadness of Lolita's story, as Humbert later realizes, is that she hasn't had the childhood he casually evokes here in metaphor: only the mud and the spoiled picnic, followed by her escapade with Quilty and sudden adulthood. Just one gag after another.

Lolita may well be happier than Humbert (or we) can imagine, but she seems stunned and flattened, almost erased by the life she has led, and for Humbert, of course, this scene is dominated by the thought that the whole sad story is his work, that he has brought Lolita to this. He compares his hands to those of Dick Schiller and thinks: 'I have hurt too much too many bodies with my twisted poor hands to be proud of them'. We remember his hitting Lolita, twisting her wrist; his tormenting of his first wife, Valeria. Trying to make small talk, he almost asks Lolita about one of her old class-mates in Ramsdale, 'I wonder sometimes what has become of the little McCoo girl . . .?', but doesn't, for fear of Lolita's responding, 'I wonder what has become of the little Haze girl . . .' Lolita won't say this, of course, only the ventriloquism of Humbert's guilt speaks. Similarly, when Lolita starts (but does not finish) a comparison between Quilty and Humbert – 'I would sooner go back to Cue. I mean—' – it is Humbert who mentally supplies the lurid novelistic words: '*He* broke my heart. *You* merely broke my life'.

Is this sensitivity new in Humbert? It is not new in the book which is littered with expressions of compunction – entirely unavailing, not in the least acted on, to be sure. After Charlotte Haze's death and Humbert's first night with Lolita:

> More and more uncomfortable did Humbert feel. It was something quite special, that feeling: an oppressive, hideous constraint as if I were sitting with the small ghost of somebody I had just killed.[15]

At the end of their first set of all-American travels:

> We had been everywhere. We had really seen nothing. And I catch myself thinking today that our long journey had only defiled with a sinuous trail of slime the lovely, trustful, dreamy, enormous country that by then, in retrospect, was no more to us than a collection of dog-eared maps, ruined tour books, old tyres, and her sobs in the night – every night, every night – the moment I feigned sleep.[16]

There is a certain amount of narrative complication here. Humbert is 'thinking today' throughout his text, but the constraint, the sobs and the feigned sleep belong to the lived past. What he is suggesting, I think, is that guilt was always with him, but his perpetual desire and fear wouldn't allow him to concentrate on it, and in any case it was a difficult guilt, associated with a publicly identifiable crime, that of cohabitation with a minor. What he wants to evoke and renounce in his last meeting with Lolita is the guilt not of having slept with her but of having treated her as a sample or a treasure, a hoarded specimen of nymphetry, rather than as a person. It is this person, Lolita then *and* now, he insists he loves [emphasis Wood's]:

> there she was with her ruined looks and her adult, rope-veined narrow hands and her goose-flesh white arms, and her shallow ears, and her unkempt armpits, there she was (my Lolita!), hopelessly worn at seventeen, with that baby, dreaming already in her of becoming a big shot and retiring around A.D. 2020 – and I looked and looked at her, and knew as clearly as I know I am to die, that I loved her more than anything I had ever seen or imagined on earth, or hoped for anywhere else . . . You may jeer at me, and threaten to clear the court, but until I am gagged and half-throttled, I will shout my poor truth. I insist the world knows how much I loved my Lolita, *this* Lolita, pale and polluted, and big with another's child, but still grey-eyed, still sooty-lashed, still auburn and almond, still Carmencita, still mine . . .[17]

This is the end of a maniac, the projected birth of a hero. Humbert rejects his past specialization, his obsessive interest in a *class* of little girls, the charms Lolita could only grow out of: 'sterile and selfish vice, all *that* I cancelled and cursed' [emphasis Wood's]. His conversion comes far too late of course, but it would always have been too late, a one-sided love story, Tristan without Isolde. What Humbert is busily, desperately doing is to convert a ragged and tantalising tale of physical possession and loss into a great romance. This is the function of the clustering references to *Carmen*, once a tender allusion for Humbert, then an unwanted joke between him and Quilty, now a touch of literary orchestration, a hoisting of his 'poor romance' into famous sentimental company. This is not Nabokov's parody of Mérimée, it is Humbert's bid for Mérimée's help – although we may glimpse, some-where off in the margin, Nabokov's smile at Humbert's conventional taste. Humbert *is* Don Jose, Lolita *is* Carmen: a replay. *'Changeons de vie, ma Carmen, allons vivre quelque part où nous ne serons jamais séparés . . . Carmen, voulez-vous venir avec moi?'* There is a difference, though, which Humbert carefully exploits.

> I could not kill *her*, of course, as some have thought . . . Then I pulled out my automatic – I mean, this is the kind of fool thing a reader might suppose I did . . . [18]

Don Jose killed Carmen; Humbert kills the bullfighter. And Humbert's prose, of course, is more various than Mérimée's: histrionic, self-regarding ('pale and polluted', 'I looked and looked', 'my poor truth'), but also casual ('big shot') and heartrendingly exact ('rope-veined', 'sooty-lashed').

What are we to make of all this? Readers and critics have rightly focused much attention on this troubling scene. Michael Long thinks Nabokov is trying to change key and hasn't got the voice for it, as Flaubert and Joyce have: 'Its hardly possible for the hero of such an exuberant work of fictional artifice to turn, at the last, into the weep-ing figure from whom these fragments are torn'.[19] Appel and Rampton wonder whether we believe in Nabokov's new order of love; conclude that we do, albeit with difficulty.[20] I think Long gets closer to the centre of the problem. I can't believe in Humbert's new love partly because there is nothing in his self-portrait to suggest he can rise to it, and partly because he is protesting too much, hooked on his version of *Carmen*, too anxious for us to see the change in him ('You may jeer at me, and threaten to clear the court . . .'). I can't believe in his repent-ance because the language of his renunciation is the language of gloating – as indeed his language throughout, however guilty he feels or says he felt, is full of relished remembrance, like that of Dante's lovers Paolo and Francesca enjoying the rerun of what took them down to hell.

> She was only the faint violet whiff and dead echo of the nymphet I had rolled myself upon with such cries in the past; an echo on the brink of a russet ravine, with a far wood under a white sky, and brown leaves choking the brook, and one last cricket in the crisp weeds . . . [21]

This is (overwritten) nostalgia, not regret. Humbert calls his old vice sterile and selfish, but a *grand péché radieux*, as he also names it, can't be so easy to moralize, let alone give up. The same goes for his later intimations of remorse: his talk of his 'foul lust', 'total evil', 'bestial cohabitation'; his sense that his life with Lolita had been only a 'parody of incest'; his self-sentencing ('Had I come before myself, I would have given Humbert at least thirty-five years for rape, and dismissed the rest of the charges'); his listening to 'the melody of children at play':

> I stood listening to that musical vibration from my lofty slope, to those flashes of separate cries with a kind of demure murmur for background, and then I knew that the hopelessly poignant thing was not Lolita's absence from my side, but the absence of her voice from that concord.[22]

This perception is surely morally correct. Humbert's crime is the Jamesian one *par exellence*, the theft of another's freedom – in this case, the freedom to be the ordinary, lively, vulgar American kid we have intermittently seen. But coming from Humbert the claim seems mawkish and self-regarding, altogether too good to be true, 'dictated by some principle of compensation', as Dupee says.[23] Humbert's fussy prose, elsewhere so resourceful and acrobatic, here manages to seem both artful and hackneyed.

One of Humbert's afterthoughts is slightly more convincing, because it offers an argument and anticipates the queer moral indifference of the second generation of *Lolita*'s readers (after the outrage, the lazy tolerance – and after that, the vigilantes again):

> Unless it can be proven to me – to me as I am now, today, with my heart and my beard, and my putrefaction – that in the infinite run it does not matter a jot that a North American girl-child named Dolores Haze had been deprived of her childhood by a maniac, unless this can be proven (and if it can, then life is a joke), I see nothing for the treatment of my misery but the melancholy and very local palliative of art.[24]

We can agree that this deprivation does matter, and more than a jot; that life is not this kind of joke. But even here Humbert ends on his misery, and is still glamorizing his misdemeanours: the one thing worse than being a serious malefactor would be to be nobody, a negligible miscreant.

We might go further and say that while Humbert writes wonderfully about his own deviance, he can't write himself straight; and that the thinness of his repentance is a measure of the weird, lingering humanity of his crime. He has been involved in 'intricately sordid situations', as Dupee says, but somehow 'his horrid scrapes become our scrapes'. Not literally or legally, we hope, but closely enough for all but saints and hypocrites. Love itself, of the least deviant kind, is scarcely less possessive or crazed than Humbert's mania.

> No matter, even if those eyes of hers would fade to myopic fish, and her nipples swell and crack, and her lovely young velvety delicate delta be tainted and torn – even then I would go mad with tenderness at the mere sight of your dear wan face, at the mere sound of your raucous young voice, my Lolita.[25]

The wan face, the raucous voice, the eyes like myopic fish, the velvety delicate delta are the notations of a desperate love, and Humbert writes here the purest, most precise Nabokovian prose. What we question is not his passion but his supposed new respectability. The whole of this book has been asking us to trust Humbert's obsession, even as we are repelled by it. We can't leave off trusting it now, especially when it speaks in these accents, so lyrically mourning what it claims it won't miss.

Still it may not be necessary for us to believe what Humbert believes at the end. Indeed we may understand his crime more fully if we are sceptical about his repentance and altered love. What is unmistakable is his desire to see himself and to project himself, as supremely conscious of his grisly errors, as the sort of grovelling Dostoyevskian sinner Nabokov so detested. It is easy to confess, as Appel says, and it may actually be to Humbert's credit that he is not entirely convincing in this line, in spite of his ambitions. And of course what finally fuels this whole great scene, what makes it moving, with all its disconcerting, criss-crossing antics, is not the moral issue, important as it is. We need to work through our scepticism, I think, but then we can let it go, because we can all, without question, believe in Humbert's loss, his sense of dereliction. 'I believe in my abandonment', a figure cries in a Geoffrey Hill poem, 'since it is what I have'.[26] Humbert's loss is what he has; we can't, so to speak, take that away from him. His shabby selfishness, his alternately brilliant and inflated prose, his unavailing bid to lift himself into high romance, all add to the sadness rather than lessen it. We don't have to admire Humbert in order to feel his pain, and he does become, briefly and ambiguously, in his overacted way, the kind of character we find in Joyce and Flaubert, one whose lamentable lack of grandeur stirs us perhaps more than the grand tragedy of some others. The shift is pictured in this chapter in a beautifully placed entirely banal American word. Humbert repeats his request that Lolita/Carmen come away with him ('*Carmen, voulez-vous . . .?*'), and she says 'No honey, no'. Humbert reflects, 'She had never called me honey before'. She couldn't call him honey before because she didn't think of him fondly enough or casually enough: banality was outlawed from their life, which was only romance and torture (for him), drudgery and quarantine (for her). For a moment Humbert seems to glimpse the attraction of the acceptable and the familiar, of the way other people daily talk and live – the realm of shared feeling which inhabits cliché, and which cliché serves. Of course he can only recognise the feeling because he is excluded from it, but the recognition is something, since it matters that even this tiny and perfunctory brand of tenderness was missing from his relation with Lolita. Missing on both sides, we might add, in spite of Humbert's liking or tenderness as a word; as kindness is often missing from romantic love.

It is a very short-lived recognition though, and Humbert is soon driving off through 'the drizzle of the dying day', wrapped in an imagery of pathos and on his way to kill Quilty among the bedrooms and bathrooms of grotesque comedy, where Humbert and his style meet their extravagant match.[27] □

In common with Wood, British academic and literary critic Rachel Bowlby writes persuasively about the ethical implications of Humbert Humbert's involvement with Lolita (the stealing of her ordinary childhood). This is achieved through a sophisticated and sustained analysis of the languages of *Lolita*. Informed by theories of feminism, psychoanalysis and consumer culture, Bowlby examines the ways in which the text appears to represent a sharp division between 'Lolita's consuming American vulgarity' and Humbert Humbert's 'European intellectual superiority'.[28] As we have noted, that division was seized upon by many of the early reviewers of the novel as a way of absolving (or, at the very least, distancing) Nabokov's literary narrator from the literal cruelty of his crimes. But as Bowlby convincingly argues in her nuanced reading of the rhetoric of *Lolita*, the language of vulgar consumption and the language of literary culture turn out to be connected and conflicting in interesting and surprising ways. '*Lolita* and the Poetry of Advertising' was first published in *Shopping with Freud* (Bowlby, 1993). Let us now turn to the first extract from Bowlby's extensive chapter, in which she elaborates the ethical and moral implications of those divisions, oppositions and polarities, ostensibly registered in the novel, that have proved troublesome for critics.

■ Once again, it seems as though it is difficult to talk about ethics in relation to *Lolita* without setting up a division which renders literature, in its supposed divorce from real people and mature attitudes, irresponsible, or childish, or at best salutary (a consolation for mortality). This same impasse – the difficulty of bringing the moral and the aesthetic together – forms the starting point for Linda Kauffman's challenging reinterpretation, like Dipple's explicitly setting itself in the context of the 1980s focus on issues of child sexual abuse.[29] Kauffman seeks to avoid the stark alternatives which suggest that a text be seen either as simply copying a world awaiting transcription (the representational fallacy) or, on the other hand, as sublimely independent of the social and ethical questions its story may suggest or require. The first, habitually, would be the moralizing version of the kind exemplified by the John Ray Foreword, where the acknowledged enchantments of literature are merely added on as ornament or distraction to texts which in other ways may perfectly well tell it like it is or was – in this instance, the 'lesson-for-our-time' case history. The second version would be the supposed moral insouciance of the often-cited 'aesthetic bliss' invoked by Nabokov's Afterword (p. 332).[30] Unlike Dipple, Kauffman does not see a moral awaiting retrieval from Nabokov's text; but she suggests that it might be 'possible . . . in a double movement to analyze the horror of incest by reinscribing the material body of the child Lolita in the text and simultaneously to undermine the representational fallacy by situating the text dialogically in relation to other texts'.[31]

Reading much more against the novelistic grain than Dipple, Kauffman then finds not the compensatory immortalization of Lolita's body but its violation: 'By thus inscribing the female body in the text . . . one discovers that Lolita is not a photographed image, or a still life, or a freeze frame preserved on film, but a damaged child'.[32] Kauffman reaches this conclusion by way of recent medical literature on father–child incest, which serves more as corroboration than as intertextual counterpoint. It is as though the moral point can only be made, despite every recognition of the difficulties, by returning to a form of referential appeal – 'this is the way it is' – which once again implies that there are some things – some bodies, some acts – which although inscribed or reinscribed, in a text, none the less carry a meaning independently of it.

It is, in one sense, ironic that this should be true of incest of all crimes, since – as Lévi-Strauss demonstrated – though the prohibition is apparently a cultural universal, its specific exclusions are infinitely variable. It is worth noticing too, that Humbert is not Lolita's father in any of the ordinary ways, either biologically or adoptively – he did not bring her up – which emphasises the arbitrary aspect in all human relationships, including those that do connect blood relations: paternity is here quite literally a legal form in relation to which bodily desires and acts will come to take their meaning. Far from being a natural or obviously 'material' question of bodily affects, the incest taboo, for Lévi-Strauss, both inaugurates and epitomizes the symbolic order of human culture: 'placing' persons in relation to one another, in terms of permissions and prohibitions which are unconnected with nature.

This is not to say that Lolita is not a damaged child; but to suggest that that phrase gives too much away, from Kauffman's own point of view, to a particular normative cultural fiction, one parodied within the novel, as well as through the Ray preface, which would have it that there is a state of perfect health and wholeness – proper individuality and proper human relations – from which it is possible to make clear-cut demarcations as to just where the damages begin. The extremity of the Lolita case becomes more, not less, forceful as a critique of sexual values if it is acknowledged that it is not without relation to the sanitizing fictions of faultless human growth and relationship.

Apart from the divisions of guilt and innocence, seducer and victim, real love and perverse sexuality, there is another area in which *Lolita* seems to have suggested to its readers the existence of sharp antinomies; and in this case they are usually taken to be more or less those intended by the author. For the novel apparently stages a manifest clash between the literary values of Humbert and the vulgar, consumerly values of Lolita, which is reinforced through the familiar opposition of the European visitor and the all-American girl. In this antithesis, Lolita does not so much represent innocence and virginity as the crude embodiment of a different kind of victim: one subject to and made over in the image of a mass culture with which she has completely identified; and the narrator, far from representing the force of exploitation, can be associated with an aesthetic authenticity whose plausibility gives the novel its power, because it distracts the reader from what would otherwise appear as a simple assault.

Linda Kauffman implicitly connects these two versions of the antithesis:

> Materialist critiques of the novel could focus on the rampant consumerism of American society in 1955, since Lolita is the ideal consumer, naive, spoiled, totally hooked on the gadgets of modern life, a true believer in the promises of Madison Avenue. Yet a materialist *feminist* perspective enables one to see something that has not been noted before: Lolita is as much the object consumed by Humbert as she is the product of her culture. And if she is hooked, he is the one who turns her into a hooker.[33]

As the juxtaposition shows, consumer culture and violent seduction are seen to be discursively interchangeable, the first as 'rampant' as a rapist in commonplace critiques, and the victim in the second equivalent to a commodity and then to a prostitute. But as we shall see, the equivalences are not so straightforward: Humbert does not enjoy Lolita in the way in which she might enjoy a soda pop or a new dress; and if she is 'hooked' on consumer culture, that does not imply vulnerability so much as pleasure.[34] ☐

As we can see here, Bowlby is keen to disturb the equivalences she finds in Kauffman's interpretation that would offer up Lolita as pure victim of Humbert Humbert and American culture in equal measures. Lolita as a 'damaged' child: spoiled in every sense of the word. In the next extract, we take up Bowlby's detailed analysis of the relation between the rhetoric of consumer culture and the 'poetry of advertising'.

■ Over and over again, the language of consumption, which on the surface is spurned as obviously inferior to the traditions of great literature, seems to take over the poetic force of the novel as though against the grain of the narrator's own intentions. In one sense this is presented as an identification with Lolita's own desires, so that in the afternoon prior to picking her up from the summer camp, the fascination with the girl is shifted by an easy transfer onto 'buying beautiful things for Lo':

> Goodness, what crazy purchases were prompted by the poignant predilection Humbert had in those days for check weaves, bright cottons, frills, puffed-out short sleeves, soft pleats, snug-fitting bodices and generously full skirts! Oh, Lolita, you are my girl, as Vee was Poe's and Bea Dante's, and what little girl would not like to whirl in a circular skirt and scanties? (p. 113)

The alliteration of 'p', followed by the fashion-item list of fetishistic details in the style of magazine copy and then the concluding apostrophe, is perfect in its rhythmic precision, which naughtily makes 'Dante's' the cue for 'scanties' so that the esteemed literary lovers are effortlessly elevated or pulled down (by now the two are indistinguishable) onto the dancefloor of American teen culture.

But the poetic speed of consumption also mutates into its opposite, a state of tranquil suspension, underwater slow motion. The noisy jingle metamorphoses into a silently timeless still life, a 'quiet poetical afternoon of fastidious shopping' (p. 114):

> There is a touch of the mythological and the enchanted in those large stores where according to ads a career girl can get a complete desk-to-date wardrobe, and where little sister can dream of the day when her wool jersey will make the boys in the back row of the

classroom drool. Lifesize plastic figures of snubbed-nose children with dun-coloured, greenish, brown-dotted, faunish faces floated around me. I realized I was the only shopper in that rather eerie place where I moved about fish-like, in a glaucous acquarium. I sensed strange thoughts form in the minds of the languid ladies that escorted me from counter to counter, from rock ledge to sea-weed, and the belts and the bracelets I chose seemed to fall from siren hands into transparent water. (p. 114)

There is a distant resurfacing here of Proust's dining-room in the hotel at Balbec, seen by the outsiders peering in through the windows as an aquarium of slow, magical consumption. Here on the inside the 'eerie' atmosphere derives partly from the narrator's being out of place as a man in the women's department, but also from the literal fulfilment of the fantasy that the appeals of consumption constantly promote: that this is just for you, you are the only shopper in the world, and far from you having to do anything to obtain them, the goods will simply float effortlessly into your hands.

Elsewhere the language of consumption is focused more directly on the figure of Lolita herself, an appreciatively responsive reader:

A great user of roadside facilities, my unfastidious Lo would be charmed by toilet signs – Guys-Gals, John-Jane, Jack-Jill and even Buck's-Doe's; while lost in an artist's dream, I would stare at the honest brightness of the gasoline paraphernalia against the splendid green of oaks, or at a distant hill scrambling out – scarred but still untamed – from the wilderness of agriculture that was trying to swallow it. (p. 161)

Here the parody of the poet *manqué* is open, as he turns away from the modern necessities to find tired clichés of romanticism in the surrounding landscape, while Lo can be 'charmed' by the appurtenances of words which cover the functionally basic, the very lowest of needs, with all the variants of a cutesy kitsch.

The culmination of this ambivalent celebration of Lolita as the poetic consumer occurs at the end of another sequence of the verbal offers to which she so perfectly responds:

She believed, with a kind of celestial trust, any advertisement or advice that appeared in *Movie Love* or *Screen Land* – Starsail Starves Pimples, or 'You better watch out if you're wearing your shirt-tails outside your jeans, gals, because Jill says you shouldn't'. If a roadside sign said VISIT OUR GIFT SHOP – we had to visit it, had to buy its Indian curios, dolls, copper jewellery, cactus candy. The words 'novelties and souvenirs' simply entranced her by their trochaic lilt. If some café sign proclaimed Icecold Drinks, she was automatically stirred, although all drinks everywhere were ice-cold. She it was to whom ads were dedicated: the ideal consumer, the subject and object of every foul poster. (p. 156)

It is Lolita who is the poetic reader, indifferent to things in themselves and entranced by the words that shape them into the image of a desire which consumption then perfectly satisfies. Appearing under the sign of 'novelties and souvenirs', anything can be transmuted through that 'trochaic lilt' into an object of interest, worth attention. It is the narrator who prosaically refuses the fascination with words in themselves or words as moulding the promise of a pleasure for which a referent might then be found, as he stubbornly rejects the promise of the 'Icecold' in favour of a purely informational theory of language which suggests that words and their objects exist in an unvariable twinning of simple denomination.

This fascination with Lolita as the ideal consumer, the American girl *par excellence*, becomes the measure of her inaccessibility to Humbert whose distance in this respect is signalled by his insistence on his own separation from the world that is Lolita's. The language of consumption is represented as being at once the culmination of the poetic tradition and a reprehensible attempt to imitate it. And the infiltration of high and low language goes in both directions, so that advertising interferes with the purity of poetry, but at the same time poetry acquires its modern form in the everyday aestheticization of a culture of images.

These tensions are intimately bound up with the framing of the narrative of the book, somewhere between a legal defence and a psychiatric case history, in which the narrator purports to be accounting for what he did to Lolita. In this text, it is not the woman but the masculine narrator whose sanity is in question, and the early period of his life is reconstructed as a conscious series of pre-Lolitas leading up to the girl herself as perverse fulfilment of the condition that must be satisfied in order for him to desire. Annabel Leigh, the first love who dies, immobilizes his desire in the image of a pubescent beauty doomed to end, and it is she who will come to figure as the poetic ideal impossible to attain in reality. Annabel's desires are perfectly in harmony with the boy's; nothing comes between them except the normal constraints of grown-up intruders and the exceptional curtailment of her untimely disappearance.[35]

Valeria, the temporary wife, is represented, as Charlotte Haze will be later and to some extent Rita too, as of no particular erotic interest, serving only as a decoy or fall-back for the continuing quest to recover and possess an Annabel/Lolita. But between Annabel and Valeria is the Paris streetwalker whose distinctive walk evokes something of 'the nymphic echo' (p.24). Monique is poised halfway between Annabel and Lolita in other ways than biographically. Like Annabel, she is not significantly different in age from Humbert and there is a degree of shared pleasure, so that 'my last vision that night of long-lashed Monique is touched up with a gaiety that I find seldom associated with any event in my humiliating, sordid, taciturn love life' (p.25). But at the same time, like Lolita, Monique is a proto-consumer:

> She looked tremendously pleased with the bonus of fifty I gave her as she trotted out into the April night drizzle with Humbert Humbert lumbering in her narrow wake. Stopping before a window display she said with great gusto: *'je vais m'acheter des bas!'* and never may I forget the way her Parisian childish lips exploded on *'bas'*, pronouncing it with an appetite that all but changed the 'a' into a brief buoyant bursting as in *'bot'*. (p.25)

The frank exchange of money for love here endows Monique with the power to satisfy her 'appetite' as a consumer of *'des bas'* – combining the femininity of stockings as an article of narcissistic adornment, hugging the skin, with the 'low' emphasis that descends even further in the climactic *bot* of the foot. After this, Monique loses for Humbert what she gains for herself: their next date 'was less successful, she seemed to have grown less juvenile, more of a woman overnight' (p.25).

It is low consumption which makes this girl a woman and puts her at a distance from the man by providing another source of satisfaction. In being not (yet) a woman, but absolutely a consumer, Lolita then represents for Humbert another version of this division between the purity of pre-womanhood and the baseness of consumption. She herself is wholly and simply the narcissistic girl-consumer, sexually neither pure nor mature (these are not the categories which make sense from her point of view). Humbert's crime, as he recognises, is to breach her self-containment by introducing his own utterly incompatible terms of desire. Before the first night he sleeps with her, Humbert clearly declares that their respective scenarios are not the same:

> Since (as the psychotherapist, as well as the rapist, will tell you) the limits and rules of such girlish games are fluid, or at least too childishly subtle for the senior partner to grasp – I was dreadfully afraid I might go too far and cause her to start back in revulsion and terror. (p.119)

The acknowledgement is pragmatic rather than principled: it does not detract from his being 'agonizingly anxious to smuggle her into the hermetic seclusion of The Enchanted Hunters' (p. 119).

In the explicit separation it invokes, this scene replays and extends the one . . . when Humbert masturbates on the sofa in her mother's house with an oblivious Lolita: 'What I had madly possessed was not she but my own creation, another, fanciful Lolita; . . . The child knew nothing' (p. 66). The difference between the 'senior partner' and the 'child' is that one is aware of the difference, of the double perspective, and the other has no access to it. There is fantasy on each side – on Humbert's, for his poetic nymphet embodied in the modern American image of the girl; on Lolita's, for the movie-star hero resembling Humbert whose picture she pins to her bedroom wall – but Lolita's has none of the insistence and exclusiveness of his. The problem is not that such a discrepancy should exist at all (to imagine that it might not, that fantasies are normally or even ideally complementary, would be to accept, on the model of Lolita's high-school training, that human communication is normally faultless). Humbert's crime is to force his version on Lolita in a way that deprives her irrevocably of her 'girlish games' (p. 119) and their ordinary sequels, happy or not.

It is only after this violation that Lolita starts to bargain, as though in acknowledgement that only money can serve provisionally as a regulating standard between the otherwise incommensurable positions in which she and her 'father' are situated. If he can have her, she can have whatever she wants that money can buy. This is the forced contract which is instigated by the array of goods that Humbert buys Lolita on the 'quiet poetical afternoon of fastidious shopping' (p. 114) before he goes to fetch her from the camp; the bribe is followed, the next day, by the compensation, the first of Humbert's numerous lists of commodities:

> I bought her four books of comics, a box of candy, a box of sanitary pads, two cokes, a manicure set, a travel clock with a luminous dial, a ring with a real topaz, a tennis racket, roller skates with white high shoes, field glasses, a portable radio set, chewing gum, a transparent raincoat, sunglasses, some more garments – swooners, shorts, all kinds of summer frocks. At the hotel we had separate rooms, but in the middle of the night she came sobbing into mine, and we made it up very gently. You see, she had absolutely nowhere else to go. (p. 149)

Here the bare list of things almost unadorned by adjectives or amplifications, just the necessary equipment for the motoring tour to come, is already some way from the dreamy strangeness of the previous afternoon, 'a touch of the mythological and the enchanted in those large stores' (p. 114).

Lolita demonstrates – more enchantingly perhaps than any other novel – that advertising has its poetry, that far from being incompatible, advertising language and literary language share an assumption that objects of all kinds acquire their desirability through the words and the implied stories in which they are represented. There is no separation of form between Humbert's literary world and Lolita's consumerly world; the gap is rather in the incompatibility of the particular wishes and dreams which make them up. Lolita, 'as glad as an ad' (p. 170), is the modern attraction for the literary seeker after the latest embodiment of youthful female perfection, but by depriving her of her premature 'girlish games' he turns her story into something never shown in the happy world of advertisements.[36] □

Bowlby's intellectual concerns about the cultural representation of femininity, and the ways in which females become associated with extremes of cultural value (from the highest form of inspiration to the lowest form of vulgarity), are shared by Elisabeth Bronfen. Bronfen's discussion of *Lolita* appears as a section in a long chapter entitled 'The Dead Beloved as Muse' in *Over Her Dead Body: Death, Femininity and the Aesthetic* (1992). It is part of Bronfen's enterprise to explore the possibility of recovering 'feminine' versions of self-authorisation. In this regard, we might recall the ways in which Bowlby identifies consumer culture as a potential site of self-pleasure for Lolita. As suggested by the titles of Bronfen's chapter and book, however, she is primarily concerned with the representation of femininity and death in art and literature. The underlying proposition of her book is that '[Western] culture uses art to dream the deaths of beautiful women'.[37] Informed by theories of psychoanalysis, semiotics and feminist literary criticism, Bronfen's argument takes the form of 'an elaborate presentation and analysis of the many facets of the feminine-death-figure'. Her interest in *Lolita* is focused quite specifically on the 'plethora of allusions to the conjunction of femininity and death – dead mothers'.[38] In the following extract Bronfen offers an original interpretation of the famous and frequently discussed scene of masturbation in which H. H. 'safely' solipsises 'his' Lolita.

■ At certain moments in the narrative, H.H. unwittingly articulates the difference between the beloved he possesses and the actual girl. In the very first sexualised encounter between them, the dual figure I am concerned with underlines the scene. With both listening to a popular song about Carmen and her lover's wish to kill her with a gun, H.H. experiences masturbatory ecstasy in the seeming ignorance of the girl who inspires it: 'What I had madly possessed was not she, but my

own creation, another, fanciful Lolita – perhaps, more real than Lolita
. . . floating between me and her, and having no will, no consciousness
– indeed, no life of her own' (p. 62).[39] The ideal beloved is not only
created in reference to literary predecessors, as a cliché or dead
metaphor of representations of feminine figures of death, nor is she
herself merely understood as a mental corpse. Rather, in the process,
the actual Dolores Haze is also 'safely solipsized', equally lacking a
life of her own, because superseded and effaced by his 'creation . . .
more real'.[40]

His ecstasy shows him caught between the actual Dolores, absent
because beyond the solipsism of his image-repertoire, and the double,
the fanciful Lolita. What Nabokov discloses is that possessing her
body as an image he has created means being blind to the fact that her
actual body is there, that her subjectivity contradicts his allegorising
reduction. Seeing only the image of his own creation he can oversee
that his contact is indeed with the material body of a girl. He can
delude himself into believing that his incursion involves only an
image. Pushing her outside the frame of his vision, he denies her presence in that she is outside the parameters of the world he creates in the
same way that the imagined body supplanting her also has no life of
her own, because totally his creation. The duplicity of his behaviour, a
form of violent gazing, is that by denying her actual presence and her
subject position, he deludes himself into believing that he has touched
an image not a body. In doing so he not only violates the body but also
denies that any violation has occurred. What this leaves undecided for
the reader is whether s/he chooses to read only the surface H.H. offers,
or whether s/he chooses also to focus on that beneath the confession
and his own self-parody.

The resistance of the real body of the girl to H.H.'s imaginary
appropriation again comes to the fore in the scene where he picks her
up at the summer camp after her mother's death. For a second she
seems to him 'less pretty than the mental imprint' he had cherished,
but as his glance turns into a longer gaze he adds 'I overtook my prey
. . . and she was my Lolita again – in fact, more of my Lolita than ever'
(p. 111). In such moments H.H. unwittingly, or consciously, reflects on
the way the real, the alterity of the girl, must be silenced or transformed to fit his image. [In post-structuralist discourse, 'alterity' is taken
to mean otherness.] Narrative moments where the real disrupts the
unity of his narcissistically informed memory text are also found in his
reference to the sobs he hears every night, once he feigns sleep, and
which he leaves uncommented (p. 173), or in the description of her
innocence, frankness and kindness when she plays tennis, which contradicts the cruel and crafty deceitfulness he wishes to attribute to her.
Or when a 'chance combination of mirror aslant and door ajar' gives

him a view of Dolores's disappointed face because he will not let her go out alone, he briefly realises that 'an outside world . . . was real to her'. In these moments he acknowledges the existence of her desires in a world beyond his fancy.

Of course these moments, where he acknowledges that he does not know a thing about her, that he has in fact been ignoring her states of mind, are repeatedly recuperated by such statements that describe their life as a 'parody of incest' (p. 286). Here the real facticity and materiality disrupt the parody of freely floating signifiers in the same narrative gesture that articulates the occlusion of the feminine subject position, precisely because this is coterminous with an attempt to use the trope of the beloved to efface real death. [In using the term 'facticity', Bronfen is drawing attention to the conflict in the text between the events of the narrative, the content, and H.H.'s rhetorical transformations of what 'actually' happens.] Unlike Carl Proffer, who suggests that Humbert invokes 'Carmen' or 'Bluebeard' to signal premonitions of Lolita's death as red herrings meant to play with the literate reader, I argue that these allusions duplicitously point to the real effacement of the feminine subject that grounds this representation and are used to veil the figural murder of Dolores Haze that does occur in the text.

These false leads are not only part of the process that turns the actual girl into a trope, 'my Lolita', but because they result in a frustration of the reader's expectation, where an expected murder is shown not to occur, they shift the focus away from the figural murder that underwrites the entire system of representation. I follow Shute's cue that Nabokov's parody 'appeals to something other than itself', a disengenuous [sic] strategy whereby it simultaneously invokes and negates the psychoanalytic economies of desire.[41] I would merely add not only that the act of citation and parody, like the fetish, simultaneously effaces and leaves intact the theme of love as repetition, but that what is equally effaced and left wholly visible is the feminine subject position in its alignment with death as that which grounds and disrupts the illusory portrait of the artist as an autonomous man.[42] □

Bronfen's point here about the 'illusory portrait of the artist as an autonomous man' is directly related to the artistic pretensions and delusions of the narrator of *Lolita*, H.H. However, charges of artistic pretension and delusions of autonomy have a particular resonance for Nabokov himself. Like his creation H.H., he is frequently invoked in these terms. As we have seen, the 1980s inaugurated a rush of claims to revoke those charges, but they are not yet laid to rest. In the following extract from Frederick Whiting's marvellous analysis of the cold-war cultural context of *Lolita*, the question of Nabokov's aesthetic project is once again addressed. The broad framework of Whiting's extended analysis of the text, and in particular the social, sexual and critical context, can be inferred from his title, '"The Strange Particularity of the Lover's Preference": Pedophilia, Pornography, and the Anatomy of Monstrosity in *Lolita*', the first part of which is a citation from Trilling's discussion in the 1950s. In many ways there are affinities between Whiting's reading and Linda Kauffman's reading of the novel in the 1980s. However, whereas Kauffman's reading of *Lolita* is informed by a feminist under-standing of late twentieth-century debates about child sexual abuse, Whiting draws particular attention to the different issue of child molest-ation, and public scares about child molesters in the 1950s. What the two arguments clearly share is a passionate concern to expose some of the troubled and troubling assumptions about sexuality, 'morality' and art that so fervently underscore critical attitudes of the 1950s.

■ . . . On the face of it, it seems difficult to imagine a more exemplary expositor of formalist aesthetics than Nabokov or a more hospitable literary critical environment than the one in which *Lolita* emerged. But if we consider *Lolita*'s critical reception in light of the period's anxieties about pedophilia and pornography, the matter-of-fact assertions of critical principles acquire a confessional air. Humbert's confession shares with real-life testimony delivered before HUAC an uncanny ability to engender further confessions. Professional critics and casual readers alike felt compelled not only to reveal where they stood with respect to Humbert and his strange desire but to deliver as well their own literary loyalty oaths and pledges of aesthetic allegiance. And just as Humbert's confession, in its very obedience, eventually exposes the incoherence of the sexual and legal formalisms that enjoin and struc-ture it, so the confessions of *Lolita*'s critics and creator problematize the tenets of literary formalism they seek to champion.

At one extreme is a quite remarkable sort of critical repression that leads not only to a denial of any effective linkage between art and political anxiety but to a denial of the political anxiety itself. John Hollander's assertion that *Lolita* is about 'Mr. Nabokov's love affair with the romantic novel' rather than Humbert's 'love affair' with a twelve-year-old is predicated not upon the aesthetic advantages of the former but on the impossibility of the latter. He founds this impossi-bility upon the colorable assertion that there is, in effect, no real category of deviant to which Humbert belongs ['colourable' – US 'colorable' – means 'specious', 'plausible', or 'counterfeit'. I think Whiting's intention veers towards 'specious', which means 'superficially plausible but actually wrong']:

> But there is something more here, surely, some better way for the reader to escape (if he must) the too-serious acceptance of the

suburb of heterosexuality in which Humbert dwells. His particular Lecherville has, as far as I know, no well-known clinically
respectable name of long standing (Old Can't-tell-the-players-
without-a-scorecard Krafft-Ebing has to resort to 'violation of
persons under the age of fourteen' for his map).[43]

Hollander is here concerned not only to suggest that the book is not
about pedophilia but that, in effect, there is no such thing as pedophilia
for it to be about. Rather, his 'suburb of heterosexuality' offers up the
image of a benign peripheral area presumably disarmed in Hollander's
mind by its convenient proximity, hardly commuting distance, to the
sexual center of the city. The absence of clinical nomenclature, of
respectable road signs at the city limits, he seems to suggest, indicates
that the town has been incorporated rather than that he is a man
without a map. Given the general prominence of the issue of child
molesting during the period, Hollander's description of this sexual
geography has about it a note of uneasy nostalgia for a time when the
erotic terrain was less complicated, when the pedophile as a discrete
form of sexual subjectivity, a species with a particular set of inner dis-
positions, didn't exist. Instead, there were only those who committed
forbidden acts.

What with Hollander is a patent antagonism toward considering
Lolita's connection to contemporary sexual anxieties becomes in the
hands of a more self-conscious and socially concerned critic like
Trilling intelligent ambivalence and introspection. His essay is, in
effect, an investigation in which he is both confessor and confessee of
his own reluctance to acknowledge Humbert's monstrosity. He allows
from the outset that the social anxieties Hollander wishes to ignore
necessarily position *Lolita*'s readers: 'The response [to sexual relations
between an adult male and a girl] is not reasoned but visceral. Within
the range of possible heterosexual conduct, this is one of the few prohibitions which still seem to us to be confirmed by nature itself'.
Indeed, according to Trilling, these anxieties are important because
they extend beyond the social and are rooted in the immutable order
of nature. Humbert's monstrousness consists not in his criminal acts
but in violating that order. In light of this realization, however,
Trilling feels himself oddly complacent: 'I was plainly not able to
muster up the note of moral outrage'. He speculates that his reluctance
can be traced, at least in part, to contemporary legal and psychiatric
attempts to explain pedophilia: 'Pathology naturalises the strange
particularity of the lover's preference'. The observation highlights a
persistent feature of theorizations of monstrosity – the disarming of the
monster's affective threat through causal explanation. By making the
pedophile a distinct species of erotic identity with an anomalous

mechanism of desire and a discrete etiology, medicine and law could contain it and bring it within the orderly operation of nature. But if in the course of his ruminations Trilling manages to avoid the kind of blunt denial that characterizes confessions like Hollander's, he is nonetheless led to kindred repressions: 'Perhaps his [Humbert's] depravity is the easier to accept when we learn that he deals with a Lolita who is not innocent, and who seems to have very few emotions to be violated'![44]

Indeed, the imperative to confess that *Lolita* produced extended even to its author, who was ordinarily supremely indifferent to the reception of his work. In 'On a Book Entitled *Lolita*', an afterword written to accompany the novel's American debut, Nabokov defends himself against allegations of pornography and un-Americanism . . . That Nabokov should not only go to the trouble of responding to public concerns but that he should choose to have his response published with the novel belies the critical indifference he sought to affect. Although he was spared the court appearance that the novel's troubled publication history had threatened, public opinion nevertheless made Nabokov's confession necessary.[45] His explanation was a separation of moral and artistic concerns ostensibly as crisp as Hollander's (elsewhere in the afterword Nabokov altered Hollander's formulation of his love object from the romantic novel to the English language). He dispatched with characteristically corrosive invective the type of readers who 'would pronounce *Lolita* meaningless because it does not teach them anything':

> I am neither a reader nor a writer of didactic fiction, and despite John Ray's assertion, *Lolita* has no moral in tow. For me a work of fiction exists only insofar as it affords me what I shall bluntly call aesthetic bliss, that is a sense of being somehow, somewhere, connected with other states of being where art (curiosity, tenderness, kindness, ecstasy) is the norm . . . (p. 316)[46]

Here as elsewhere in his essays and interviews, Nabokov appears to validate dichotomies such as moral versus aesthetic and literature-of-ideas versus true-art in order to explain his life and work, always vehemently eschewing the first term and valorizing the second. Implicit in these oppositions is a clean separation of public and private spheres. Unlike the public moralism of the literature of ideas, the aesthetic bliss that true art produces is measurable only in the private response of the individual reader. Hence, Nabokov's position seems no more than a particularly polemical expression of the traditional liberal democratic argument for the separation of spheres. And in maintaining it, he seems concerned only with safeguarding the rights and protections belonging to the private. This insistence undoubtedly accounts for the perception that Nabokov was indifferent to Humbert's monstrous deeds and the period's anxieties about them.

However, the separation of morality and aesthetics, public and private, form and content that Nabokov seems to delineate is hardly as straightforward as critics have claimed. In the first place, the split between moral and aesthetic concerns in the passage above is far less neat than the rhetoric at first suggests. The first three terms that Nabokov places in parenthetical apposition to aesthetic bliss – curiosity, kindness, and tenderness – import into his purely aesthetic model the very moral register he seems bent on avoiding.[47] All three are qualities that, insofar as they are necessary to recognize oneself as part of a larger collective, regulate the ability to occupy a moral perspective at all. Their publicness stands in marked contrast to the connotations of privacy that surround the last term in the series, ecstasy. Moreover, both ecstasy and the term it is intended to define, bliss, seem odd choices in view of Nabokov's argument here. His definition arises, after all, in the course of his attempt to distinguish *Lolita* from ordinary pornography. Yet these terms suggest a blurring of the boundary between pure and impure, spiritual and sensual, upon which Nabokov seems to insist.

Significantly, both terms are also mainstays of Humbert's vocabulary for his experience of nymphets. And while this commonality has led moralist critics to insist upon the monstrous similarities between Humbert and Nabokov, there are risks in too precipitately identifying Humbert and his creator. If the uneasy coexistence of moral and aesthetic conceptual registers within Nabokov's parentheses leads us to question the formalism he seems to be espousing, there is evidence in the novel that he was not unaware of the difficulties. A fact that has received astonishingly scant critical attention (call this repression) is that Humbert is not a writer of fiction but a literary critic, a professor of English and French literature. With this fact in mind, it is difficult to ignore the parallels between the fixing of identity that his confession attempts and his claim to some measure of redemption by immortalizing Lolita through art. Such immortality is, after all, the logical extension of the reduction of Lolita to formal features that has characterized his account of her all along. And in view of the incoherence of that account, I read its linkage with literary formalism at the novel's close as a mark of Nabokov's ambivalence concerning the politics of critical formalism, if not a cautionary comment.[48] □

What is important about all of these essential readings from the 1990s is that they contain the potential for reading *Lolita* in nuanced and complex ways that allow for, and give credence to, all the ambiguities, contradictions and complications that make the novel what it is: an iconic, canonic, controversial twentieth-century text. We can respond to the finely drawn character of Lolita as a typically ordinary adolescent American girl (with all that that entails), as well as to the cultural geography of America in a particular moment of its history; we can draw on the wide range of critical approaches now at our disposal in order to analyse the intricacies of the languages, the structural deviations of the narrative, the relation to literary history both invoked and (importantly) reproduced by the novel; and, at the same time, we can acknowledge that something bad happens in the book. Indeed, the sense of working through and accounting for the full effects of the ethical *and* literary ambiguities and contradictions is where almost fifty years of unremitting critical attention to *Lolita* come to rest – for the moment, at least.

The last extract in this chapter comes from David Rampton. Rampton has written widely on Nabokov, and, as Whiting and Rorty have noted, he is one of the critics responsible for rescuing Nabokov from the isolations of formalism in the 1980s (see the discussion of Rorty in chapter four of this Guide). In particular, Rampton argues for a reconsideration of the ethical terms of *Lolita*. In the 1990s he brings the critical discussion of *Lolita* up to date in *Vladimir Nabokov* (1993). Through a brilliantly engaged reading, Rampton calls attention to the novel as a 'moving account of a magnificent obsession that explores the boundaries of one consciousness, one world, not the interaction of two'.[49] As we have seen, the focus of critical attention in the 1990s has moved closer to detailed readings of what happens to Lolita in the text, and to the question of why H.H.'s narrative has in different ways proved so seductive over time. It seems appropriate, then, to bring this Readers' Guide to a close with a fine reading of the ending of *Lolita*, a text that continues to fascinate, to provoke and to trouble readers and critics alike.

■ At the end of the novel, as Humbert is about to be arrested, he recalls 'a last mirage of wonder and hopelessness' that he witnessed while searching for Lolita. From a mountain road he surveys a small mining town in a distant valley below. The visual impression, as always lovingly and unforgettably etched by Nabokov, is here superseded by the aural:

> Reader! What I heard was but the melody of children at play, nothing but that, and so limpid was the air that within this vapor of blended voices, majestic and minute, remote and magically near, frank and divinely enigmatic – one could hear now and then as if released, an almost articulate spurt of vivid laughter, or the crack of a bat, or the clatter of a toy wagon . . . . I stood listening to that musical vibration from my lofty slope, to those flashes of separate

> cries with a kind of demure murmur for background, and then I knew that the hopelessly poignant thing was not Lolita's absence from my side, but the absence of her voice from that concord. (p. 306)[50]

This is a great conclusion, because it resolves key issues for certain readers, and leaves in suspense all the tensions that so intrigue others. It says that Humbert has robbed Lolita of her childhood; thus he stands condemned, self-condemned. The lyrical evocation reinforces the intensity, and the allusion to a final harmony from which the discordant Humbert is excluded suggests that he remains marginal to the end. The text has also come more or less full circle, back to the days when he listened in on Lolita and her friends at Ramsdale. Those less interested in finality will seize on other aspects of the ending, on the ways in which, whatever his intentions, Humbert undermines his own attempts at imposing closure. Nietzsche's observation that those who despise themselves nevertheless esteem themselves as self-despisers hovers ominously over such passages. According to this view, the voices are 'frankly enigmatic' because they say different things to different people. Humbert's regret for Lolita's loss of her childhood is a threnody for time passing, including the loss of his own childhood, not a confrontation with his guilt. ['Threnody' means 'a song of lamentation'.] She was hardly a child when she met him, and he took from her, not playtime with friends and their 'toy wagons', but the possibility of normal adult experience. Besides, 'American childhood' has been revealed in the course of his narrative to be something rather different from the innocent play described here: 'the Miranda twins had shared the same bed for years, and Donald Scott . . . had done it with Hazel Smith in his uncle's garage, and Kenneth Knight . . . used to exhibit himself wherever and whenever he had a chance' (pp. 138–9) – so runs Lolita's account of her coevals. The passage, seen in this light, represents one more appeal to an illusory Lolita by a deluded Humbert.

The coda of the novel will support such opposed readings as well. In it, Humbert says goodbye to Lolita, who is no longer living when the authorities publish Humbert's book, and promises her an immortality of sorts in the work of art he has created. This is a more profound and moving sincerity for many, different in kind from the self-serving and self-regarding effusions that characterize earlier parts of the text. 'I am thinking of aurochs and angels, the secret of durable pigments, prophetic sonnets, the refuge of art', says Humbert. The aurochs is a species of extinct buffalo, the angel an imaginary creation of religious mystics, yet they live on in accounts that describe them, as do the faces of those memorialized in an artist's 'durable pigments', or the beloved figure in the world's great love poems.

For others, Humbert's threats, contained in the very last lines of the book, to kill by slow torture Lolita's husband if he mistreats her are much more to the point. Sexual jealousy and possessiveness have always been Humbert's subject. According to this view, even when he condemns himself to thirty-five years for rape, he is engaging in a rhetorical flourish only, since his posing as ultimate judge and jury was what got him and Lolita into so much trouble in the first place. In fact, the very life/art antithesis his last words introduce is suspect, since this tidy distinction is precisely the one the novel has worked so hard to subvert. Only notional creatures can find solace in the immortality offered by sonneteers and portrait artists eager for exhorbitant commissions, and thus Humbert contents himself in the end by ascribing a hackneyed bookish reality to the person whose independent reality he has never been able to acknowledge. The plausibility of such different accounts is surely one of the main reasons the novel continues to be so popular.

The above description of *Lolita* is accurate as far as it goes, but it downplays the novel's self-reflexive qualities, its elaborate games, its interrogation of the status of the novel and of fiction itself. Recent movements in literary criticism have sought to 'undermine the referential status of language', subvert 'received ideas about the text, the context, the author, the reader', undo 'the very comforts of mastery and consensus that underlie the illusion that objectivity is situated somewhere outside the self', 'show the text resolutely refusing to offer any privileged reading', serve as the antithesis of any mode of reading that subscribes to 'traditional values and concepts', and to prove that meaning is 'ultimately indeterminate'.[51] Any critic who attempts to approach texts in these ways would seem to have found the ideal text in *Lolita* . . .

Theoretically minded readers would explore at greater length the ways in which Humbert's narrative unwittingly subverts itself. For example, by presenting us with a 'father' who is the 'lover' of his 'daughter', and a 'child' who is denied a childhood. It presents an ominous gap or silence at the heart of the book after Charlotte is killed, the counterpart to the gap left by the silence about sex itself. Critics concerned about the logocentrism of Western culture might adduce comments like 'Repeat until the page is full, printer', in Humbert's ostentatiously 'written' text, as evidence for his assigning a priority to the written as opposed to the spoken confession, and a preference for writing over speech that subverts the traditional position of these two in Western thought. So too with the culture/nature dichotomy. When Humbert insists: 'I have but followed nature. I am nature's faithful hound', he reminds us that *Lolita*'s revision of sexuality reveals the vacuity of the attempt to divide up experience into these conventional categories. His argument is in one sense a case of preposterous special pleading, since for genetic reasons nature works against incest by natural selection; but the standards of conduct set by parents and children and the limits of desire are cultural constructs whose assumptions his story seeks to undercut. It is true that such criticism can divert attention from material that is equally relevant. For example, after his comment about nature, quoted above, Humbert says, 'Why then this sense of horror that I cannot shake off?' As so often in Nabokov, here the subversion is accompanied by a reversion to traditional morality. Of course, such pronouncements need have no special status, and one can easily imagine a critique that reveals them to be simply elaborate parodies of an ideology that requires moralistic tags to conclude its stories. But the point is that an appeal to internal evidence cannot by itself resolve such questions. The values that inform any set of critical criteria may well be contingent, in the sense that they are human creations and not eternal laws; our task is to determine how well such criteria perform the function we have set for them.[52] □

NOTES

INTRODUCTION

1 Alfred Appel Jr, 'An Interview with Vladimir Nabokov' rpt, in L.S. Dembo, ed., *Nabokov: The Man and his Work* (Madison: University of Wisconsin Press, 1967), pp. 19–44. [*Appel's Note:*] This interview was conducted on September 25, 27, 28, 29, 1966, at Montreux, Switzerland . . . Since Mr. Nabokov does not like to talk off the cuff (or 'Off the Nabocuff', as he said) no tape recorder was used. Mr. Nabokov either wrote out his answers to the questions or dictated them to the interviewer; in some instances, notes from the conversation were later recast as formal questions-and-answers. The interviewer was Nabokov's student at Cornell University in 1954 . . .

2 Vladimir Nabokov, letter to Graham Greene, 31 December 1956. Dmitri Nabokov and Matthew J. Bruccoli, eds, *Vladimir Nabokov: Selected Letters 1940–1977* (London: Weidenfeld and Nicolson, 1990), pp. 197–8.

3 Norman Page, ed., *Nabokov: The Critical Heritage*, The Critical Heritage Series (London: Routledge, 1982), p. 13.

4 D. Nabokov and Bruccoli (1990), p. 198, f.n.1.

5 See letter from Graham Greene to Nabokov, January 1957, D. Nabokov and Bruccoli (1990), p. 198.

6 For an indispensable reading of the Chatterley trial and its links with the response in England to *Lolita*, see Rachel Bowlby, 'Lady Chatterley: the obscene side of the canon', in Bowlby, *Shopping with Freud*, (London: Routledge, 1993), pp. 28–9; a different version, '"But she could have been reading *Lady Chatterley*"', appears in Karen R. Lawrence, ed., *Decolonizing Tradition: New Views of Twentieth-Century 'British' Literary Canons* (Urbana: University of Illinois Press, 1991). Bowlby argues that 'the ambivalent status of [those] books hovering uncertainly on what came to be defined as a critical boundary between "literature" and "obscenity" [was] derived in some indissociable way from the dubious figure of a woman and her sexual character. Situated on the verge between two equally untenable verdicts, depravity or respectability, she stands in for the book, a surrogate object of attack or defence'.

7 Annette Michelson, '*Lolita*'s Progeny', *October* 76, Spring 1996, pp. 3–14.

8 Vladimir Nabokov, letter to *Life International*, 2 April 1959; D. Nabokov and Bruccoli (1990), pp. 286–7. [*Nabokov and Bruccoli's Note:*] An altered text of this letter was published in the 6 July 1959 issue of *Life International* along with a letter from Maurice Girodias.

9 Andrew Field, *Nabokov: His Life in Art* (London: Hodder and Stoughton, 1967), p. 336; cited in David Packman, *Vladimir Nabokov: The Structure of Literary Desire* (Columbia: University of Missouri Press, 1982), p. 46.

10 Alfred Appel Jr, ed., T*he Annotated 'Lolita': Vladimir Nabokov* (New York: McGraw-Hill, 1970), p. xxxiv. [*Editor's Note:*] Appel offers this as a humorous proof of the failure of *Lolita* as pornography. But it does raise a more serious point about the idea of the pornographic reader (who can neither read properly nor speak properly, in this version) and the literary reader who recognises literature when he sees it.

11 Appel (1970), pp. xxxiv–xxxv.

12 Vladimir Nabokov, letter to Maurice Girodias, 14 December 1956, in D. Nabokov and Bruccoli (1990), pp. 196–7.

13 Walter Minton, telegram to Vladimir Nabokov, 3:46p.m., 18 August 1958, in D. Nabokov and Bruccoli (1990), p. 257.

14 Frederick Whiting, '"The Strange Particularity of the Lover's Preference": Pedophilia, Pornography, and the Anatomy of Monstrosity in *Lolita*', *American Literature*, 70: 4 (December 1998), p. 851.

15 Whiting (1998), p. 852.

16 Vladimir Nabokov, *Lolita* (1955; Harmondsworth: Penguin, 1980), p. 309.

17 Nabokov (1980), p. 310.

18 Vladimir Nabokov, *The Enchanter*, trans. Dmitri Nabokov (London: Picador, 1986), p. 126.

19 Vladimir Nabokov, *Poems and Problems*

(London: Weidenfeld and Nicolson, 1972).
20 Even the most cursory glance at
'Lilith' reveals a familiar Nabokovian
assembly of persons and tropes: male narrator, 'naked little girl', 'russet armpits',
'pomelled lust', and 'spilled . . . seed'.
21 'Lilith' and *Lolita* have first-person
male narrators. *The Enchanter* has a third-
person narrator, but one whose subject is
always the male protagonist.

CHAPTER ONE

1 Norman Page, ed., *Nabokov: The Critical
Heritage* (London: Routledge, 1982), p. 16.
2 Jackson R. Bryer and Thomas J. Bergin
Jr, 'Vladimir Nabokov's Critical Reputation
in English: A Note and a Checklist',
Wisconsin Studies, VIII (Spring 1967),
reprinted in L.S. Dembo, ed., *Nabokov the
Man and his Works: Studies* (Madison:
University of Wisconsin Press, 1967),
pp. 225–74.
3 Alfred Appel Jr, ed., *The Annotated 'Lolita'*
(1970; Harmondsworth: Penguin, 1991),
p. xxxv. [*Appel's Note:*] In a manner similar
to Joyce's, Nabokov four years later paid
his careful respects to Prescott, though not
by name, by having the assassin Gradus
carefully read *The New York Times*: 'A hack
reviewer of new books for tourists,
reviewing his own tour through Norway,
said that the fjords were too famous to
need (his) description, and that all
Scandinavians loved flowers' (*Pale Fire*,
p. 275). This was actually culled from the
newspaper.
4 [*Editor's Note:*] For a useful summary of
the critical formations and general literary
developments, see 'Periods of American
Literature' in M.H. Abrams, *A Glossary of
Literary Terms*, seventh edition (1957; Fort
Worth: Harcourt Brace, 1999), pp. 208–9.
On receiving an inscribed copy of the first
edition of the *Glossary* from Abrams,
Nabokov pronounced it 'a neat, clear,
precise, and scholarly piece of work', then
suggested numerous corrections on which
Abrams did not act. See Nabokov, letter
to Meyer Abrams, 6 January 1958,
D. Nabokov and Bruccoli (1990), pp. 240–4.
5 Margaret Mead, *Coming of Age in Samoa:
A Study of Adolescence and Sex in Primitive*

Societies (1928; Harmondsworth: Penguin,
1966). [*Editor's Note:*] The allusion to
Mead's anthropological work is interesting
from another aspect and that is the role of
the anthropologist or ethnographer as an
observer of other cultures. In these terms,
H.H. could be described as also an ethnographer of 1950s America.
6 Lionel Trilling,'The Last Lover: Vladimir
Nabokov's *Lolita*', *Griffin*, VII (August
1958), pp. 4–21, reprinted in *Encounter*
(October 1958), pp. 9–19, reprinted in
Page (1982), pp. 92–102.
7 Lionel Trilling, 'Freud: Within and
Beyond Culture' (1955) reprinted in
*Beyond Culture: Essays on Literature and
Learning* (London: Secker and Warburg,
1966), pp. 89–118.
8 On the controversies surrounding
Freud's so-called abandonment of the
seduction theory, see Jacqueline Rose,
'"Where does the misery come from?":
psychoanalysis, feminism and the event',
in R. Feldstein and J. Roof, eds, *Feminism
and Psychoanalysis* (Ithaca: Cornell University Press, 1989).
9 Betty Friedan, *The Feminine Mystique*
(1963; London: Gollancz, 1965).
10 Trilling, reprinted in Page (1982),
pp. 95–6.
11 Trilling, reprinted in Page (1982),
pp. 98, 101.
12 Trilling, reprinted in Page (1982),
pp. 92–4, 94, 94–5, 102.
13 Trilling, reprinted in Page (1982),
p. 94.
14 Vladimir Nabokov, *Lolita* (1955;
Harmondsworth: Penguin, 1980).
15 F.W. Dupee, 'A Preface to Lolita',
Anchor Review (June, 1957), pp. 1–14,
reprinted in Page (1982), pp. 84–91.
[*Editor's Note:*] Dupee does not include
page references to *Lolita*. It is also worth
noting that the selection from *Lolita*
published in *Anchor Review*, and introduced by Dupee, was not chosen by
Nabokov: 'I approve in advance whatever
selection you make'. See Vladimir
Nabokov, letter to Jason Epstein, 1 October
1956, D. Nabokov and Bruccoli (1990),
p. 191; 'There was considerable enthusi-
asm among the Doubleday editors for
Lolita, though we were all apprehensive

about possible legal consequences. As I recall, Ken McCormack, the editor-in-chief at the time, would have agreed to publish it if Douglas Black, the president of the company, authorized it. But Black was so strongly opposed that he refused even to read the manuscript'. Jason Epstein to Sally Dennison, 23 February 1982; Dennison, (*Alternative*) *Literary Publishing* (Iowa City: University of Iowa Press, 1984), p. 175.

16 Dupee, reprinted in Page (1982), pp. 88–91.

17 Howard Nemerov, 'The Morality of Art', *Kenyon Review*, XIX (Spring 1957), pp. 313–14, 316–21, reprinted in Page (1982), pp. 91–2.

18 [*Editor's Note*:] Although referring only briefly to Nabokov, Alan Sinfield's discussion of what he refers to as the reinvention of modernism in 1950s America, and its concomitant decline in Britain, is pertinent to Amis's discussion of style. See Alan Sinfield, *Literature, Politics and Culture in Postwar Britain* (Oxford: Blackwell, 1989), pp. 184–5: On the one hand, 'younger literary intellectuals . . . were sensitive in their own way to Englishness, and saw Modernism as a foreign fashion that had had its day'. On the other hand, 'New York stole the idea of Modern Art. In other forms similarly, techniques and affiliations to Modernism were developed from the later 1940s: Beat and confessional poetry; novels by Vladimir Nabokov . . .'

19 Kingsley Amis, review of *Lolita* by Vladimir Nabokov, *Spectator* (November 1959), pp. 635–6, reprinted in Page (1982), pp. 102–7. [*Editor's Note*:] Amis does not include page references to *Lolita*. It seems unclear as to whether he is quoting from the new British issue of *Lolita* or the Olympia Press edition. Amis, reprinted in Page (1982), p. 104.

20 Amis, reprinted in Page (1982), pp. 102–7.

21 [*Editor's Note*:] For an extremely informative account of the broader social–sexual context of the 1959 Act, see chapter thirteen, 'The Permissive Moment' in Jeffrey Weeks, *Sex, Politics and Society: The regulation of sexuality since 1800*,

second edition (1981; London: Longman, 1989).

22 Walter Allen, review of *Lolita* by Vladimir Nabokov, *New Statesman* (7 November, 1959), p. 632, reprinted in Page (1982), p. 107.

23 V. S. Pritchett, review of Vladimir Nabokov's *Lolita*, *New Statesman* (10 January 1959), reprinted in Page (1982), p. 14.

CHAPTER TWO

1 [*Josipovici's Note*:] That essay was written in 1956. Since then a good deal of the early work has been translated, but there are still one or two novels behind which the author can hide from non-Russian-reading critics.

2 Gabriel Josipovici, *The World and the Book: A Study of Modern Fiction* (Basingstoke: Macmillan, 1994), pp. 201–2.

3 Josipovici (1994), p. 203.

4 Josipovici (1994), p. 205.

5 Josipovici (1994), pp. 201–2, 203, 205, 220.

6 Page Stegner, *Escape into Aesthetics: The Art of Vladimir Nabokov* (London: Eyre and Spottiswoode, 1967), p. vii.

7 [*Stegner's Note*:] There is an interesting article in *Literature and Psychology*, X, pp. 97–101 by Elizabeth Phillips, 'The Hocus Pocus of *Lolita*', that notes a number of parallels between Humbert and Poe, and attempts to demonstrate that Nabokov is parodying Mme Marie Bonaparte's *The Life and Works of Edgar Allan Poe: A Psycho-Analytic Interpretation* (London, 1949). [*Editor's Note*:] Stegner gives no date for the reference to Phillips and I have been unable to trace the article.

8 Vladimir Nabokov, *Lolita* (New York: G. P. Putnam's Sons, 1958).

9 [*Editor's Note*:] *Vladimir Nabokov, Speak Memory* (London: Victor Gollancz, 1951).

10 Stegner (1967), pp. 108–115.

11 Carl R. Proffer, *Keys to Lolita* (Bloomington: Indiana University Press, 1968), 'Foreword'.

12 [*Proffer's Note*:] Among the writers who have influenced Nabokov (no matter how testily he denies it) are Gogol and

Bely, both of whom were exponents and practitioners of prose-poetry.

13 [*Proffer's Note*:] I find 'a mobile Adam's apple' in Speak, Memory, p.36.

14 [*Proffer's Note*:] In *The Gift* he used an analagous Russian alliteration: *szadi nee zamedlennymi zigzagami, Dar* (New York: Chekhov, 1952), p. 39.

15 Proffer (1968), pp.82–3.

16 Alfred Appel Jr, '*Lolita*: The Springboard of Parody', in L.S. Dembo, ed., *Nabokov: The Man and his Work* (Madison: University of Wisconsin Press, 1967), pp. 106–143.

17 Appel Jr (1967), p.107.

18 Vladimir Nabokov, *Lolita* (New York: G.P. Putnam's Sons, 1958).

19 [*Appel's Note*:] The reader-manipulation effected by the two 'false endings' on the last page of the story 'Signs and Symbols' (in Nabokov's *Dozen*) telescopes the methods of the Nabokovian trap-play and thus provides an excellent introduction to the monstrous trap that is *Lolita*.

20 [*Appel's Note*:] This involuted process is best described by Jorge Luis Borges in 'Partial Magic in the *Quixote*', in *Labyrinths* (Norfolk, 1962).

21 [*Appel's Note*:] *Ombre* is played in Canto III of *The Rape of the Lock*. For a summary of the 'game' in *Lolita*, so uncannily accurate that Nabokov must have had [Canto III] in mind, see lines 87–100.

22 [*Appel's Note*:] Apologies for the game-element in Nabokov should not have to be made. Those who find the play-concept antithetical to 'seriousness' would do well to read J. Huizinga's *Homo Ludens*.

23 Appel Jr, (1967), pp.117–23.

24 Appel Jr, (1967), pp.107, 117–23, 126–7.

25 [*de Rougemont's Note*:] This 'geographic' part of the book suggests a parody of Nils Holgersson's journey across Sweden.

26 Denis de Rougemont, *Love Declared: Essays on the Myths of Love*, trans. Richard Howard (New York: Pantheon: 1963), pp.48–54.

27 Martin Green, 'The Morality of Lolita', *The Kenyon Review*, XXVIII (June 1966) No. 3, p.352.

28 Green (1966), pp.352, 374–7.

CHAPTER THREE

1 Vladimir Nabokov, letter to Alfred Appel Jr, 28 March 1967, *Vladimir Nabokov: Selected Letters 1940–1977*, Dmitri Nabokov and Matthew J. Bruccoli, eds, (London: Weidenfeld and Nicolson, 1989), pp.407–8; For a further reference to Diana Butler's article, see Nabokov's letter to Page Stegner (on receiving a copy of *Escape into Aesthetics*), 14 October 1966, D. Nabokov and Bruccoli (1989), pp.392–3. 'You should have been warned that Mrs. Butler's article is pretentious nonsense from beginning to end'. Diana Butler, '*Lolita* Lepidoptera', *New World Writing* (Philadelphia: Lippincott, 1960).

2 Vladimir Nabokov, *The Annotated 'Lolita'*, edited, introduced and annotated by Alfred Appel Jr (Harmondsworth: Penguin, 1995), p.xxvii.

3 [*Appel's Note*:] I have elsewhere discussed the novel as a novel, as well as an artifice; see my article, '*Lolita*: The Springboard of Parody', *Wisconsin Studies in Contemporary Literature*, VIII (Spring 1967), pp.204–41. Reprinted in L.S. Dembo, ed., *Nabokov: The Man and his Work* (Madison: University of Wisconsin Press, 1967). [*Editor's Note*:] See chapter two for a discussion of this article.

4 *Nabokov*, Appel Jr, ed., (1995), p.xii.

5 [*Editor's Note*:] The page references in this passage are to the 1995 edition of *The Annotated 'Lolita'*.

6 *Nabokov*, Appel Jr, ed., (1995), pp.xxvii, xii, lvii.

7 Julia Bader, *Crystal Land: Artifice in Nabokov's English Novels* (Berkeley: University of California Press, 1972), p.81.

8 [*Bader's Note*:] For a general summary of 'clues and allusions' see C.R. Proffer, Keys to *Lolita* (Bloomington: Indiana University Press, 1968). See Diana Butler on the butterfly theme, '*Lolita* Lepidoptera', *New World Writing* No. 16 (Philadelphia: 1960), pp.58–84. See Lionel Trilling on the troubadour theme, 'The Last Lover: V.N.'s *Lolita*', *Encounter*, XI, 4 (1958), pp.9–19. See Conrad Brenner on the 'perversion' of conventional subjects in Nabokov's works, 'Nabokov: The Art of

the Perverse', *New Republic,* June 23 (1958), pp. 18–21. See G.D. Josipovici on parody as a means of turning words into emotion, '*Lolita*: Parody and the Pursuit of Beauty', *Critical Quarterly,* VI (1964), pp. 35–48. See A.E. Dubois on 'Poe and *Lolita*', *College English Assn. Critic,* XXVI: 6 (1964), pp. 1, 7, which is an article worthy of Kinbote himself and ends with this statement: 'I somehow feel insulted. But certainly *Lolita* should be added to the bibliography of reflections about Poe'.

9 Bader (1972), pp. 57–9.

10 Vladimir Nabokov, *Lolita* (New York: Putnam, 1958).

11 [*Editor's Note:*] Bader's phrase 'tampering with her [Lolita's] magic' demonstrates the impossibility of trying to keep apart the idea of Lolita as Humbert's illusory, 'artistic' creation, and the sense of a 'real' girl in the text who is represented as being 'tampered' with.

12 [*Editor's Note:*] Vladimir Nabokov, *Lolita* (Harmondsworth: Penguin, 1980), pp. 166–7.

13 [*Bader's Note:*] The shifting aspect of *Lolita* is discussed by several critics, most suggestively by Carol T. Williams, 'Nabokov's Dialectical Structure', in L.S. Dembo, ed., *Nabokov: the Man and his Works: Studies* (Madison: University of Wisconsin Press, 1967), pp. 176–82. [This is discussed] in greater detail by Alfred Appel Jr, in *The Annotated 'Lolita'* (New York: McGraw-Hill, 1970) both in the far-ranging Introduction and in the painstakingly assembled Notes.

14 Bader (1972), pp. 57–9, 75–81.

15 [*Editor's Note:*] For more on the psychoanalytic implications of Bader's insight, see under the entry 'Wish (Desire)' in J. Laplanche and J.-B. Pontalis, *The Language of Psychoanalysis* (London: Karnac Books, 1988), pp. 482–3. 'Desire appears in the rift which separates need and demand; it cannot be reduced to need since, by definition, it is not a relation to phantasy; nor can it be reduced to demand, in that *it seeks to impose itself without taking the language or the unconscious of the other into account,* and insists upon absolute recognition from him' [emphasis editor's].

16 G.M. Hyde, *Vladimir Nabokov: America's Russian Novelist,* Critical Appraisals Series (London: Marian Boyars, 1977), p. 7.

17 Hyde (1977), p. 12.

18 R.D. Laing, *The Divided Self: An Existential Study in Sanity and Madness* (Harmondsworth: Penguin, 1990).

19 [*Editor's Note:*] A number of writers will later draw attention to the lack of psychoanalytic criticism of *Lolita,* particularly in this period. Sometimes this is attributed to the effect of Nabokov's fierce and unremitting warnings that Freudians should keep out of his books. It would take us too far away from the immediate discussion of *Lolita* to explore this fully. But there is a case to be made that psychoanalytic interests inform many of the interpretations referenced in this Guide, both directly and indirectly. Hyde's essay is especially useful here because he at once reveals his interests and then withdraws them for most of his textual analysis. For a discussion of Nabokov's opposition to psychoanalysis in general and Freud in particular, see Jeffrey Berman, *The Talking Cure: Literary Representations of Psychoanalysis* (New York: New York University Press, 1985). For an account of the way Nabokov invokes psychoanalysis only to negate it, see J.P. Shute, 'Nabokov and Freud: The Play of Power' in *Modern Fiction Studies,* 30: 4, Winter 1984, pp. 637–650.

20 [*Hyde's Note:*] Vladimir Nabokov, *Lolita* (London: Weidenfeld and Nicolson, 1959), p. 178. Nijinsky was not an invert, but the creature of one (Diaghilev).

21 [*Hyde's Note:*] Lionel Trilling perhaps puts this too emphatically, but he was essentially right. [*Editor's Note:*] It is on precisely this point about love that Linda Kauffman quarrels with Trilling. See chapter four of this Guide.

22 [*Hyde's Note:*] D.H. Lawrence, *Studies in Classic American Literature* (New York: Doubleday Anchor, 1955). If Nabokov is an American novelist, he is one in the sense in which Poe was an American poet: both invented new terrains and peopled them with old monsters.

23 [*Hyde's Note:*] Lawrence (1955), p. 74. Nabokov is himself a scientist in something like this sense, though not, like Poe

and Humbert, a vivisectionist.

24 [*Hyde's Note*:] Lawrence (1955), p.78.

25 [*Hyde's Note*:] Lawrence (1955), p.85.

26 [*Hyde's Note*:] One of the many allusions to the literature of the decadence, which knew Poe not only by direct acquaintance but also transmitted via Baudelaire and Mallarmé.

27 [*Hyde's Note*:] Bizet's opera, with its *femme fatale* heroine and yearning for an ultimate love (which is death, merging, loss of self) is an evident motif in *Lolita*. A rare musical allusion: Nabokov does not care for music.

28 [*Hyde's Note*:] T.S. Eliot, *The Waste Land*, lines 411–416; *The Complete Poems and Plays* (London: Faber, 1969). It is odd how often Eliot crops up in Nabokov's work: he is wantonly disparaging about him, but in this novel – despite the facile parody of Eliot attributed to Humbert on p. 18 – seems closer than usual to Eliot's pessimism.

29 [*Editor's Note*:] The use of parentheses in Hyde's reading is fascinating, since they often contain crucial insights into the novel. In particular, the idea that Lolita's sexuality and her seduction game is not in any sense comparable with Humbert's sexuality and his scheming seduction anticipates critical readings of the 1980s and the 1990s. See especially the extracts from Michael Wood and Rachel Bowlby in chapter five.

30 [*Hyde's Note*:] Here, too, it is a phallus, 'aching to be discharged', see Nabokov (1959), p.284.

31 [*Hyde's Note*:] Scott Fitzgerald, *The Great Gatsby* (Harmondsworth: Penguin, 1971), p.29.

32 [*Hyde's Note*:] Humbert's pills are magic bullets, but also nothing more than a mild sedative. The facts constantly fall short of Humbert's fantasies.

33 [*Hyde's Note*:] On p.192 he sees himself as 'a shabby emigré'.

34 Hyde (1977), pp.116–22.

35 Julian Moynahan, *Vladimir Nabokov*, University of Minnesota Pamphlets on American Writers Number 96 (Minneapolis: University of Minnesota Press, 1971), p.34.

36 Moynahan (1971), p.5.

37 Moynahan (1971), pp.5, 34, 35–6.

38 For more on the representation of dead mothers and daughters in *Lolita*, see Elisabeth Bronfen's marvellous reading in *Over Her Dead Body: Death, Femininity and the Aesthetic* (Manchester University Press, 1992). Importantly, given the later readings, which stress the theft of Lolita's childhood, Bronfen draws attention to the often unnoticed fact that the death of the mother allows 'his beloved' to be severed from her family history. In effect, H.H. can then be father and mother to Lolita.

39 Vladimir Nabokov, *Lolita* (New York: McGraw-Hill, 1970).

40 Douglas Fowler, *Reading Nabokov* (Ithaca: Cornell University Press, 1974), pp.148–51.

41 [*Fowler's Note*:] Nabokov's poem, 'The Ballad of Longwood Glen', discussed in the Epilogue [to Fowler's book], is another example of the triumph of indifference.

42 Fowler (1974), pp.164–6.

43 Fowler (1974), pp.164–6, 172–5.

CHAPTER FOUR

1 Ellen Pifer, *Nabokov and the Novel*, (Cambridge, Mass.: Harvard University Press, 1980), p.169.

2 Against the general grain of the 1980s project to 'recover' Lolita's story is David Packman's idea that readers have been distracted by the apparent reality of the 'sensational subject matter'. See David Packman, *Vladimir Nabokov, The Structure of Literary Desire* (Columbia: University of Missouri Press, 1982), p.46

3 Pifer (1980), p.165.

4 Vladimir Nabokov, *The Annotated 'Lolita'*, Alfred Appel Jr, ed. (New York: McGraw-Hill, 1970).

5 [*Pifer's Note*:] Possessing a steadier moral sense and a kinder heart, Nabokov's own poet, John Shade, would undoubtedly receive Humbert's glorification of the poet's morality with wry scepticism . . . See Vladimir Nabokov, *Pale Fire* (Harmondsworth: Penguin, 1991).

6 [*Pifer's Note*:] 'In art, an individual style is essentially as futile and as organic as a

fata morgana', said Nabokov in an interview by Arlene Talmey, *Vogue*, reprinted in Vladimir Nabokov, *Strong Opinions* (London: Weidenfeld and Nicolson, 1974), p. 153.

7 [*Pifer's Note:*] Interview by Herbert Gold, reprinted in Nabokov (1974), p. 94.

8 [*Pifer's Note:*] Interview by Kurt Hoffman, Bayerischer Rundfunk, October 1971, reprinted in Nabokov (1974), p. 193.

9 Pifer (1980), pp. 164–71.

10 Richard Rorty, *Contingency, Irony, and Solidarity* (Cambridge: Cambridge University Press, 1989), p. 141

11 Rorty (1989), p. 141.

12 Rorty (1989), p. 141.

13 Rorty (1989), p. 144.

14 Kingsley Amis (1959), pp. 635–6; reprinted in Page (1982).

15 [*Editor's Note:*] It is interesting to note that Rorty's reappraisal of *Lolita* seems to overlook the question of the sexual narrative. Sex is displaced to a footnote in which it is suggested as a metaphor for something else. The effect of this displacement from the body of Rorty's writing is to erase the detail of what is inflicted on Lolita. In regard to Kauffman's reading of the novel in terms of sexual politics, and the symptomatic response of male critics to the character of Lolita, Rorty's reading seems to dispense with the particular narrative of sexual persecution under the general heading of 'cruelty'. The relation between the initial response to *Lolita* and the trial of *Lady Chatterley's Lover* has already been noted in the introduction to this Guide. The further connection to be made here between Rorty's displacement, the displacement of 'sex' from many of the influential readings of *Lolita* (notably Trilling's *cri de coeur* that the novel was about love, not sex), and the *Chatterley* trial is the way in which sex disappears: 'a beauty which cancels lust'; see Jonathan Dollimore, 'The Challenge of Sexuality' in Alan Sinfield, ed., *Society and Literature: 1945–1970, The Context of English Literature* (London: Methuen, 1983).

16 [*Editor's Note:*] This famous comment of Nabokov's on the character of Humbert

was originally made in an interview. This is published in the collection of articles and interviews, Nabokov (1974), p. 94.

17 [*Editor's Note:*] Rorty's notes are particularly detailed and lengthy. I have taken the liberty of editing the footnotes when the content is not closely related to the topic of *Lolita*. [*Rorty's Note:*] The background of this definition of art is interesting. Since Nabokov seems never to have forgotten anything, it is likely that a snide remark to Wilson about 'the stale Bolshevik propaganda which you imbibed in your youth' was an allusion to an equally snide remark Wilson had made eight years previously. Simon Karlinsky, ed., *The Nabokov–Wilson Letters* (New York: Harper, 1979), p. 304; December 13 1956; p. 211; November 15 1948; p. 214; November 21 1948. . . . . . .

18 [*Rorty's Note:*] Contrast Nabokov's list of the characteristics of art with what Baudelaire tells us is the norm in Cythera, namely, 'order, beauty, voluptuous luxury and calm'. This was also the norm of the country houses of Nabokov's childhood, islands in the middle of what Nabokov says was a 'to be perfectly frank, rather appalling country'. Vladimir Nabokov, *Speak Memory: An Autobiography Revisited* (New York: Pyramid, 1968), pp. 85–6. Nabokov's definition gives a new twist to the slogan 'art for art's sake', and to the relation between art and morality. Baudelaire's description of the Cytheran norm does not mention any relation to other human beings, except perhaps voluptuous enjoyment. But Nabokov does.

19 [*Editor's Note:*] Rorty's invocation to the artistry of Humbert's writing is in keeping with many critical responses to the novel. However, as Frederick Whiting notes (see chapter five of this Guide), this is to overlook the ordinary matter of Humbert's occupation. He is in fact a professor of English and French literature.

20 [*Rorty's Note:*] Nabokov might have included Lenin on this list. But he might not have, since he must have suspected that he and Lenin himself had more in common than either did with Paduk or Gradus. Lenin, I think, hovers in the back-

ground of Nabokov's consciousness as the terrifying O'Brien figure [in George Orwell's *Nineteen Eighty-four*] – the man who will rule the world because he combines Paduk's cruelty with something uncomfortably like Nabokov's brains. . . . . . .

21 [*Rorty's Note*:] He knows not only that Humbert is wrong when he says that 'poets never kill' but that it is pointless to say, with Kinbote, that 'the one who kills is *always* his victim's inferior'. For 'inferiority' means nothing here – it is one of those machine-made general ideas. If we could specify in what respect murderers were always inferior to their victims, in what respect, for example, Humbert is inferior to Quilty or O'Brien to Winston, then we might have said something useful. But all we can say is that they are *morally* inferior – and if that is what we mean, it would be better to say, 'Thou shalt not kill', and have done with it. Nabokov's point about general ideas is that once the concrete detail is left behind, everything quickly blurs together and the result might as well be left unsaid. See Vladimir Nabokov, *Pale Fire* (New York: Berkeley, 1968), p. 157.

22 [*Rorty's Note*:] What makes Humbert and Kinbote such interesting people is that, although they rarely react to people in predictable ways, they are not oblivious to other people. Not only are they *intensely*, albeit selectively, curious, but their own minds find a 'kind of twisted pattern in the game', a motif in the lives of others. The question of whether that pattern was really there is as bad a question as that of whether an artist 'truly represents' human emotions. Once the artist has done his work, it is as much 'there' as the pattern which conventional moral discourse finds in the same story of joy and suffering . . . . People react to intolerable ecstasy or hopeless longing or intense pain as best they can, and once we leave the realm of action for that of writing, it is no service to anyone to ask whether a reaction was 'appropriate'. For appropriateness is a matter of taking up a place within a preestablished and familiar pattern. The curiosity which Nabokov thought essential to art consists in never being content with such a pattern.

23 [*Rorty's Note*:] I shall use a footnote to say something about why I take *Lolita* and *Pale Fire* as Nabokov's acme. I am urging that we think of these two novels as revolving around the same theme as Nabokov's early novel *The Gift* – namely, around the choice between tenderness and ecstasy which those gifted with artistic talent face, the necessity that they be only *selectively* curious. Compared to these two later novels, however, *The Gift* is didactic, a set of illustrations for some general ideas. The trajectory of Nabokov's career, like that of Heidegger's, was shaped by the attempt to avoid being didactic, to avoid the use of words which had been tarnished, reduced to near transparency, by common use . . . The two great novels have a distinctively Nabokovian idiosyncrasy which the earlier novels (except perhaps for *Invitation to a Beheading*) lack, and a perfection of form which the later novels lack.

24 [*Rorty's Note*:] Humbert's nympholepsy and Kinbote's homosexuality are made so plausible and interesting (so 'charming', to use the word that everyone in *Bleak House* uses about Skimpole) that – probably just as Nabokov intended – they arouse questions in his readers' minds about Nabokov's own views on sex. I take these to be just more of Nabokov's celebrated false leads. There is certainly something of Nabokov himself in these monsters, but it has nothing in particular to do with any particular sort of sex. Sexual obsessions are just handy examples of a more general phenomenon.

25 Vladimir Nabokov, *Lolita* (Harmondsworth: Penguin, 1980).

26 [*Editor's Note*:] The note that follows is lengthy. However, as it appears to be integral both to Rorty's general argument about incuriosity, and to his analysis of this particular aspect of the text, I am citing it in full. [*Rorty's Note*:] The town of Kasbeam is described as seen from a nearby hilltop, in terms which anticipate those used at the climactic moment, just before the end of the novel, when Humbert looks down from another hill to another 'toylike' town, the one from which rises the 'melody of children at play'. Then

Humbert realizes that 'the hopelessly poignant thing was not Lolita's absence from my side, but the absence of her voice from that concord' (p. 306). This is the moment which produces what Humbert has earlier called the 'unbelievable, unbearable, and, I suspect, eternal horror that I know *now*' (p. 167). Humbert, writing his story as he dies of heart disease, describes that horror when he writes: 'Alas I was unable to transcend the simple human fact that whatever spiritual solace I might find, whatever lithophanic eternities might be provided for me, nothing could make my Lolita forget the foul lust I had inflicted upon her. Unless it can be proven to me – to me as I am now, today, with my heart and my beard, and my putrefaction – that in the infinite run it does not matter a jot that a North American girl-child named Dolores Haze had been deprived of her childhood by a maniac, unless this can be proven (and if it can, then life is a joke), I see nothing for the treatment of my misery but the melancholy and very local palliative of articulate art. To quote an old poet:

The moral sense in mortals is the duty
We have to pay on mortal sense of beauty.'
(p. 281)

The old poet is Nabokov himself. I am suggesting that he hoped that poets had to pay this duty, but was not sure, and thus not sure that life was not a joke.

I am not sure whether 'cost me a month of work' means that Nabokov rewrote the sentence about the barber for a month, or that his associations with the idea of not noticing the death of another's child kept him writing for a month, or that some actual encounter with another's (perhaps an actual barber's) suffering kept him from writing for a month. It is typical of Nabokov to let his reader guess.

27 [*Rorty's Note*:] Just before giving his definitions of 'aesthetic bliss' and of 'art' in the Afterword, Nabokov says, 'I am neither a reader nor a writer of didactic fiction, and despite John Ray's assertion, *Lolita* has no moral in tow' (p. 313).

28 Rorty (1989), pp. 141, 144, 158–64.

29 Appel Jr (1970).

30 Elizabeth Dipple, *The Unresolvable Plot: Reading Contemporary Fiction* (London: Routledge, 1988), pp. 73–4.

31 Field, Andrew, *VN: The Life and Art of Vladimir Nabokov* (London: Macdonald, 1987), p. 140.

32 Gladys M. Clifton, 'Humbert Humbert and the Limits of Artistic License', in J. E. Rivers and Charles Nicol, eds, *Nabokov's Fifth Arc: Nabokov and Others on his Life's Work* (Austin: University of Texas Press, 1982), p. 164.

33 Appel Jr (1970), p. 11.

34 Clifton (1982), pp. 153, 164.

35 Linda Kauffman, 'Framing Lolita: Is There a Woman in the Text?' in Patricia Yaeger and Beth Kowaleski-Wallace, eds, *Refiguring the Father: New Feminist Readings of Patriarchy* (Carbondale: Southern Illinois University Press, 1989), p. 131.

36 [*Kauffman's Note*:] Thomas Molnar, 'Matter-of-Fact Confession of a Non-Penitent', *Chronicles of Culture* 2 (January–February 1978), pp. 11–13.

37 Vladimir Nabokov, *Lolita* (1955; New York: Berkeley Books, 1977).

38 [*Kauffman's Note*:] Alfred Appel Jr, '*Lolita*: The Springboard of Parody', Dembo, ed., (1967), p. 121, emphasis added.

39 [*Kauffman's Note*:] Judith Fetterly, *The Resisting Reader: A Feminist Approach to American Fiction* (Bloomington: Indiana University Press, 1978), p. xii.

40 [*Editor's Note*:] See especially Roland Barthes, *The Pleasures of the Text* (London: Jonathan Cape, 1976). For a useful summary of the significance of the term in feminist discourse, see the entry in Elizabeth Wright, ed., *Feminism and Psychoanalysis: A Critical Dictionary* (London: Blackwell, 1992), pp. 185–8.

41 [*Kauffman's Note*:] Claude Lévi-Strauss, *The Elementary Structures of Kinship* (1949; repr. Boston: Beacon, 1969), p. 115. [*Editor's Note*:] The formulation of the incest taboo as the universal rule of culture, in Claude Lévi-Strauss's theory of kinship structures, has been important for feminist theories of gender and the position of women in culture. This particular aspect of Kauffman's argument invokes Gayle Rubin's ground-breaking essay, 'The traffic in women: notes on the

"political economy" of sex' (1974) in Rayne R. Reiter, ed., *Toward an Anthropology of Women* (New York: Monthly Review Press, 1975), pp. 157–210. For a critical overview of Rubin's argument, see Judith Butler's excellent entry on 'Gender' in Elizabeth Wright, ed., *Feminism and Psychoanalysis: A Critical Dictionary* (London: Blackwell, 1992), pp. 140–5.

42 [*Kauffman's Note:*] Patrocinio Schweickart, 'Reading Ourselves: Towards a Feminist Theory of Reading' in Elizabeth A. Flynn and Patrocinio Schweickart, eds, *Gender and Reading: Essays on Readers, Texts, and Contexts* (Baltimore: Johns Hopkins University Press, 1985), pp. 31–62.

43 [*Kauffman's Note:*] Jacques Lacan, *Ecrits: A Selection*, trans. Alan Sheridan (New York: Norton, 1977). See especially Chapter 1 on the mirror stage.

44 [*Kauffman's Note:*] Frederick W. Shilstone, 'The Courtly Misogynist: Humbert Humbert in *Lolita*', *Studies in the Humanities* 8 (June 1980): pp. 5–10.

45 [*Kauffman's Note:*] Alfred Appel, 'An Interview with Vladimir Nabokov', in L.S. Dembo, ed., *Nabokov: The Man and His Work* (Madison, Milwaukee: University of Wisconsin Press, 1967), pp. 19–44 [emphasis added].

46 [*Kauffman's Note:*] Henry James, *The Art of the Novel*, introd. Richard P. Blackmur (New York: Scribner's, 1934), p. 172. For a discussion of the tale as an elegiac reaccentuation of sentimental fiction, see Linda Kauffman, *Discourses of Desire: Gender, Genre, and Epistolary Fictions* (Ithaca: Cornell University Press, 1986), Chapter 5.

47 [*Kauffman's Note:*] Henry James to Dr Louis Waldstein, October 21 1898, in Robert Kimbrough, ed., *The Turn of the Screw* (New York: Norton, 1966), p. 110.

48 [*Kauffman's Note:*] For evidence that James's governess murders Miles, see Kauffman (1986), Chapter 5.

49 [*Kauffman's Note:*] Edgar Allan Poe, 'Lenore', in *Poetry and Tales* (New York: Library of America, 1934), p. 69.

50 [*Kauffman's Note:*] Vladimir Nabokov, *Lectures on Literature*, ed. Fredson Bowers, introd. John Updike (New York: Harcourt Brace Jovanovich, 1980), p. 83.

51 [*Kauffman's Note:*] See James R. Pinnells, 'The Speech Ritual as an Element of Structure in Nabokov's *Lolita*', *Dalhousie Review* 60 (Winter 1980–81): pp. 605–21. Pinnells points out that in the speech rituals in *Lolita*, two realities come in conflict: average reality and Humbert's solipsism. Lolita is seldom allowed to speak in her own voice, but when she does, she effectively shatters Humbert's fantasies and exposes his lies, distortions, and duplicity.

The best example of Pinnells' thesis is the scene at the Enchanted Hunters Motel, when Humbert speaks euphemistically about fathers and daughters sharing hotel rooms: '"Two people sharing one room, inevitably enter into a kind – how shall I say – a kind –" "The word is incest", said Lo (pp. 110–11)'.

52 [*Kauffman's Note:*] Judith Lewis Herman, *Father–Daughter Incest* (Cambridge: Harvard University Press, 1981), p. 4.

53 Kauffman, in Yaeger and Kowaleski-Wallace (1989), pp. 131, 133–42.

CHAPTER FIVE

1 Michael Wood, *The Magician's Doubts: Nabokov and the Risks of Fiction* (London: Chatto and Windus, 1994), p. 140.

2 Wood (1994), p. 141.

3 Vladimir Nabokov, *Lolita* (1955; Harmondsworth: Penguin, 1980), p. 131. [*Editor's Note:*] Wood notes that all further references are to this edition of Lolita. He gives no page numbers after this first one.

4 Nabokov (1980), see note 3.

5 Nabokov (1980), see note 3.

6 [*Wood's Note:*] F. W. Dupee, 'A Preface to *Lolita*' in *The King of the Cats* (University of Chicago Press, 1984), p. 119.

7 Nabokov (1980), see note 3.

8 [*Wood's Note:*] Plato, *Phaedrus*, trans. W. C. Helmhold and W. G. Rabinowitz (Bobbs-Merrill, 1956), pp. 69–70.

9 [*Wood's Note:*] Derrida's famous claim: Jacques Derrida, *Of Grammatology*, trans. Gayatri Chakravorty Spivak (1967; Baltimore: Johns Hopkins University Press, 1976), p. 158. [*Editor's Note:*] The phrase appears in the chapter ' . . . That Dangerous Supplement . . . ', and like all

of Derrida's claims is difficult to summarise or simplify. In the context in which Wood invokes it here, it is best understood as a comment on writing and its relation to representation. The words in and of the text cannot represent things-in-themselves. However, Wood glosses this notion by suggesting that the practice of literature *per se*, and Nabokov's *Lolita* in particular, involves the representation of certain kinds of experience through which we come to understand the world.

10 Wood (1994), pp. 103–6.

11 Wood (1994), p. 116.

12 Wood (1994), p. 117.

13 David Rampton, Vladimir Nabokov (Cambridge University Press, 1984), p. 114.

14 Nabokov (1980), see note 3.

15 Nabokov (1980), see note 3.

16 Nabokov (1980), see note 3.

17 Nabokov (1980), see note 3.

18 Nabokov (1980), see note 3.

19 [Wood's Note:] Michael Long, Marvell, Nabokov (Oxford: Clarendon Press, 1984), p. 150.

20 [*Wood's Note*:] Alfred Appel Jr, '*Lolita*: The Springboard of Parody' reprinted in L.S. Dembo, ed., *Nabokov: The Man and his Work* (Madison: University of Wisconsin Press, 1967), p. 128. Rampton (1984), pp. 114–15.

21 Nabokov (1980), see note 3.

22 Nabokov (1980), see note 3.

23 Dupee (1984), p. 125.

24 Nabokov (1980), see note 3.

25 Nabokov (1980), see note 3.

26 Geoffrey Hill, 'Funeral Music', 1968: *Collected Poems* (Harmondsworth: Penguin, 1985), p. 75.

27 Wood (1994), pp. 103–6, 116, 117, 135–42.

28 Rachel Bowlby, *Shopping with Freud* (London: Routledge, 1993), pp. 4–5.

29 [*Bowlby's Note*:] Elizabeth Dipple, *The Unresolvable Plot: Reading Contemporary Fiction* (New York: Routledge, 1988), pp. 74, 82. Linda Kauffman, 'Framing Lolita: is there a woman in the text?', in Patricia Jaegar and Beth Kowaleski-Wallace, eds, *Refiguring the Father: New Feminist Readings of Patriarchy* (Carbondale: University of Illinois Press, 1989), pp. 131–52.

30 Vladimir Nabokov, *Lolita* (1955; reprinted London: Corgi Books, 1969).

31 [*Bowlby's Note*:] Kauffman (1989), p. 133.

32 [*Bowlby's Note*:] Kauffman (1989), p. 148.

33 [*Bowlby's Note*:] Kauffman (1989), p. 141.

34 Bowlby (1993), pp. 50–3.

35 [*Editor's Note*:] For a reading of the congruity of Humbert/Annabel and the incongruity of Humbert/Lolita, see Thomas R. Frosch, 'Parody and Authenticity in *Lolita*', in J.E. Rivers and Charles Nicol, eds, *Nabokov's Fifth Arc: Nabokov and Others on his Life's Work* (Austin: University of Texas Press, 1982), pp. 171–87.

36 Bowlby (1993), pp. 4–5, 50–3, 65–71.

37 Elisabeth Bronfen, *Over Her Dead Body: Death, Femininity and the Aesthetic* (Manchester University Press, 1992), p. xi.

38 Bronfen (1992), p. 371.

39 Vladimir Nabokov, *Lolita* (1955; Harmondsworth, Penguin, 1980).

40 [*Editor's Note*:] For another reading that focuses on Humbert's 'purely onanistic act', but situates it in relation to the novel's vision of America, see John Haegert, 'Artist in Exile: The Americanization of Humbert Humbert', in *ELH* 52, 1985, pp. 777–94.

41 [*Bronfen's Note*:] J.P. Shute, 'Nabokov and Freud: The Play of Power', *Modern Fiction Studies* 30: 4, p. 648.

42 Bronfen (1992), pp. xi, 371, 379–80.

43 John Hollander, 'The Perilous Magic of Nymphets', *Partisan Review* XXIII (Fall 1956), pp. 559–60.

44 [*Whiting's Note*:] Lionel Trilling, 'The Last Lover: Vladimir Nabokov's Lolita', *Griffin*, VII (August 1958), pp. 4–21, reprinted in *Encounter*, (October 1958), pp. 9–19.

45 [*Whiting's Note*:] Although proceedings to ban the novel were initiated in France, *Lolita* was never charged with obscenity in the United States. [*Editor's Note*:] As I understand it, the proceedings to ban the novel in France pertained directly to the exporting of English-language editions to Britain.

46 Vladimir Nabokov, *Lolita* (1955; New York: G.P. Putnam's, 1958).

47 [*Whiting's Note*:] I am hardly the first to recognise the moral dimension of Nabokov's aesthetic model here. Richard Rorty remarks upon these terms in his excellent discussion of Nabokov's aesthetics and his preoccupation with immortality. Ellen Pifer and David Rampton both argue for the centrality of moral concerns in Nabokov's work. See Richard Rorty, *Contingency, Irony and Solidarity* (Cambridge: Cambridge University Press, 1989); Ellen Pifer, *Nabokov and the Novel* (Cambridge: Cambridge University Press, 1980); and David Rampton, *Vladimir Nabokov: A Critical Study of the Novels* (Cambridge: Cambridge University Press, 1984).

48 Frederick Whiting, '"The Strange Particularity of the Lover's Preference": Pedophilia, Pornography, and the Anatomy of Monstrosity in *Lolita*', *American Literature*, 70: 4 (December 1998), pp. 851–5.

49 David Rampton, *Vladimir Nabokov*, Macmillan Modern Novelists (Basingstoke: Macmillan, 1993), p. 96.

50 Vladimir Nabokov, *Lolita* (1955; Harmondsworth: Penguin, 1980).

51 [*Rampton's Note*:] J. Hillis Miller, Vincent B. Leitch, Barbara Johnson, Christopher Norris and Jonathan Culler, quoted in John M. Ellis, *Against Deconstruction* (Princeton, N.J.: Princeton University Press, 1989), pp. 68–9, 124.

52 Rampton (1993), pp. 96, 99–102.

SELECT BIBLIOGRAPHY

1. Major works by Vladimir Nabokov

Novels written in Russian and translated into English

Mary (Berlin: Slovo, 1926; New York: McGraw-Hill, 1970; London: Weidenfeld and Nicolson, 1971).

King, Queen, Knave (Berlin: Slovo, 1928; New York: McGraw-Hill, 1968; London: Weidenfeld and Nicolson, 1968).

The Defense (Berlin: Slovo, 1930; New York: Putnam's, 1964; London: Weidenfeld and Nicolson, 1964).

Glory (Paris: Sovremennye Zapiski, 1932; New York: McGraw-Hill, 1971; London: Weidenfeld and Nicolson, 1972).

Camera Obscura (Berlin: Sovremennye Zapiski, 1932; London: John Long, 1936). Revised as *Laughter in the Dark* (Indianapolis: Bobbs-Merrill, 1938).

Despair (Berlin: Petropolis, 1936; London: John Long, 1937; New York: Putnam's, 1966).

The Eye (Berlin: Russkie Zapiski, 1938; New York: Phaedra, 1965; London: Weidenfeld and Nicolson, 1966).

Invitation to a Beheading (Paris: Dom Knigi, 1938: New York: Putnam's, 1959; London: Weidenfeld and Nicolson, 1960).

The Gift (New York: Chekhov, 1952; New York: Putnam's, 1963; London: Weidenfeld and Nicolson, 1963).

The Enchanter (New York: Putnam's, 1986; London: Picador, 1986). Translated by Dmitri Nabokov.

Novels written in English

The Real Life of Sebastian Knight (Norfolk, Conn.: New Directions, 1941).

Bend Sinister (New York: Henry Holt, 1947; London: Weidenfeld and Nicolson, 1960).

Lolita (Paris: Olympia, 1955; New York: Putnam's, 1958; London: Weidenfeld and Nicolson, 1959).

Pnin (Garden City, N.Y.: Doubleday, 1957; London: Heinemann, 1957).

Pale Fire (New York: Putnam's, 1962; London: Weidenfeld and Nicolson, 1962).

Ada or Ardor: A Family Chronicle (New York: McGraw-Hill, 1969; London: Weidenfeld and Nicolson, 1969).

Transparent Things (New York: McGraw-Hill, 1972; London: Weidenfeld and Nicolson, 1973).

Look at the Harlequins! (New York: McGraw-Hill, 1974; London: Weidenfeld and Nicolson, 1975).

Collected short stories

Nabokov's Dozen (Garden City, N.Y.: Doubleday, 1958; London: Heinemann, 1959).

Nabokov's Quartet (New York: Phaedra, 1966; London: Weidenfeld and Nicolson, 1967).

A Russian Beauty and Other Stories (New York: McGraw-Hill, 1973; London: Weidenfeld and Nicolson, 1973).

Tyrants Destroyed and Other Stories (New York: McGraw-Hill, 1975; London: Weidenfeld and Nicolson, 1975).

Details of a Sunset and Other Stories (New York: McGraw-Hill, 1976; London: Weidenfeld and Nicolson, 1976).

Drama

The Waltz Invention (New York: Phaedra, 1966; London: Weidenfeld and Nicolson, 1967).

Lolita: A Screenplay (New York: McGraw-Hill, 1974).

The Man From the USSR and Other Plays (New York: Harcourt Brace Jovanovich/Bruccoli Clark, 1984; London: Weidenfeld and Nicolson, 1985).

Poems

Poems (Garden City, N.Y.: Doubleday, 1959; London: Weidenfeld and Nicolson, 1961).

Poems and Problems (New York: McGraw-Hill, 1971; London: Weidenfeld and Nicolson, 1972).

Memoirs

Conclusive Evidence (New York: Harper, 1951; London: Victor Gollancz, 1951).

Speak, Memory: An Autobiography Revisited (New York: Putnam's, 1966; London: Weidenfeld and Nicolson, 1967), revised and expanded version of *Conclusive Evidence*.

Translations

Alice in Wonderland (Berlin: Gamayun, 1923).

Three Russian Poets: Translations of Pushkin, Lermontov and Tiutchev (Norfolk, Conn.: New Directions, 1944).

A Hero of Our Time. A Novel by Mikhail Lermontov (Garden City, N.Y.: Doubleday, 1958).

The Song of Igor's Campaign (New York: Random House, 1960; London, Weidenfeld and Nicolson, 1961).

Eugene Onegin. A Novel in Verse by Aleksandr Pushkin, 4 vols (New York: Bollingen Foundation, 1964; London: Routledge and Kegan Paul, 1964).

Lectures and criticism

Nikolai Gogol (Norfolk, Conn.: New Directions, 1944).

Lectures on Literature (New York: Harcourt Brace Jovanovich/Bruccoli Clark, 1980; London: Weidenfeld and Nicolson, 1981).

Lectures on 'Ulysses' (New York: Bruccoli Clark, 1980).

Lectures on Russian Literature (New York: Harcourt Brace Jovanovich/Bruccoli Clark, 1981; London: Weidenfeld and Nicolson, 1982).

Lectures on 'Don Quixote' (New York: Harcourt Brace Jovanovich/Bruccoli Clark, 1983; London: Weidenfeld and Nicolson, 1983).

Letters

The Nabokov–Wilson Letters: Correspondence Between Vladimir Nabokov and Edmund Wilson 1940–1971, ed. Simon Karlinsky (New York: Harper and Row, 1971; London: Weidenfeld and Nicolson, 1979).

Perepiska s sestroy [Correspondence with His Sister] (Ann Arbor, Mich.: Ardis, 1985).

Vladimir Nabokov: Selected Letters 1940–1977, eds Matthew Bruccoli and Dmitri Nabokov (New York: Harcourt Brace Jovanovich/Bruccoli Clark, 1990; London: Weidenfeld and Nicolson, 1990).

Collected interviews

Strong Opinions (New York: McGraw-Hill, 1973; London: Weidenfeld and Nicolson, 1974).

2. Biographical studies

Boyd, Brian, *Vladimir Nabokov: The Russian Years* (Princeton: Princeton University Press, 1990).

Boyd, Brian, *Vladimir Nabokov: The American Years* (Princeton: Princeton University Press, 1991).

Field, Andrew, *Nabokov: His Life in Art* (London: Hodder and Stoughton, 1967).

Field, Andrew, *Nabokov: His Life in Part* (London: Hamish Hamilton, 1977).

Field, Andrew, *VN: The Life and Art of Vladimir Nabokov* (London: Macdonald, 1987).

3. Bibliographies

Bryer, Jackson R. and Thomas J. Bergin, Jr, 'Vladimir Nabokov's Critical Reputation in English: A Note and a Checklist', reprinted in Dembo (1967), pp. 225–74.

Field, Andrew, *Nabokov: A Bibliography* (New York: McGraw-Hill, 1973).

Juliar, Michael, *Vladimir Nabokov: A Descriptive Bibliography* (New York: Garland, 1986).

Parker, Stephen Jan, 'Nabokov Bibliography', *The Nabokovian* (Lawrence: University of Kansas, 1984–). Formerly *The Vladimir Nabokov Research Newsletter*, published twice yearly 1978–84.

Schuman, Samuel, *Vladimir Nabokov: A Reference Guide* (Boston, Mass.: G.K. Hall, 1979)

Zimmer, Dieter E., *Vladimir Nabokov: Bibliographie des Gesamtwerks* (Hamburg: Rowohlt, 1963).

4. Selected critical studies

Alexandrov, Vladimir E., *Nabokov's Otherworld* (Princeton: Princeton University Press, 1991).

Appel, Alfred, Jr, ed., *The Annotated 'Lolita': Vladimir Nabokov* (New York: McGraw-Hill, 1970).

Appel, Alfred, Jr, *Nabokov's Dark Cinema* (New York: Oxford University Press, 1974).

Appel, Alfred, Jr, and Charles Newman, eds, *Nabokov: Criticism, Reminiscences, Translations, and Tributes* (London: Weidenfeld and Nicolson, 1971).

Bader, Julia, *Crystal Land: Artifice in Nabokov's English Novels* (Berkeley: University of California Press, 1972).

Bloom, Harold, ed., *Vladimir Nabokov, Modern Critical Views* (New York: Chelsea House, 1987).

Bloom, Harold, ed., *Vladimir Nabokov's LOLITA, Modern Critical Interpretations* (New York: Chelsea House, 1987).

Dembo, L. S., ed., *Nabokov: the Man and his Works: Studies* (Madison: University of Wisconsin Press, 1967).

Fowler, Douglas, *Reading Nabokov* (Ithaca: Cornell University Press, 1974).

Gibian, George and Stephen Jan Parker, eds, *The Achievements of Vladimir Nabokov: Essays, Studies, Reminiscences* (Ithaca: The Center for International Studies, Cornell University, 1985).

Grabes, H., *Fictitious Biographies: Vladimir Nabokov's English Novels* (The Hague: Mouton, 1977).

Grayson, Jane, *Nabokov Translated: A Comparison of Nabokov's Russian and English Prose* (Oxford: Oxford University Press, 1977).

Green, Geoffrey, *Freud and Nabokov* (Lincoln: University of Nebraska Press, 1988).

Hyde, G. M., *Vladimir Nabokov: American Russian Novelist* (London: Marian Boyars, 1977).

Moynahan, Julian, *Vladimir Nabokov University of Minnesota Pamphlets on American Writers Number 96* (Minneapolis: University of Minnesota Press, 1971).

Packman, David, *Vladimir Nabokov: The Structure of Literary Desire* (Columbia: University of Missouri Press, 1982).

Page, Norman, ed., *Nabokov: The Critical Heritage* (London: Routledge, 1982).

Pifer, Ellen, *Nabokov and the Novel* (Cambridge: Harvard University Press, 1980).

Proffer, Carl, *Keys to Lolita* (Bloomington: Indiana University Press, 1968).

Quennell, Peter, ed., *Vladimir Nabokov: A Tribute to His Life, His Work, His World* (London: Weidenfeld and Nicolson, 1979).

Rampton, David, *Vladimir Nabokov: A Critical Study of the Novels* (Cambridge: Cambridge University Press, 1984).

Rampton, David, *Vladimir Nabokov* Macmillan Modern Novelists (Basingstoke: Macmillan, 1993).

Rivers, J. E. and Charles Nicol, eds, *Nabokov's Fifth Arc: Nabokov and Others on his Life's Work* (Austin: University of Texas Press, 1982).

Roth, Phyllis, ed., *Critical Essays on Vladimir Nabokov* (Boston: G.K. Hall, 1984).

Rowe, William Woodin, *Nabokov's Spectral Dimensions: The Other World in His Works* (Ann Arbor, Mich.: Ardis, 1981).

Stegner, Page, *Escape into Aesthetics: The Art of Vladimir Nabokov* (New York: Dial, 1966).

Stuart, Dabney, *Nabokov: The Dimensions of Parody* (Baton Rouge: Louisiana State University Press, 1978).

Toker, Leona, *Nabokov: The Mystery of Literary Structure* (Ithaca: Cornell University Press, 1989).

Wood, Michael, *The Magician's Doubts: Nabokov and the Risks of Fiction* (London: Chatto, 1994).

5. Selected reviews and critical articles

Amis, Kingsley, review of *Lolita* by Vladimir Nabokov, *Spectator* (November 1959), pp. 635–6, reprinted in Page (1982).

Appel, Alfred, Jr, ed., Vladimir Nabokov Issue, *Triquarterly*, 17 (Winter 1970).

Bell, Michael, '*Lolita* and Pure Art', *Essays in Criticism*, 24 (1974), pp. 169–84.

Brand, Dana, 'The interaction of aestheticism and American consumer culture in Nabokov's *Lolita*', *Modern Language Studies*, 17: 2 (Spring 1987), pp. 14–21.

Butler, Diana, '*Lolita* Lepidoptera', in *New World Writing*, no. 16 (1960), pp. 58–84.

Clifton, Gladys M., 'Humbert Humbert and the Limits of Artistic License', in J.E. Rivers and Charles Nicol, eds, *Nabokov's Fifth Arc: Nabokov and Others on his Life's Work* (Austin: University of Texas Press, 1982).

Dupee, F.W., '*Lolita* in America', *Encounter* (February 1959), pp. 30–5, reprinted in Page (1982).

Ermarth, Elizabeth, 'Conspicuous Construction: Or, Kristeva, Nabokov, and the Anti-Realist Critique', *Novel*, 21 (1988), pp. 330–9.

Green, Martin, 'The Morality of *Lolita*', *Kenyon Review* XXVIII (June 1966), pp. 352–77.

Haegert, John, 'Artist in Exile: The Americanization of Humbert Humbert', *ELH* 52 (1985), pp. 777–94.

Hollander, John, 'The Perilous Magic of Nymphets', *Partisan Review* XXIII (Fall 1956), pp. 557–60.

Levine, Peter, '*Lolita* and Aristotle's Ethics', *Philosophy and Literature* 19: 1 (April 1995), pp. 32–47.

Michelson, Annette, '*Lolita*'s Progeny', *October* (Spring 1996), pp. 3–14.

Modern Fiction Studies, 25, 3 (1979), Vladimir Nabokov Special Issue.

Nemerov, Howard, 'The Morality of Art', *Kenyon Review*, XIX (Spring 1957), pp. 313–14, pp. 316–21, reprinted in Page (1982).

Russian Literature Triquarterly, 24 (1991) Vladimir Nabokov Special Issue.

Shute, J.P., 'Nabokov and Freud: The Play of Power', *Modern Fiction Studies*, 30.4 (Winter 1984), pp. 637–50.

Tamir-Ghez, Nomi, 'The Art of Persuasion in Nabokov's *Lolita*', *Poetics Today: Theory and Analysis of Literature and Communication*, 1 (1979), pp. 65–83.

Trilling, Lionel, 'The Last Lover: Vladimir Nabokov's *Lolita*', *Griffin*, VII (August 1958), pp. 4–21, reprinted in *Encounter*, (October 1958), pp. 9–19; reprinted in Page (1982).

Whiting, Frederick, '"The Strange Particularity of the Lover's Preference": Pedophilia, Pornography, and the Anatomy of Monstrosity in *Lolita*', *American Literature*, 70: 4 (December 1998), pp. 833–62.

6. Chapters in books

Berman, Jeffrey, *The Talking Cure: Literary Representations of Psychoanalysis* (New York: New York University Press, 1985), pp. 211–38.

Bowlby, Rachel, *Shopping with Freud* (London: Routledge, 1993), pp. 46–71.

Bronfen, Elisabeth, *Over Her Dead Body: Death, Femininity and the Aesthetic* (Manchester: Manchester University Press, 1992), pp. 371–81.

Dipple, Elizabeth, *The Unresolvable Plot: Reading Contemporary Fiction* (New York: Routledge, 1988), pp. 67–83.

Josipovici, Gabriel, *The World and the Book: A Study of Modern Fiction*, 2nd edn (London: Macmillan, 1979), pp. 201–20.

Kauffman, Linda, 'Framing Lolita: Is There a Woman in the Text?', in Yaeger and Kowaleski-Wallace (1989), pp. 131–52.

Rorty, Richard, *Contingency, Irony, and Solidarity* (Cambridge: Cambridge University Press, 1989), pp. 41–68.

Rougemont, Denis de, *Love Declared: Essays on the Myths of Love*, trans. Richard Howard (New York: Pantheon, 1963), pp. 49–54.

Seidel, Michael, *Exile and the Narrative Imagination* (New Haven, Conn.: Yale University Press), pp. 164–96.

Tanner, Tony, *City of Words: American Fiction 1950–70* (London: Jonathan Cape, 1971), pp. 33–49.

Yaeger, Patricia and Beth Kowaleski-Wallace, eds, *Refiguring the Father: New Feminist Readings of Patriarchy* (Carbondale: Southern Illinois University Press, 1989), pp. 131–52.

7. Selected reviews of *The Enchanter*

Jenkins, Alan, 'First Throb Of The Enchanted Hunter', review of *The Enchanter* by Vladimir Nabokov, trans. Dmitri Nabokov, *Times Literary Supplement*, 16 January 1987: p. 4372.

Merrill, Robert, review of *The Enchanter* by Vladimir Nabokov, trans. Dmitri Nabokov, *Resources for American Literary Study*, 18: 2 (1992): pp. 279–81.

Pritchett, V. S., 'The Magician's Trick', review of *The Enchanter* by Vladimir Nabokov, trans. Dmitri Nabokov, *New York Review of Books*, 34: 4 (1987): p. 9.

Thibault, Paul J., review of *The Enchanter* by Vladimir Nabokov, *Queens Quarterly*, 95: 4 (1988): pp. 902–3.

8. *Lolita* on Film

Corliss, Richard, *Lolita,* BFI Film Classics (London: BFI, 1994).
Kael, Pauline, *'Lolita', I Lost it At the Movies* (New York: Bantam Books, 1966).
Sinclair, Marianne, *Hollywood Lolitas: The Nymphet Syndrome in the Movies* (New York: Holt, 1988).

ACKNOWLEDGEMENTS

The editor and publisher wish to thank the following for their permission to reprint copyright material: McGraw-Hill (for material from *The Annotated 'Lolita': Vladimir Nabokov*); University of California Press (for material from *Crystal Land: Artifice in Nabokov's English Novels*); Routledge (for material from *Shopping with Freud; The Unresolvable Plot: Reading Contemporary Fiction*; and *Nabokov: The Critical Heritage*); Manchester University Press (for material from *Over Her Dead Body: Death, Femininity and the Aesthetic*); University of Wisconsin Press (for material from *Nabokov: the Man and his Works: Studies*); Cornell University Press (for material from *Reading Nabokov*); *The Kenyon Review* (for material from 'The Morality of *Lolita*'); Marian Boyars (for material from *Vladimir Nabokov: America's Russian Novelist*); Macmillan (for material from *The World and the Book: A Study of Modern Fiction*; and *Vladimir Nabokov*); Southern Illinois University Press (for material from *Refiguring the Father: New Feminist Readings of Patriarchy*); University of Minnesota Press (for material from *Vladimir Nabokov*); Harvard University Press (for material from *Nabokov and the Novel*); Cambridge University Press (for material from *Contingency, Irony, and Solidarity*); Pantheon (for material from *Love Declared: Essays on the Myths of Love*); Eyre and Spottiswoode (for material from *Escape into Aesthetics: The Art of Vladimir Nabokov*); *American Literature* (for material from '"The Strange Particularity of the Lover's Preference": Pedophilia, Pornography, and the Anatomy of Monstrosity in *Lolita*'); Chatto and Windus (for material from *The Magician's Doubts: Nabokov and the Risks of Fiction*).

There are instances where we have been unable to trace or contact copyright holders before our printing deadline. If notified, the publisher will be pleased to acknowledge the use of copyright material.

The editor wishes to thank Duncan Heath for his generous editorial support, Nicolas Tredell for his excellent reading skills, and Jacqueline Dobbyne for her careful copy-editing.

Christine Clegg is a lecturer in Cultural Studies and English Literature at the University of East London. She has contributed to *Feminist Review, Fragmenté* and *Soundings* and has recently co-edited a special issue of *New Formations* on 'Childhood'.

INDEX